Freedom

Awarded the Johnsonian Prize in Philosophy, 1990

FREEDOM

A COHERENCE THEORY

CHRISTINE SWANTON

Hackett Publishing Company, Inc.
Indianapolis / Cambridge

Copyright © 1992 by Christine Swanton

All rights reserved

Printed in the United States of America

For further information, please address

   Hackett Publishing Company
   P.O. Box 44937
   Indianapolis, Indiana 46244–0937

Library of Congress Cataloging-in-Publication Data

Swanton, Christine, 1947–
   Freedom: a coherence theory/Christine Swanton.
      p.   cm.
   Includes bibliographical references and index.
   ISBN 0–87220–129–5 (cloth: alk. paper)

1. Liberty   I. Title.
JC585.S846   1992
323. 44–dc20   91-21282
                                                                                CIP

The paper used in this publication meets the minimum requirements of American National Standard for Information Sciences—Permanence of Paper for Printed Library Materials, ANSI Z39.48-1984.

Contents

Acknowledgments vi

Introduction vii

PART I METHODOLOGY

Chapter 1   The Essential Contestedness View 1
Chapter 2   Coherence Theory: Wide Reflective Equilibrium 11

PART II THE BACKGROUND THEORY

Chapter 3   A Defeasibility Account of Freedom 31
Chapter 4   Limitations in Practical Activity 49

PART III CONCEPTIONS OF FREEDOM

Chapter 5   Rival Conceptions of Freedom 61
Chapter 6   Coherence in the Core Area 76

PART IV THE FREEDOM PHENOMENA

Chapter 7   Unavailability of Actions 89
Chapter 8   Ineligibility of Actions 104
Chapter 9   Heteronomy 118
Chapter 10 Executive Failure 136
Chapter 11 Significance of Actions 162
Chapter 12 Conflicts of Freedom 178

CONCLUSION 191

ENDOXA CONCERNING FREEDOM 193

Index 195

Acknowledgments

This work arose in part from my D. Phil. thesis, "Freedom and Equality," submitted to the University of Oxford in 1976. I remain grateful for the conscientious and helpful supervision of Brian Barry and Alan Ryan. Since that time I have been indebted to Nicholas Denyer for inspiration on Aristotelian coherence theory, and to both Nick and Jeremy Waldron for much conversation about freedom and other areas of political and moral philosophy. My very grateful thanks are due also to Rosalind Hursthouse and to Robert Young, who read and sent critical comments on the penultimate draft. Finally, my sincere thanks to Jenny Diepraam, who typed the manuscript despite the pressures of departmental office duties.

I am grateful for permission for reprinting material as follows:

Sections of Chapter 10 originally appeared as "Weakness of Will as a Species of Executive Cowardice," *Canadian Journal of Philosophy* 20 (1991), pp. 123–140.

Sections of Chapter 1 originally appeared as "On the Essential Contestedness of Political Concepts," *Ethics* 18 (1985), pp. 68–65. © 1985 by The University of Chicago. All rights reserved.

Sections of Chapter 11 originally appeared in "The Concept of Interests," *Political Theory* 8 (1980), pp. 83–101.

Chapter 6 has its origin in "The Concept of Overall Freedom," *Australasian Journal of Philosophy* 57 (1979), pp. 337–349.

A section of Chapter 8 originally appeared in *Australasian Journal of Philosophy* 67 (1989), pp. 472–475 under the title of "Robert Stevens on Offers."

Introduction

A survey of the literature on political and social freedom reveals an amazing amount and variety of disagreement over its nature. In short, anyone attempting to elucidate this nature has to face the fact that the concept of freedom is highly contested. Let me illustrate by just two examples.

The first concerns a dispute about a putative distinction between freedom and ability. Maurice Cranston[1] claims: "Truly there is little point in 'being free to do' unless we 'have the power to', but it certainly does not follow from this that the one is identical to the other" (*ibid*, p. 27). There are those who reject the distinction between freedom and power or ability, however. According to R. H. Tawney:[2] "It [freedom] means the ability to do, or refrain from doing, definite things, at a definite moment, in definite circumstances, or it means nothing at all" (*ibid.*, p. 228). John Dewey[3] says: "To say that a man is free to choose to walk, while the only walk he can take will lead him over a precipice, is to strain words as well as facts" (*ibid.*, p. 304).

The second example of disagreement is the question of whether impediments not imposed by human contrivance can deprive of freedom. According to D. D. Raphael:[4] ". . . we may speak of freedom from want, or of freeing mankind from the scourge of cancer, when we mean that the impediments to which we refer, although not imposed by human action, are capable (we hope) of being removed by human action" (*ibid.*, p. 115).

S. I. Benn and R. S. Peters[5] disagree. To allow a concept of freedom as the effective removal of limitations to people's choice, they claim, is to trivialize the concept of freedom (*ibid.*, p. 212).

The question naturally arises: How should a theorist approach the problem of apparently intractable dispute? One ap-

1. *Liberty: A New Analysis* (London: Longmans, 1953).
2. *Equality* (London: Unwin, 1964).
3. *Human Nature and Conduct* (New York: Holt, 1922).
4. *Problems of Political Philosophy* (London: Macmillan, 1970).
5. *Social Principles and the Democratic State* (London: Allen and Unwin, 1959).

proach, inspired by John Rawls,[6] has been to search for a core concept or schema of freedom on which protagonists do, or could, agree. Rival conceptions of freedom are thus to be understood as interpretations of a single "core concept" of freedom. Unfortunately, controversies concerning the nature of freedom not only are many and various, but are also many-layered, occurring at the highest level of generality. There is not even agreement on the formal structure of that property. There appear to be three views either implicit or explicit in the literature.

(1) Gerald MacCallum[7] has made a persuasive attempt to provide a core concept of freedom with his "triadic schema," viz., x is (is not) free from y to do (not do, become, not become) z. In this schema, 'x' ranges over agents, 'y' ranges over such "preventing conditions" as "constraints, restrictions, interferences, and barriers," and 'z' ranges over "actions or conditions of character or circumstances" (*ibid.*, p. 314). For MacCallum, all disputes concerning the nature of freedom are to be interpreted as disagreements about the proper range of the term variables 'x', 'y', and 'z'. For example, the two disputes mentioned above can be understood as disputes about the proper range of the 'y' variable.

(2) Secondly, there is the view that, at least in certain contexts, freedom is a dyadic relation between agents and obstacles. In the introduction to *Four Essays on Liberty*,

---

6. *A Theory of Justice* (Cambridge: Harvard, 1971) [hereafter TJ]. Rawls claims that the 'common element' in rival 'conceptions' of justice is the role played by the various conceptions in determining rules for assigning basic rights and duties, and the proper nonarbitrary balancing of competing claims to the advantages of social life. According to Rawls:

> "Men can agree to this description of just institutions since the notion of an arbitrary distinction and of a proper balance, which are included in the concept of justice, are left open for each to interpret according to the principles of justice that he accepts" (TJ, 5).

The idea that a *conception* of a political ideal x is an interpretation of the concept of x in Rawls's sense is taken over by Steven Lukes in his *Power: A Radical View* (London: Macmillan, 1974). Here he claims that there is a "common core" or primitive notion of power (viz., A exercises power over B when A affects B in a "non-trivial or significant manner", p. 26), which underlies the various rival accounts of power.

7. "Negative and Positive Freedom," *The Philosophical Review*, LXXVI (1967): 312–34.

Isaiah Berlin[8] makes the following claim in a footnote: "It has been suggested that liberty is always a triadic relation: one can only seek to be free from X to do or be Y; hence 'all liberty' is at once negative and positive, or, better still, neither (see MacCallum). This seems to me an error. A man struggling against his chains or a people against enslavement need not consciously aim at any definite further state. A man need not know how he will use his freedom; he just wants to remove the yoke. So do classes and nations" (*ibid.*, p. xliii).

(3) Thirdly, a large group of theorists appear to understand freedom as a monadic property of agents. For such theorists, a free agent is one who possesses the appropriate personality—is self-realized, self-actualized, in a stage of harmony, rational, autonomous in any one of a number of senses of these notions. According to views of this type, to say of an agent that he is free is not necessarily to have in mind some assignable obstacles from which the person is free. To be free just is a matter of having a certain kind of character, having certain kinds of desires, and so forth.

A defense of a favored conception of freedom is thus beset with problems of methodology. There is a multitude of conceptions of freedom that defy even attempts at classification;[9] no agreed upon conceptual core and no consensus on the value of freedom. Hence the theorist must self-consciously address questions of methodology. In presenting a theory of justice, Rawls stands out as a shining example of one who realizes the importance and difficulties of methodological questions. In general, by contrast, theorists of the nature of freedom plunge ahead, usually offering yet another definition de novo, without attempting to discover sensible features in rival conceptions or the point of such conceptions.

I shall avoid this defect here by presenting and deploying a coherence theory—a version of "wide reflective equilibrium" (WRE). My major thesis is that a suitable coherence theory of freedom can perceive the strengths of, and reconcile, a wide

8. (New York: Oxford, 1969).
9. Cf., e.g., the criticism that has attended Berlin's classification of conceptions of freedom as "negative" and "positive."

variety of competing conceptions of freedom, including the three views above. The favored version of wide reflective equilibrium is presented and defended in chapter 2, and is deployed in the subsequent chapters. In chapter 1, I discuss an influential skeptical view that suggests the pointlessness of justifying favored conceptions of contested ideals. This is the view that freedom, justice, and other concepts are not only contested but "essentially" so.

PART I
Methodology

CHAPTER 1
The Essential Contestedness View

(i) *The Thesis of Essential Contestedness*

The view that freedom and other ideals such as justice are essentially contested is important, not only because the view has enjoyed some vogue since W. B. Gallie's influential article "Essentially Contested Concepts,"[1] but also because it suggests the pointlessness of developing a theory of the nature of freedom. In this chapter, I first describe the view that freedom is essentially contested, then outline the serious problems posed by that view for the justificatory enterprise, and, finally, face those problems, arguing that, even if freedom is essentially contested, the justification of conceptions of freedom is a crucially important enterprise.

A reasonably precise characterization of the "essential contestedness" view requires a distinction between the concept of an item x (such as freedom) and a conception of x. Essential contestedness theorists believe that an essentially contested concept is not vague or ambiguous; rather, there is just one concept that is itself essentially contested. According to these theorists, one can consistently believe that there is one concept of x and that there are rival "conceptions" of x—or, in Gallie's terms, "uses" of the concept of x (*ibid.*, p. 189).

---

1. *Proceedings of the Aristotelian Society*, LVI (1955–56): 167–98.

The precise nature of the distinction between a concept of x and conceptions of x may be characterized in various ways. There are three views either implicit or explicit in the recent literature on moral and political ideals.

(1) The concept of x is provided by a schema or canonical form. One example is MacCallum's schematic characterization of freedom. As explained above, freedom, according to MacCallum, should be regarded as "always one and the same triadic relation" (*op. cit.*, p. 312) represented by the following schema: "x is (is not) free from y to do (not do, become, not become) z (*op. cit.*, p. 314). For MacCallum, all disputes concerning the nature of freedom are to be interpreted as disagreements about the proper range of the variables 'x', 'y', and 'z' in his triadic schema. These disputes could be understood by the essential contestedness theorist as yielding different *conceptions* of freedom.

(2) A specification of the *concept* of x encapsulates a common content (as opposed to structure) of rival conceptions of x. For example, according to Rawls, the common element in rival conceptions of justice is the role played by the various conceptions in determining rules for assigning basic rights and duties, and the proper nonarbitrary balancing of competing claims to the advantages of social life. Unlike schemas, the specification of such a concept does not contain the definiendum in the definiens; nonetheless, the "common element" is described in a manner sufficiently broad to be susceptible of a number of interpretations. Thus, according to Rawls: "Men can agree to this description of just institutions since the notion of an arbitrary distinction and of a proper balance, which are included in the concept of justice, are left open for each to interpret according to the principles of justice that he accepts" (TJ, 5).

The idea that a conception of x is an interpretation of the concept of x in Rawls's sense is taken over by Steven Lukes in his *Power: A Radical View*,[2] where he argues that power is an essentially contested concept. Here he claims that there is a "common core" or primitive no-

---

2. New York: Macmillan, 1974.

tion of power (namely, *A* exercises power over *B* when *A* affects *B* in a "nontrivial or significant manner") which underlies the various contested views of power (*ibid*., pp. 26–7; p. 27, fn. 1).

(3) The *concept* of *x* is "derived" from an "exemplar" of *x* to which the concept of *x* paradigmatically applies. In describing his model of an essentially contested concept, namely, the champion team at bowling, Gallie claims that the method and style of playing of the teams is "derived from a process of imitation and adaptation from an *exemplar*, which might have the form either of one prototype team of players, or of a succession (or tradition) of teams . . . This exemplar's way of playing must be recognized by all the contesting teams (and their supporters) to be 'the way the game is to be played'" (*op. cit.*, p. 176).

Whichever one of the above views is adopted, essential contestedness theorists agree that essentially contested concepts do possess a "common core," but that detailed specifications of this core are essentially contested. I shall follow Rawls's usage in calling the "common core" the *concept* and the contested "interpretations" of that core *conceptions*.

Armed with the distinction between a concept of an ideal *x*, and conceptions of *x*, I am now in a position to characterize the view that certain political concepts are "essentially contested." I might begin with the following often cited passage from Gallie's "Essentially Contested Concepts": "There are concepts which are essentially contested, concepts the proper use of which inevitably involves endless disputes about their proper uses on the part of their users" (*op. cit.*, p. 169). This passage makes two main points: (1) proper use of the concepts in question involves recognition by the users of the concept that use is "contestable, and will, as a rule, be actually contested"; and (2) these contests are in the nature of the case inevitable.

Thus the essential contestedness views to be described contain two main theses, which I shall term the thesis of contestedness and the thesis of *essential* contestedness. The former thesis I label C:

C: There is at least one concept, central to political theory, which is such that (a) that concept admits of a variety of "interpretations" or "uses," and (b) is such that its proper use is disputable, and conceptions are deployable both "aggressively and defensively" against rival conceptions (*op. cit.*, p. 172; emphasis added).

Second, Gallie makes the point that contests about proper use are "inevitable" and "endless." Both Gallie and later theorists ground this inevitability and endlessness not merely in features of the human psyche—for example, its proneness to remain "engagé" despite inability to effect universal conversion to a point of view—but in features of the concept itself—features that render contests incapable of being rationally settled.

This is the thesis of *essential* contestedness, of which there are ontological and epistemological versions. The ontological version is:

P_0: There is at least one concept C of x, central to value theory, which admits of a variety of "interpretations" (namely, conceptions of x), and which is such that no interpretation of C is the *best* conception of x.

Given that a putative correct or best conception of x would generate a unique set of truth conditions for assertions involving C, then, according to P_0, there is no such set of truth conditions. Lukes[3] appears to embrace this ontological version of the essential contestedness view. He claims:

With respect to our knowledge of the world, truth is distinguishable from error because there are *non-relative truth conditions*, non-relative principles of reasoning and ways of justifying claims to such knowledge that are objectively better than other ways. By contrast, moral judgments may be incompatible but equally rational, because criteria of rationality and justification in morals are themselves relative to conflicting and irreconcilable perspectives (*ibid.*, 172).

Of course, Lukes's claim about moral judgments does not itself entail P_0: his claim entails P_0 only on the assumption, which he makes, that essentially contested concepts are embedded in *moral* theoretical perspectives.

---

3. "Relativism: Cognitive and Moral," *Proceedings of the Aristotelian Society*, suppl. 48 (1974): 165–89 (italics added).

The epistemological version of the essential contestedness thesis is:

> P_E: There is at least one concept C of x, central to political theory, which admits of a variety of interpretations (namely, conceptions of x) and which is such that for any interpretation C_i of C, there is no warrant for the belief that C_i is the *best* conception of x.

Gallie appears to adopt the epistemological version in the following explication of an essentially contested concept: "It is quite impossible to find a *general principle* for deciding which of two contestant uses of an essentially contested concept really 'uses it best'" (*ibid.*, p. 189).

Assuming that truth conditions are not necessarily to be identified with assertibility conditions, P_E is compatible with the falsity of P_0. Given that assumption, there may be a best conception of x without its being possible to justify any claim to have discovered such a conception. Gallie, in the passage cited above, claims merely that it is impossible for us to find a general principle for justifying claims that a conception is the best; he does not claim that there is no best conception.

(ii) *Problems for Our Enterprise*

I have described above two essential contestedness views: the conjunction of C and P_0, and the conjunction of C and P_E. There are two problems posed by these views, which appear to suggest that any attempt at justifying a favored conception of freedom is doomed to failure. I shall discuss in turn each of these problems.

The first problem is this. We accept, with the essential contestedness views, the truth of C. Yet the truth of C raises the possibility that putative *rival* conceptions may not be conceptions of the same ideal at all. Terms putatively referring to a single ideal may be multiply ambiguous. If 'freedom' is multiply ambiguous, however, one should not attempt to justify a conception of freedom as best: the one term merely refers to different ideals.

The essential contestedness view itself suggests a way out of the problem raised by C. 'Freedom' and other terms referring to other putatively essentially contested concepts are not multiply ambiguous, since common to the rival conceptions is an uncontested "core concept" of which the rival conceptions are interpretations. Lukes makes explicit the need to postulate a "core concept" that underlies contested conceptions of an ideal: "Contests . . . are after all, contests over something: essentially contested concepts must have some common core; otherwise, how could we justifiably claim that the contests were about the same concept?" (*ibid.*, p. 187). If there is no common core concept, he argues, then 'freedom' is multiply ambiguous: contests about the correct conception of freedom would be pointless since the contestants are "not in the same event."

I believe, however, that the resolution to our problem suggested by the essentially contested views is dubious. It may be charged that the "core concept" is a fiction designed for the purposes of the essential contestedness view; for is not the supposed concept in the same boat as the conceptions: not only in being contested, but in being essentially so? As I have indicated in the introduction, theorists have disputed proposed "core concepts" of freedom. It could be replied, however, that though the core is contested—C applies to the core—it is not *essentially* contested. This is, of course, a possibility, but it is difficult to see why P_E and P_0 should apply to conceptions and not to the core. What is the principle for settling disputes about the core which is not available in the case of contested conceptions?

I shall not pursue this unpromising line of thought, since Lukes's reason for postulating uncontested core concepts is misguided. Showing why it is misguided will also resolve our problem posed by the truth of C. Certainly, if disputants about the nature of freedom are to be engaged in a genuine contest, they must be arguing about the same ideal. It cannot be the case that freedom, for example, is multiply ambiguous. If the contestants are arguing about the nature of the same ideal, however, is it necessary that there be a single concept of that ideal common to all the contested conceptions of it? More generally, is it necessary that terms referring to freedom all possess the same meaning? I shall say not.

According to some philosophers of language, the fact that terms lack a common meaning does not entail that they lack a

Chapter 1 The Essential Contestedness View

common referent.[4] For example, a theory of reference could be proposed in which rival theories are deemed to refer to the same thing by virtue of their agreement on sufficiently many "samples." In the case of freedom, for example, they may agree on sufficiently many sample instances of utterances containing the word 'free' and cognates as being what Aristotle[5] would term the *endoxa*: the "common conceptions" on a subject acceptable to the "many or the wise." For example, theorists could agree that the many or the wise would accept the following sample utterance *as an endoxon*, even if they wished to reject its truth in a fully fledged theory of freedom: "A traveler who handed over his money having yielded to the demands of a highway robber threatening, 'Your money or your life', was not free in that situation." Yet those same theorists would differ on how to resolve tensions between, and puzzles generated by, the *endoxa*: for example, the tension between the above judgment and the following generalization believed by many of "the wise": "One cannot be unfree to do something one actually does."[6] Given this, there will be (and is) disagreement on how the *endoxa* will be accommodated, if at all, in a fully fledged theory of freedom. Hence, although there may well be a high level of agreement on what is to count as the *endoxa*, there is little reason to believe that, when different theories attempt to construct conceptions of freedom in which tensions between the *endoxa* are resolved, there will be a "core concept" of freedom common to all.

I conclude that the first problem posed for our enterprise by the essential contestedness views can be resolved. One may sensibly speak of contested conceptions referring to the same

---

4. See, e.g., Peter Smith, *Realism and the Progress of Science* (New York: Cambridge, 1981), pp. 7–8.
5. *Tolpica* 1.1.100b. 21–13. For more on this notion, see G.E.L. Owen, "Tithenai ta Phainomena," in *Articles on Aristotle*, Jonathan Barnes, Malcolm Schofield, and Richard Sorabji, eds., vol. 1: *Science* (London: Duckworth, 1975), pp. 113–26; and Martha Craven Nussbaum, "Saving Aristotle's Appearances," in *Language and Logos Studies in Ancient Greek Philosophy*, Malcolm Schofield and Nussbaum, eds. (New York: Cambridge, 1982), pp. 267–93. (A longer version of this paper is ch. 8 of Nussbaum's *The Fragility of Goodness* (New York: Cambridge, 1986).
6. See, e.g., W. A. Parent, "Some Recent Work on the Concept of Liberty," *American Philosophy Quarterly*, xi (1974): 149–67, p. 160.

ideal without assuming the existence of a common meaning—viz., a core concept common to those conceptions.

There is a second problem raised by the essential contestedness views which appears to render unviable the justification of a favored conception of freedom. To adopt P_0 or P_E, it appears, is to presuppose that contests about the nature of our conception of freedom are rationally unsettlable. If this is so, however, what becomes of the justificatory enterprise?

The problem can be resolved only by clarifying further the nature of the thesis of rational unsettlability. On one account of this thesis it means: (1) there is no criterion for settling disputes about the nature of freedom. The truth of P_0 and P_E does not entail (1), however. It entails only a second interpretation of the thesis of rational unsettlability, viz., (2) there is no criterion for settling disputes about which is the *best* conception of freedom.

Interpretation (2) of the thesis of rational unsettlability is compatible with the view that there are criteria for rejecting inferior conceptions. Indeed interpretation (2) *must* be adopted by the essential contestedness views to avoid a charge of incoherence. Assume that P_E and P_0 are understood in the light of interpretation (1). It will then be objected that there is an inconsistency between C, on the one hand, and P_E and P_0, on the other. To adopt C is to presuppose that there is a point to contests about the nature of so-called essentially contested concepts. Furthermore, a contest has point only if there exists some criterion for settling it. To adopt P_0 or P_E, the objection continues, is to presuppose that there is no such criterion. I shall claim, however, that P_E and P_0 should be understood in the light of interpretation (2), in which case the charge of incoherence is avoided.

Unless the distinction between interpretations (1) and (2) is borne in mind, it is easy to accuse the essential contestedness views of incoherence. For example, in his review of Lukes's *Power: A Radical View*, Brian Barry[7] accuses Lukes of a "central tension" in his application of the essential contestedness view to the concept of power. According to Barry, Lukes argues that power is *essentially* contested: debates about the proper use of "power" involve irresolvable value conflict. Yet Lukes gives point to the contests by suggesting the existence of criteria for settling them: in particular he claims that the "one-dimensional" and "two-dimensional" conceptions of power are

---

7. "The Obscurities of Power," in *Government and Opposition*, X (1975): 250–4.

Chapter 1 The Essential Contestedness View 9

"blind" and "superficial" and that the "three-dimensional" conception of power is thereby "superior."

Lukes's claim is consistent with the thesis of rational unsettlability, however, for it clearly is to be understood in the light of interpretation (2). Given this, the essential contestedness view can meet the charge of incoherence. P_E and P_0 and C do not entail that all possible interpretations of an essentially contested concept of x will inevitably be the subject of "endless" dispute once thought about. This *would* imply that there is no point to contests; for not only can no consensus on a best conception of x emerge, but no conception of x can be rejected on the grounds that some other conception of x is better than it. The theses of essential contestedness, as stated, are weaker than this: though there is no best conception, or none knowable to be the best, some conceptions may nonetheless be better than others. While affording no criterion for determining the best wheat, contests have point because they separate the wheat from the chaff; and this separation is an endless process because political theorists are always in the habit of adding to the chaff. Thus there need be no tension, let alone incoherence, in Lukes's view: he may favor one conception of power because it is superior to certain other salient conceptions, while denying that there is a single best conception of power; for he denies any notion of moral truth or verisimilitude against the background of which the notion of "single best conception" makes sense.

I conclude that the essential contestedness views not only do not impugn the justificatory enterprise, but must indeed allow for such an enterprise to avoid a charge of incoherence. In the above, I have not argued that the essential contestedness views are false.[8] It is my view, however, that those espousing the essential contestedness views downplay the importance of justification because of their efforts to deny the existence of transcendent perspectives, such as Rawls's notorious Archimedean point (TJ, 260-3, 584), or Ronald Dworkin's[9] "Hercules": a lawyer of "superhuman skill, learning, patience and acumen" who considers all possible points of view and coheres them in a way that best "justifies and reconciles" them.

8. I have argued elsewhere, however, that arguments proposed for its truth fail. See my "On the 'Essential Contestedness' of Political Concepts," *Ethics*, XCV (1985): 811-27.
9. See "Hard Cases," in *Taking Rights Seriously* (Cambridge: Harvard, 1977), esp. p. 105.

Even if it is pointless to seek and defend a *best* conception of an ideal, it is not pointless to seek consensus on the elimination of inadequate and inferior conceptions. Indeed, I believe this is Lukes's view properly interpreted. If this is indeed the case, however, the problem of justification of conceptions has not been eliminated: it has simply been sidestepped. The view that political and moral concepts are essentially contested tells us nothing about the methodology required to sort out superior conceptions from inferior conceptions.

Chapter 2

Coherence Theory: Wide Reflective Equilibrium

(i) Introduction

The methodology to be adopted in this work is a version of coherence theory labeled by Norman Daniels "wide reflective equilibirum" (WRE). This kind of methodology has been defended by Kai Nielsen[1] as a very promising development in the search for a device for increasing our ability to choose between competing moral conceptions. Nonetheless, this confidence will be seen as misplaced unless serious issues are resolved. Unclarities surround the questions:

   (i) What is the claimed epistemological role for WRE?
   (ii) What version of WRE is to be employed?

I shall resolve these unclarities in a way that supports Nielsen's claim. First, however, I should specify in broad terms what the method of WRE is.

Daniels provides the following succinct summary of WRE, which he regards as a development of the account in Rawls's *A Theory of Justice*:

> A wide reflective equilibrium is a coherent triple of sets of beliefs held by a particular person; namely, (a) a set of considered moral judgments; (b) a set of moral principles; and (c) a set of relevant background theories, which may include both moral and nonmoral theories. We collect the person's initial moral judgments, which

---

1. "Grounding Rights and a Method of Reflective Equilibrium," *Inquiry*, XXV (1982): 227–306.

may be particular or general, and filter them to include only those of which he is relatively confident and which have been made under conditions generally conducive to avoiding errors of judgment. We propose alternative sets of moral principles which have varying degrees of "fit" with the moral judgments. Rather than settling immediately for the "best fit" of principles with judgments, which would give us only a narrow equilibrium, we advance philosophical arguments that reveal the strengths and weaknesses of the competing sets of principles (that is, competing moral conceptions). I construe these arguments as inferences from relevant background theories (I use the term loosely). Assume that some particular set of arguments wins and the moral agent is thus persuaded that one set of principles is more acceptable than the others (and perhaps than the conception that might have emerged in narrow equilibrium). The agent may work back and forth, revising his initial considered judgments, moral principles, and background theories, to arrive at an equilibrium point that consists of the triple—(a), (b), and (c).[2]

Of course, it need not be assumed that this definition of WRE is definitive. In particular, the most satisfactory conception of the items falling under (i)—described as "considered judgments"—is open to debate. I myself shall reject the Rawls-Daniels conception (see section (iii)).

Consider now the claimed epistemological role for WRE. The role claimed by Nielsen is limited. It is not claimed that WRE is a "doxastic decision procedure" in Alvin Goldman's[3] sense—i.e., a device whose proper use yields right results (relative to the appropriate epistemic goal). Nielsen states merely that WRE enables us to make progress. It is not assumed that WRE en-

2. "Two Approaches to Theory Acceptance in Ethics," in David Copp and David Zimmerman, eds., *Morality, Reason and Truth* (Ottawa: Rowman and Allenheld, 1985): 121. See also Daniels, "Wide Reflective Equilibrium and Theory Acceptance in Ethics," *Journal of Philosophy*, LXXVI (1979): 256–82; "Reflective Equilibrium and Archimedean Points," *Canadian Journal of Philosophy*, X (1980): 83–103; and "Some Methods of Ethics and Linguistics," *Philosophical Studies*, XXXVII (1980): 21–36.

3. "The Internalist Conception of Justification," in *Midwest Studies in Philosophy*, V, Peter A. French, Theodore E. Uehling, Jr., Howard K. Wettstein, eds. (Minneapolis: Minnesota UP, 1980): 27–51.

ables us to choose the best conception, or even that there is a best conception. In short, the method may simply allow the rejection of relatively bad conceptions, or the retention of several adequate conceptions. This indeed is my own view: there is no single *best* way of cohering the relevant phenomena.

It is also important to distinguish the idea that WRE is a *device* for enabling theorists to make progress, from the idea that WRE constitutes a justification for moral conceptions. As William G. Lycan[4] and others point out, a normative theory of justification of belief may not be usable by a given knower to determine whether or not her beliefs are justified. This distinction enables us to undercut a criticism of WRE made by Paul Thagard.[5] According to Thagard, the fact that an agent's beliefs are in an appropriate kind of *equilibrium* is irrelevant to the issue of justification of those beliefs. Even if the appropriate criteria of justification are *coherentist*, the fact that agents are in equilibrium adds nothing to the justification of those beliefs. Conversely, if the criteria of justification are met, then agents ought to be in equilibrium whether or not they are so. As Thagard puts it: "Reflective Equilibrium would be . . . a mere epiphenomenon of the justified acceptance of the theory" (*op. cit.*, p. 40). This criticism loses its force, however, if WRE is seen as a device or tool for making progress rather than as constitutive of the criteria for progress. The struggle to achieve equilibrium in the right kind of way is seen as a method of *achieving* the appropriate kind of coherence. The attainment of equilibrium suggests a natural stopping place in the search for coherence, and a disruption of equilibrium—by, e.g., the input of new data or acquaintance with new or refined alternative theories—a natural restarting place.[6]

This defense of WRE may leave one dissatisfied, however. If we are to believe Nielsen that WRE is an "exciting new development," should it not do more than this? Should it not furnish standards of justification in the quest for progress? Indeed it

4. "Epistemic Value," *Synthese*, LXIV (1985): 137–64, esp. pp. 139–140.
5. "From the Descriptive to the Normative in Psychology and Logic," *Philosophy of Science*, XLIX (1982): 24–42.
6. Cf. Rawls's claim in TJ that a reflective equilibrium "is not necessarily stable." "It is liable to be upset by further examination of the conditions which should be imposed on the contractual situation and by particular cases which may lead us to revise our judgments" (TJ, 20–1).

should. But WRE needs to be supplemented by a fuller theory of coherentist justification. WRE *as such* is a tool for making progress: a fuller theory of justification must spell out what counts as *appropriate* coherence, and this is not reducible to the attainment of equilibrium. Standards of appropriate coherence are developed in section (iv).

A further unclarity surrounds the issue of the claimed epistemological role for WRE. This unclarity stems from an ambiguity in the notion of "rival moral conception," between: (A) rival moral conceptions are competing moral theories providing realist accounts of the nature of value and disvalue, in which it is assumed that the nature of value is not determined by "our" conception of it (whatever that may be); (B) rival moral conceptions are competing accounts of the structure of our value *conceptions* (as opposed to the structure of value).

This ambiguity is serious because WRE is sometimes criticized as an inappropriate epistemology where the epistemic goal is the justification of a realist value ontology. It does not follow from the truth of this criticism, however, that, given value realism, WRE has no role at all to play in value theory. On the contrary, I shall argue, it is a suitable epistemology for uncovering the structure of our value conceptions.

Discovering the structure of our conception of justice is the task Rawls arguably set himself in *A Theory of Justice*, though it was not until "The Independence of Moral Theory"[7] that Rawls clearly separated the two possible tasks of WRE: that of justifying a realist moral theory as true, and that of uncovering the structure of our moral conceptions:

> I suggest that for the time being we put aside the idea of constructing a correct theory of right and wrong, that is, a systematic account of what we regard as objective moral truths. Since the history of moral philosophy shows that the notion of moral truth is problematical, we can suspend consideration of it until we have a deeper understanding of moral conceptions . . . So provisionally we may bracket the problem of moral truth and turn to moral theory: we investigate the substantive moral conceptions that people hold, or would

---

7. *Proceedings and Addresses of the American Philosophical Association*, XLVIII (1974–75): 5–22.

hold, under suitably defined conditions. In order to do this, one tries to find a scheme of principles that match people's considered judgments and general convictions in reflective equilibrium (*ibid.*, p. 7).

(ii) *The Epistemological Role of Wide Reflective Equilibrium*

In the last section, I claimed that the epistemological role for WRE (provided it is supplemented by standards of appropriate coherence) is the justification of a value conception in sense (B). The nature of this role requires further clarification, however, in light of the fact that the nature of the relation between (A) and (B) is itself problematic. Various "internal realists" may undermine the distinction, arguing that the difference is apparent only when a defense of a moral conception in sense (B) invokes a justificatory circle which is narrow—as in narrow reflective equilibrium (NRE). An adequate defense, however, is one invoking a suitable WRE embracing sufficiently rich empirical theory, and in that case no distinction between (A) and (B) can be forged.

I shall not assume the truth of an internal realist view, and shall claim that a successful prosecution of our task—that of uncovering the structure of our conception of freedom—need not presuppose a defense of a (realist) account of the value of freedom, or an account of that to which 'freedom' in fact refers. Achieving our goal certainly requires the articulation of a background theory that will contain empirical hypotheses, but the role of the background theory is to provide an adequate explication of the perceived[8] role that value plays in our classification of phenomena.

The differences between the various epistemological tasks alluded to in the previous paragraph will be clarified by describing the possible conceptions of the relation between value terms and the world. I understand the notion of a value term as follows. I shall say that 'F' is a value term if users of 'F' intend to refer to a property believed by them to be valuable and that the

---

8. I use the term 'perceived' to indicate that explication of the point of the collocation must make essential reference to our beliefs (considered judgments understood in a sense to be explained), whether or not these are "true." I do not suggest that this point is perspicuous to all who successfully employ the concept of freedom.

intended *point* of collocating things as F is that Fs have the distinctive value which Fs are believed to possess. In this sense, 'freedom', 'justice', and 'courage' are value terms.

In developing a conception of the relation between 'F' and being F, it is necessary to distinguish three things:

(a) F's being valuable.
(b) The referent of F.
(c) The "F phenomena."

The F phenomena are that heterogeneous set of observable manifestations of F whose classification as being F is motivated by the following belief—the phenomena in question are valuable in a distinctive kind of way (or cluster of ways). For example, where 'F' is 'being of a humble disposition', the F phenomena include various kinds of self-effacing, self-deprecating, and retiring behavior. Nielsen's claim that WRE increases our ability to choose between competing moral conceptions can now be unpacked into three possible claimed tasks for such an epistemology. These are: (i) the identification of the F phenomena, which involves the identification of the classificatory interests that give the rationale for the classification of the F phenomena; (ii) the identification of the referent (if any) of F; and (iii) the identification of the nature of the value (if any) of F.

It is important to distinguish these three tasks because they need not be regarded as identical. Whether they are or not depends on different views about what constitutes F-ness. These views may be distinguished broadly as follows:

(1) There is a necessary connection between being F and being valuable, but no necessary connection between being F and the F phenomena.
(2) There is a necessary connection between being F and the F phenomena, but no necessary connection between being F and being valuable.
(3) There is a necessary connection between being F and the F phenomena, and a necessary connection between being F and being valuable.
(4) There is no necessary connection between being F and the F phenomena, nor between being F and being valuable.

On view (1), the F phenomena do not fix the reference of 'F'. If our classificatory interest in classifying the F phenomena as F

Chapter 2 Coherence Theory

turns out to be based on a *mistaken* belief that those phenomena are valuable, then 'F' may refer, but not to what we take 'F' to refer. 'F' would refer to that property (if such exists) of which the relevant reference-fixing descriptions of F are true. Among these descriptions is the description of F as valuable.

To illustrate, let us assume that a set of phenomena, $(P_1 \ldots P_n)$ (phenomena involving the treatment of people as equals), are the justice phenomena because of a presumed connection between $P_1 \ldots P_n$ and an aspect of human flourishing. Furthermore, it is assumed that human flourishing is valuable, and that justice is *necessarily* valuable because, necessarily, human flourishing takes place only in just societies. It turns out, however, that $P_1 \ldots P_n$ are not associated with human flourishing, properly understood. (Let us assume, for example, that Nietzsche's theory of human self-realization is correct, and that humans do not realize themselves if treated as equals.[9]) If $P_1 \ldots P_n$ turn out not to be valuable then, although 'justice' might refer, it would not refer to what we take it to refer.

According to views of type (2), there is a necessary connection between being F and the F phenomena. The connection is guaranteed by the fact that being F accounts in some way for the F phenomena forming a "genuine," though heterogeneous, group. A corollary of view (2) is that, if (it turns out) the F phenomena are not justifiably collocated (form a genuine group), then 'F' does not refer.

There are two major views about how being F accounts for the genuineness of the collocation of the F phenomena. On the first view, the F phenomena form a genuine group by being causally related to F. On the second view, the F phenomena form a genuine group in that being F answers to a particular classificatory interest. Specifically, being F is that property possessed by the F phenomena which answers to the particular needs and interests that give point to the collocation of the F phenomena.

> (2A) The first view is illustrated by the views of John Campbell and Robert Pargetter.[10] According to them, being good is a second-order property: specifically, being

---

9. For the contrast between Nietzsche's views and various egalitarian views, see Nielsen, "Grounding Rights and a Method of Reflective Equilibrium."

10. "Goodness and Fragility," *American Philosophy Quarterly*, XXIII (1986): 155–65.

good is having some property that is causally responsible for the goodness phenomena. That proposition is itself a necessary truth "discovered by philosophical analysis" (*ibid.*, p. 163). By contrast, "the property which is responsible for the goodness-phenomena is G" is a contingent truth "discovered by empirical research" (*ibid.*).

One may compare their view with the following account of the reference of 'multiple sclerosis'. The point of classifying a heterogeneous set of symptoms (the multiple sclerosis phenomena) as symptoms of a single disease (multiple sclerosis) is the hypothesis that there is a single causal agent whose effects are the production of suitable clusters of these symptoms in human beings. Multiple sclerosis is thus deemed to be whatever disease is causally responsible for the multiple sclerosis phenomena. If there is no such agent, then 'multiple sclerosis' fails to refer.

(2B) The second view is illustrated by the work of Julius Kovesi[11] and Robert Ewin.[12] According to them, the necessary connection between being F and the F phenomena is of quite a different kind. Certainly, being F is that property which explains why the F phenomena are classified as F, but this explanation is not given by a causal hypothesis linking the F phenomena with being F. Being F is not whatever causes the F phenomena, nor whatever the F phenomena themselves cause. Rather, the explanation is located in the needs and interests that give point to the classification. For example, take the disvalue term 'being dirty'. Being dirty does not refer to whatever causes disease, but is rather whatever property is appropriately connected with the "role played by disease in human wants and interests." According to Ewin,

> Disease gives a point to the classification *dirty*, but is not itself that classification. It explains why certain elements count as making something dirty, but is not itself one of those ele-

---

11. *Moral Notions* (London: Routledge and Kegan Paul, 1967).
12. *Cooperation and Human Values* (Brighton: Harvester, 1981).

ments. Beyond that, the concept ranges in fairly obvious ways. Some things are dirty because they look dirty. Spitting on the floor is dirty, so we have reason for avoiding it rather than for creating more unnecessary work with a bottle of antiseptic. 'Dirty' is not equivalent to 'causes disease,' but we can understand the notion *dirty* (let alone such notions as *clean dirt*) only if we see it in the context of disease and the role played by disease in human wants and needs (*ibid.*, p. 15).

According to views of type (3), there is a necessary connection between being F and the F phenomena, and a necessary connection between being F and being valuable. Views of this type are conventionalist in the sense that no wedge is driven between our interest in classifying a group of phenomena as F (involving a belief that these phenomena are valuable in a distinctive way) and their being really valuable. The F phenomena are necessarily valuable by virtue of our taking them to be so.

Views of type (3) differ about the nature of the relation between being F and the F phenomena. First, conventionalist views can be allied to Campbell and Pargetter's position. Indeed, they give an example of a conventionalist view of the nature of the "goodness phenomena" according to which those phenomena are necessarily valuable (because 'good' means "valuable"), and relations of people believing objects to be good on becoming aware of those objects are to count as the goodness phenomena. It should be remembered, however, that, even though on this view there are necessary connections between being good, the goodness phenomena, and being valuable, the discovery of the property responsible for the goodness phenomena is a matter for "empirical research." Second, conventionalist views can be allied to Ewin's position. His view does not *entail* a conventionalist position, for the belief giving the point to the classification of the F phenomena (viz., the belief that they are associated with a distinctive value, say) could be contingent. If the belief were false, 'F' would still refer to that property appropriately connected with the F phenomena, but 'F' would not denote something valuable. If the belief were necessarily true, however, 'F' would necessarily denote something of value.

According to view (4), there is no necessary connection between being F and the F phenomena, nor is F necessarily valuable. On this view, the referent of F is that property which is constitutive of the nature or essence of the F phenomena. Assume that this property is G. Then the claim that F = G is a necessary truth. The claim that F is associated with the F phenomena is not, however. We might illustrate this with the following example. Take the value term 'humility'.[13] Assume that the humility phenomena (self-effacing and self-deprecating behavior) are associated with a character trait in human beings having a physiological basis G. On this Kripkean account, the proposition 'Humility is G' is a necessary truth, but the connection between humility and the humility phenomena is not. In other possible worlds, the humility phenomena may not be associated with G. Nor is it necessarily true that humility is valuable. Humility is necessarily G, but G is not necessarily valuable. G is the basis of the humility phenomena in this world, but our beliefs that the humility phenomena are valuable may be false. It may be, for example, that such phenomena do not encourage meaningful fulfilling social relations, but invite aggression and oppression.

We are now in a position to specify more clearly the main thesis of this chapter. As I stated earlier, Nielsen's claim that WRE increases our ability to choose between competing moral conceptions must distinguish between three possible tasks for such an epistemology: (i) the identification of the F phenomena, which involves the identification of the classificatory interests that give the rationale for the classification of the F phenomena; (ii) the identification of the referent (if any) of F; and (iii) the identification of the nature of the value (if any) of F.

Our thesis is that WRE is a suitable epistemology for the first of these tasks, even if not for the latter two. That is, WRE enables us to make progress in choosing between rival accounts of the F phenomena and the relevant classificatory interests. In short, I have claimed, WRE is a "device for increasing our ability to choose between competing moral conceptions" in sense (B) above: that is, in a sense that does not involve commitment to the idea that our conceptions answer to what is true. In *that* sense, justifying an account of a conception of F is not neces-

---

13. I here assume that we *take* humility to be a virtue, being connected in some way with human flourishing.

Chapter 2   Coherence Theory

sarily tantamount to giving an account of the referent of '*F*'; nor is it necessarily tantamount to giving a realist account of the distinctive value (if any) of *F*.

It may be objected at this point that justifying an account of a conception of freedom cannot be separated from giving an account of its referent, for the following reason. Given the contestedness of 'freedom'—contestedness that exists at the deepest level—there is no meaning common to the rival conceptions. Indeed, this point has already been canvassed. If this is so, however, how can one be sure that 'freedom' is not simply an ambiguous term, where differing conceptions all denote differing ideals instead of being better or worse accounts of a single ideal? My reply in chapter 1 was to claim that 'freedom' may nonetheless be *deemed* to refer to one ideal by virtue of the existence of agreement on what counts as the *endoxa* of the one thing—freedom. But if this is so, the objection concludes, the two tasks—that of reference and conception determination—cannot be separated.

The fact that giving an account of freedom presupposes that 'freedom' is *deemed* to have a single referent, however, does not entail that the two tasks are identical. The defense of a conception may make essential reference to beliefs about reference, but these beliefs need not determine *actual* reference on a suitable nondescriptivist account of reference.

We finally consider an objection of Joseph Raz[14] to the view that WRE is a suitable epistemology for uncovering the structure of our moral conceptions in the sense specified above. According to Raz, the theorist's role in uncovering the structure of our conceptions is described thus by Rawls:

> One thinks of the moral theorist as an observer, so to speak, who seeks to set out the structure of other people's moral conceptions and attitudes. Because it seems likely that people hold different conceptions, and the structure of these conceptions is in any case hard to delineate, we can best proceed by studying the main conceptions found in the tradition of moral philosophy. . . .[15]

If this is *all* the theorist is doing, however, then the following claim of Raz that WRE has no role to play is hardly surprising:

---

14. "The Claims of Reflective Equilibrium," *Inquiry*, XXV (1982): 307–30.
15. "The Independence of Moral Theory," p. 7 (cited in Raz, p. 314).

"[WRE] is dispensable in favour of deriving coherent moral conceptions from the writings of moral philosophers where they are to be found more or less ready made" (*op. cit.*, p. 314).

Being a "moral observer," however, is not all that the moral theorist does in endeavoring to reveal the structure of a conception of F. Why is this? One of the tasks of this kind of theorist is the identification of the F phenomena. This identification, in turn, presupposes an understanding of the rationale for collocating a heterogeneous set of phenomena as F. The completion of this task is no easy matter, however. As we have already noted, it has been frequently observed that our value conceptions, such as freedom and justice, are highly contested, and at the deepest level. We have also noted that even those theorists for whom these concepts are *essentially* contested believe that the terms 'justice' and 'freedom', for example, are not multiply ambiguous.[16] Nor is it assumed by those theorists that all value conceptions are as good as each other in the sense that there is nothing to choose between them as explications of our conceptions. Even where it is denied that there is a *best* conception of F, it is generally affirmed that some conceptions are superior to others.[17] Given this, the construction of a "superior" conception of F is not simply a matter of observing what people ordinarily say, or what this or that philosopher says. It is a matter of giving a superior account of the nature of the F phenomena, and of the rationale for collocating certain phenomena as F.

In section (iv), I shall offer criteria for evaluating accounts as superior. We shall see there that such an account is not, and cannot be, a mere exercise in "descriptive metaphysics" where "everything is left as it is." Rather, much theoretical work is needed to provide consistency in our account of the F phenomena, and to rationalize the favored way of providing consistency by offering a convincing and sufficiently deep explanation of our interest in their collocation.

(iii) *The Nature of Wide Reflective Equilibrium*

This section elaborates the account of WRE. A major area of contention is the nature of what Daniels and Rawls call the

---

16. See Gallie, "Essentially Contested Concepts."
17. See, e.g., Lukes's *Power: A Radical View*; see further above, ch. 1.

"considered judgments." These are the judgments which form the "data" in the account of our conception of F, and which are "pruned and adjusted" when WRE is reached. It is the pruned and adjusted judgments that give the final characterization of the F phenomena. There are three candidates for *initial* characterizations of the F phenomena.

(i) The "considered judgments" of the theorist himself (as described by Daniels, see above, pp. 11–12). (These are judgments in which the theorist is relatively confident, and which are made under conditions generally conducive to avoiding errors of judgment.)
(ii) Judgments on which there is consensus across a relevant community. For Jane English[18] these judgments are likely to be highly specific, such as "a detailed story about stealing a loaf of bread to save one's dying mother". For Nielsen[19] the judgments are general and "truisms," such as the (prima facie) wrongness of torturing the innocent, lying, breaking faith with people.
(iii) What Aristotle calls the *endoxa* (i.e., the "common conceptions" on a subject acceptable to the "many or the wise").

Given that my task is to offer an account of a highly contested concept, rather than of a "thin" moral concept such as prima facie wrongness, there are serious problems with (i) and (ii). Even where WRE as opposed to NRE is employed, rendering coherent the beliefs of the theorist may reveal nothing more than the structure of the theorist's own possibly idiosyncratic conception of F. If only judgments of type (i) are included in the "data" to be cohered, there is a danger that important points of view, included in the endoxa, but disbelieved by the theorist *in advance of the reasoning involved in attaining reflective equilibrium*, will not be included.

The problem with (ii) is that, in the area of contested concepts such as freedom, consensus on even paradigm cases is often very hard to find, as we shall see below. Nor is there, *pace* Rawls, MacCallum, and Lukes, always (if ever) consensus on a

---

18. "Ethics and Science" (paper written for 1978 International Congress of Philosophy).
19. "On Needing a Moral Theory," *Metaphilosophy*, XIII (1982): 97–116, esp. p. 99.

core or schematic concept of F.[20] The best place to start is where Aristotle starts—with the endoxa. The endoxa, being the beliefs of "the many or the wise," are not the beliefs of the theorist, nor are they beliefs of the theorist about what "we ordinarily say." As the literature on, e.g., justice and freedom reveals with depressing regularity, the latter beliefs are in considerable conflict. A theorist such as Parent[21] may *claim*, by an appeal to "ordinary usage," that an agent who hands over money at gunpoint is free (in a political and social sense) and has merely had his "will undermined." Nonetheless, the denial of the claim is an endoxon, for it is believed not only by the many but also by many of the wise as well. The endoxa are a much more reliable guide to our conceptions than are the ordinary language intuitions of any individual philosopher. Indeed, they "record our usage and the structure of thought and belief which usage displays."[22] Where F is contested, the endoxa reveal that fact right at the outset. All the relevant data are before us in the initial stages, and it is the task of the theorist to determine what is reasonable in the rival viewpoints. The confronting of initial characterizations of the F phenomena by rival conceptions of F (as is recommended by the method of WRE) is of little use if those characterizations are highly selected in such a way as not to reveal the contestedness of F.

It may now be asked: Why WRE? Why not simply set out the endoxa given that they record "our usage and the structure of thought and belief"? The answer is, of course, that the endoxa exhibit considerable tension and cannot provide in their raw form a coherent conception of F. According to Nussbaum,

> The *phainomena* present us with a confused array, often with direct contradiction. They reflect our disagreements and ambivalences. The first step [in theory construction] must, therefore, be to bring conflicting opinions to the surface and set them out clearly, marshalling the considerations for and against each side, showing clearly how the adoption of a certain position on one

---

20. See further above, and my "Is the Difference Principle a Principle of Justice?" *Mind*, XC (1981): 415–21, and "The Concept of Overall Freedom," *Australasian Journal of Philosophy*, LVII (1979): 337–49.
21. "Freedom as the Non-Restriction of Options," *Mind*, LXXXIII (1974): 432–4.
22. Cf. Nussbaum, "Saving Aristotle's Appearances."

Chapter 2 Coherence Theory

issue would affect our position on others (*op. cit.*, p. 276).

As a result, the setting out of the endoxa cannot be the last word in revealing the *F* phenomena—the endoxa are the first word only. They are the first word because they "record our usage": they cannot be the last word since "the record" presents a "confused array." The theorist thus requires background theories to enable her to see the rationale of the endoxa. Once such theories have been found, the endoxa can be recast in such a way that they do not contradict each other, and in a way that preserves their point. The recast endoxa describe the *F* phenomena.

We here see that the classificatory interests that give point to the endoxa are not at all obvious. As a result, a mistake must be avoided. It must not be assumed that certain endoxa are licensed "correct" and others "incorrect" by appeals to the theorist's intuitions about what we "ordinarily say." Endoxa can be rejected only *after* WRE is completed: only after a view of the point of the classification is argued for. Until that point is reached, an endoxon remains as a datum on the grounds that it presumptively reveals something of our conception of *F*. Analogously, a symptom may presumptively be regarded as a symptom of multiple sclerosis as long as it is a member of a relevant cluster of symptoms. Only after a causal hypothesis about the cause of multiple sclerosis has been formed can the symptom be rejected as a genuine symptom of multiple sclerosis.

The employment of this analogy raises an important objection to the method of WRE. The discovery of a hitherto unknown virus may give ground for a rejection of a symptom as one of multiple sclerosis. But why should an account of the point of classifying a set of phenomena as *F* give one grounds for rejecting an endoxon? Why not say instead that the nonaccommodation of an endoxon gives one grounds for rejecting the favored account of the point of the classification? This kind of objection to WRE has been raised by David Copp.[23] He claims that, if a "considered judgment" fails to cohere with a coherent package, then that judgment impugns the status of that package as justified. For, according to Copp, in Daniels's theory, the

---

23. "Considered Judgments and Moral Justification: Conservatism in Moral Theory," in Copp and Zimmerman, eds., pp. 141–68.

lack of fit with that judgment shows that one has not reached equilibrium.

The following reply might be attempted. Copp's claim is true, *until such time* as the considered judgment is rejected. The recalcitrant judgment impugns the coherent package as justified, but only provisionally: once that judgment is discarded, then, ceteris paribus, the package is justified. This reply, however, invites another objection. If one can render a package justified by the mere act of choice to reject a judgment, then there are no objective standards of justification.[24] One can simply choose whether or not to remain in a state of disequilibrium by rejecting the judgment. The former choice results in an unjustified package, the latter in a justified one.

(iv) *The Appropriate Kind of Coherence*

In this section, we present our reply to Copp. In short, we reject the reply to Copp outlined at the end of the previous section. It is not the case that once equilibrium is reached, there is necessarily complete justification, nor is it the case that, failing equilibrium, there is necessarily complete lack of justification. Rather, there are objective standards of appropriate coherence independent of the attainment of equilibrium. Let me elaborate. It was stated in section (i) that WRE is a *device* or tool for discovering which rival conceptions of F are more or less justified (i.e., more or less accurate specifications of "our" conception of F). A description of the *device* does not itself offer standards of justification of conceptions generated by use of the device. Indeed, it cannot, for as is frequently emphasized, employment of WRE may result in several coherent packages of beliefs, and we do not want to say that all are equally well justified. Although it is argued (e.g., by Daniels[25]) that such employment should eventually result in greater convergence of belief systems, Rawls himself is skeptical of this.[26] Despite a potential lack of convergence, it is possible, however, to offer

---

24. See W. E. Cooper's attack on "constructivist" models of reflective equilibrium in "Taking Reflective Equilibrium Seriously," *Dialogue*, XX (1981): 549–55.
25. In "Wide Reflective Equilibrium and Theory Acceptance in Ethics."
26. He claims, in "The Independence of Moral Theory": "Even should everyone attain wide reflective equilibrium, many contrary moral conceptions may still be held." Nor is it the case that one will necessarily "win out over the rest" (p. 9).

standards of justification—standards of *appropriate* coherence—according to which a conception generated by one WRE is superior to one generated by another. It is even possible that a conception that belongs to a package of beliefs *not* in equilibrium is superior to one that belongs to a relatively inferior package in equilibrium. If this is possible, it is not the case that a mere act of choosing to reject a judgment will change a package from justified to unjustified. Such a choice may render a noncoherent set of beliefs coherent, but coherence of beliefs may not be the only standard of justification for conceptions in WRE.

The following dimensions of evaluation are relevant.

(a) *The degree of coherence of beliefs achieved.*

This includes coherence between the pruned and adjusted judgments, and between the pruned and adjusted judgments and the other elements of WRE. It includes also, of course, the quality of the reasoning used in achieving coherence.

(b) *The quality of the initial data.*

On our account, this includes the degree to which the endoxa are reflected in the initial judgments to be cohered. The more and the more basic the endoxa that are included, the better is the ensuing WRE, ceteris paribus; the fewer the beliefs included that are not endoxa the better is the WRE, ceteris paribus.

(c) *The extent to which the beliefs in equilibrium have been subjected to the pressure of rival viewpoints.*[27]

For example, a WRE that has considered the strengths of a large and varied range of conceptions of F is more justified, ceteris paribus, than an equilibrium that considers only a very limited range of conceptions. Thus, it is arguable that Rawls's theory of justice would be more justified if it had considered the credentials of the patterned conception of justice, "To each according to her needs"—a conception that is not included in the list of conceptions considered by parties in the "Original Position." For, Barry[28] argues, people with a maximin strategy would be concerned that the problem of pockets of poverty cannot be tackled in a society whose institutions conform to the "Difference Principle," which is a limited aggregative principle.

---

27. Cf. Brian Ellis: "An ideally rational belief system is one which is in equilibrium under the most acute pressures of internal criticism and discussion" (*Rational Belief Systems* [American Philosophical Quarterly Library of Philosophy, 1979], p. 4.

28. *The Liberal Theory of Justice* (New York: Oxford, 1973).

(d) *The extent to which the endoxa are preserved.*
As Nussbaum notes, Aristotle frequently criticizes theorists who resolve puzzles and tensions in the endoxa by rejecting them: "What all these thinkers did, evidently, was to begin in the right way, with the *endoxa*; but then they got fascinated with the internal progress of their argument and trusted the argument, even though it ended in a place incredibly remote from, and at odds with, human beliefs" (*op. cit.*, p. 277).

To illustrate this point, consider the apparent tension between the following endoxa concerning freedom.

1. One cannot be unfree to do what one in fact does.
2. In New Zealand one was until recently unfree to commit sodomy.
3. The highway robber who utters a credible threat, "Your money or your life," renders you unfree in that situation.

Some theorists are so committed to the truth of the first of these judgments *as it stands* that they reject the latter two despite the fact that belief in them is extremely prevalent. For example, Parent[29] claims that only obstacles that *prevent* performance of actions render an agent unfree: threats do not deprive an agent of freedom at all, but merely "undermine the will." On the view canvassed, however, a better theory possesses a theoretical apparatus that removes the tension between the judgments in a way that preserves the point of both. Such a theory may employ a distinction between the availability and eligibility of options, claiming that the highwayman renders the option of not yielding to his demands extremely ineligible, though still available. (Not yielding to the threat, we assume, is within his power.) If the degree of an agent's freedom is held to be a function of both availability and eligibility of options, the tension between the judgments can be resolved: the first focuses on the freedom afforded an agent by the availability of options; the latter focuses on unfreedom resultant on the rendering of options in a certain way ineligible. In short, a theory that recasts the endoxa in a way that preserves more, and more basic, endoxa is better justified than one that preserves fewer and less basic ones.

---

29. "Freedom as the Non-Restriction of Options."

There are various ways of preserving apparently incompatible endoxa. One way is to reject monistic conceptions in favor of pluralistic conceptions. For example, the principle of justice, "Do not use people merely as a means to the ends of others," could be seen as expressing a weighty prima facie obligation overrideable in given circumstances by even more weighty considerations. Alternatively, or in addition, conceptions could be given wider rather than narrower interpretations. The Kantian imperative just mentioned, for example, need not be given an interpretation as narrow as Robert Nozick's,[30] according to whom one violates the imperative if and only if one uses the entitlements of another without his consent, where entitlements are determined by a narrow libertarian conception of justice.

(e) *The extent to which preserved endoxa are shown to be reasonable.*

WRE is not just a matter of recasting endoxa so that they are rendered consistent. It must also be shown that they are worth preserving in a final conception of the ideal under investigation. This is achieved by the background theory that is designed to uncover the *point* of the endoxa. To the extent that this is not achieved, there is a temptation to downgrade the *contestedness* of ideals by speaking of ambiguity and disparate conceptions. Where desiderata (d) and (e) are both met, this temptation is yielded to as a last resort, rather than be an obvious starting point in analysis.

The relation between desideratum (e) and desideratum (d) merits discussion, for there is potential for conflict between them. The background theory provides a ground for the rejection of endoxa: endoxa are not retained if they are incompatible with the background theory, which must demonstrate their worthiness of preservation. At the same time, the background theory must construct a rationale for the endoxa which is designed to preserve as many as possible. The apparent tension is resolved by the fact that the background theory is tailored for the accommodation of as wide a range of endoxa as possible.

This solution, however, invites the charge of "gerrymandering": what kind of *justification* does the background theory provide for the retention of endoxa if its sole purpose is to preserve them in a way that coheres them? What happens to

---

30. *Anarchy, State, and Utopia* (New York: Basic, 1974).

requirement (e): the requirement that their *worthiness* to be retained is demonstrated? This criticism is met by proposing a constraint on the requirement that the background theory be "tailored" for the accommodation of the endoxa. The theory must be independently satisfying. The rationale for the retention of the endoxa is deep, and explains the significance of those endoxa. It must explain why people should want to focus on a heterogeneous range of phenomena, and invest them with a unitary significance.

On the assumption that desiderata (d) and (e) can both be met, the better theory, ceteris paribus, is the one that can *both* preserve significant, albeit conflicting, endoxa, *and* provide the most satisfying explanation of their worthiness.

To summarize. In reply to Copp, I claimed that it is not the case that reaching equilibrium—where all recalcitrant judgments have been jettisoned—results in complete justification of a package. There are standards of evaluation of appropriate coherence, other than harmony between the various elements of a package in WRE. WRE—a device for choosing between value conceptions in the sense specified—is also a powerful *justificatory* tool when supplemented by those standards. Even if this enriched WRE does not yield a doxastic decision procedure in Goldman's sense, it enables one to make progress in justifying as adequate certain value or moral conceptions, and in rejecting some packages in WRE as inferior to others. If this is true, then value conceptions such as freedom and justice are not *essentially* contested in the following strong sense of that phrase: no justificatory procedure can be employed to adjudicate between them.

PART II

The Background Theory

Chapter 3

A Defeasibility Account of Freedom

(i) Introduction

The task of this and the next chapter is to develop a background theory, the aim of which is two-fold. First, the theory must enable the coherence theorist to detect the rationale of an array of mutually incompatible endoxa, and to uncover the strengths of a bewildering variety of conceptions of freedom supported by those endoxa. WRE, it will be remembered, is not a one-way accommodation of theory to endoxa. One does not eliminate tensions among the endoxa by eliminating those less strongly believed by oneself or least supported by one's favored conception. Rather, resolving tensions involves subjecting any such "narrow" equilibrium to the pressures of rival viewpoints. As Rawls states, adherence to a favored conception comes only after consideration of those rival viewpoints. This process can be satisfactory, however, only if the strengths of those viewpoints are identified.

Second, the background theory is intended to help govern the way in which coherence is to be achieved. Coherence is governed by the need to preserve the strengths of rival conceptions of freedom, as revealed by that theory. Instead of the favored conception of freedom being derived directly from a relatively haphazard and unguided scrutiny of various "ordinary" locutions, the progress of the coherence theory as a whole is continuously governed by the background theory. Thus, appeal to the authority of the endoxa is not decisive.[1]

Rather, the point of those judgments is sought by reference to the background theory; and the need to accommodate that point will determine retention or modification of those judgments.

Rawls, too, is emphatic in his claim that definitions and "analyses of meaning" provide an insufficient base for a *theory* of the nature of an ideal such as justice:

> A theory of justice is subject to the same rules of method as other theories. Definitions and analyses of meaning do not have a special place: definition is but one device used in setting up the general structure of theory. Once the whole framework is worked out, definitions have no distinct status and stand or fall with the theory itself (TJ, p. 51).

With the conclusions of chapters 3 and 4, the aim of the background theory is realized, viz., the characterization of the point of freedom in terms sufficiently broad as to reveal the rationale and reasonableness of a wide variety of contradictory endoxa and contested conceptions of freedom, while pointing the way to a unified account of the nature of freedom.

(ii) *A Defeasibility Account of Freedom*

In this section and the next chapter, I elaborate and defend from various objections the view that the endoxa—the initial characterization of the freedom phenomena—can be understood as a reasonable collocation if the following view is held about the point of the collocation.

---

1. Cf. J. L. Austin: "Certainly, then, ordinary language is not the last word. . . . Only remember it *is* the first word"; "A Plea for Excuses," in *Philosophical Papers*, J. O. Urmson and G. J. Warnock, eds., 2nd ed. (New York: Oxford, 1970), pp. 175–204, p. 185.

Chapter 3 A Defeasibility Account of Freedom

(T): The freedom phenomena are constituted by the absence of various flaws, breakdowns, and restrictions on human practical activity, namely, those which limit the *potential* of human beings as agents.

There are two important ideas here which will be developed in this and the next section. The first is that freedom is constituted by absences of various kinds. Specifically, freedom is an absence of limitations in the practical activity of human beings characterized in its more complex manifestations by several stages: the acquisition of desires, deliberation, the formation of practical judgments and intentions, and the execution of intentions. The second idea is that the limitations constituting unfreedom are of a certain type—those breakdowns, restrictions, and flaws in practical activity which limit a human being's potential in her role as agent. The first of these ideas relates to the structure of our notion of freedom as a defeasibility concept; the second imparts substance to this structure.

The structure of our concept of freedom is best elaborated by reference to J. L. Austin's "defeasibility" conception of freedom outlined in "A Plea for Excuses." According to Austin, freedom is the absence of breakdowns and flaws of various kinds which beset our practical activity—what he tends to call "the machinery of action." This term is intended to connote the idea that action not merely embraces the physical movement but is a complex process comprising several aspects and stages. To suggest this idea, I shall speak of practical activity, which I understand to be a process that focuses desires onto the world through intentional action. I shall say a little more about the nature of practical activity before elaborating on Austin's views and defending them from criticism.

Practical activity is a process that, if successful and completed, terminates in, or is simply constituted by, intentional action. Intentional action is taken to be action of the type characterized by G.E.M. Anscombe in *Intention*:[2] "What distinguishes actions which are intentional from those which are not? The answer I shall suggest is that they are actions to which a certain sense of the question 'Why?' is given application; the sense is of course that in which the answer, if positive, gives a reason for acting" (*ibid.*, p. 9). I do not argue for this thesis, which I take to be a

---

2. 2nd ed. (New York: Blackwell, 1957).

conceptual truth. As such, it is neutral between various contingent theses about the existence or nature of intentions, which may or may not be held to *cause* intentional actions. More generally, I take Anscombe's view to be consistent with both the affirmation and the denial of the following general causalist proposition viewed as a *contingent* truth about the nature of intentional action:

> (P): *All* intentional actions are caused by mental events (event causalism), or mental acts (agent causalism), be these items introspectible or not.

Anscombe's thesis is not, however, consistent with (P) viewed as a conceptual truth concerning our "folk psychology." For it is conceptually possible that an action be intentional in Anscombe's sense even where there are no preceding mental acts or events that cause that action. I believe, however, that the subsequent discussion about the distinctive aspects of practical activity undermine the credibility of (P) viewed as a conceptual truth.

The view of intentional action outlined accords with Austin's own position that success in intentional action is not essentially characterized by the presence of a single mental item, such as an "intention" or a "volition," but by the absence of the various types of infelicity that mar the practical process. 'Freedom' connotes the absence of some of those infelicities. In more detail, his view of the structure of freedom comprises three theses.

> (1) 'Freedom' signifies a set of standards to be met by what Austin calls the "machinery of the successful act." This is what Austin means when he claims that "As 'truth' is not a name for a characteristic of assertions, so freedom is not a name for a characteristic of actions, but the name of a dimension in which actions are assessed" (*op. cit.*, p. 180). I should prefer to say that freedom is the name of a set of dimensions in which actions are assessed (see chapter 6), for the free act is an act possessing the complex property of meeting *various* standards.
>
> (2) The freedom standards to be met by what Austin calls the machinery of the act are various and complex. For, first, these standards are associated with the act viewed as a process, and concern "different parts of the machinery" of the act (*op. cit.*, p. 180). Second, the "ma-

chinery of the act" is itself complex. The notion of an act is not a simple notion, such as the making of a physical movement, but includes "the detail of the complicated internal machinery we use in 'acting'—the receipt of intelligence, the appreciation of the situation, the invocation of principles, the planning, the control of execution and the rest" (*op. cit.*, p. 171).

(3) The freedom-standards to be met by the successful act are not to be described as *presences* of items (introspectible or otherwise) that *cause* bona fide free action (such as volitions or intentions viewed as antecedent mental entities or episodes). Rather, they are to be described as *absences*, viz., the absence of "breakdowns" of "radically different kinds" which afflict the "different parts of the machinery" of the act (*op. cit.*, p. 180). For Austin, "like 'real', 'free' is used only to rule out the suggestion of some or all of its recognized antitheses" (*op. cit.*, p. 180). In short, it is 'unfree' which "wears the trousers": 'free' merely signals the *absence* of all, or some, typical breakdowns besetting practical activity.

In subsequent chapters, it will be demonstrated how an Austinian notion of freedom fulfils the task of the background theory—viz., to reveal the reasonableness of a wide variety of conflicting endoxa, and the rationale for their classification as describing the freedom phenomena. Austin's defeasibility notion has been subject to criticism, however, which we now consider.

In his article "Responsibility," Vinit Haksar[3] claims there is a central inconsistency in the defeasibility account. First, the defeasibility theorist claims that it is the various specific and heterogeneous ways of being unfree that "wear the trousers." Second, there is no way of enumerating in advance all the ways of being unfree. Given these two features, we need some kind of principle or rationale for determining when a phenomenon is a case of unfreedom—the presentation of a mere list of freedom phenomena cannot be given. If there is a single rationale for collocating a set of heterogeneous phenomena as unfree, however, then here would be "something positive that is common to

---

3. *Proceedings of the Aristotelian Society*, Supp. Volume XL (1966): 187–222.

all free actions and missing in all unfree actions, and free action would not be a defeasible concept" (*ibid.*, p. 189).

The way to resolve this apparent tension is to recognize that freedom is a *formal* property in the sense elaborated by Kovesi (*op. cit.*, pp. 1–36). A formal property is both supervenient on other properties, and defined by the *point* of the classification of objects with varying perceivable qualities in certain ways rather than others. For example, being a table is defined in terms of its role or function in the satisfaction of human needs and interests—viz., to fulfil our need for flat surfaces relative to our height when sitting. Being a table is not defined in terms of suitable clusters of (or family resemblances among) various perceivable properties (e.g., being made of wood, having four legs, having a surface parallel to the ground)—properties which Kovesi labels *material* and on which being a table is supervenient.

Freedom, too, is a formal property. The point of classifying a group of heterogeneous properties as 'free' is the perceived value those properties have in our functioning well in practical activity. As we shall see, there is a great variety of "material" properties of freedom, such as being unforced, being chosen—properties on which freedom is supervenient—but none of these properties should be seen as defining of freedom.

The recognition that freedom is a formal property allows us both to affirm that there is a single rationale for collocating a set of heterogeneous phenomena as unfree *and* to affirm that freedom is a defeasible concept. The single rationale is given by the idea of freedom as (T) which defines (in broad terms) the formal property of freedom. So *in a sense* there is something "that is common to all free actions and missing in all unfree actions." Nonetheless, freedom is a defeasible concept for the simple reason that the ways in which phenomena can fail to exemplify that formal property are multifarious and nonenumerable. Because freedom is a formal property, the principle of collocation of the "freedom phenomena" does not point to a single discriminable property that one of two otherwise identical objects can lack and the other possess. Rather, the principle merely rationalizes the collocation of a set of objects which have perhaps no material properties in common, and which cannot be exhaustively enumerated in advance. The reason 'free' is defeasible is that unfree acts are those which in various ways breach certain standards, and the ways in which those breaches are manifested

Chapter 3 A Defeasibility Account of Freedom

in specific stages of practical activity cannot be exhaustively specified in advance.

A second major criticism of Austin's defeasibility account of freedom misrepresents the nature of his account. There has been confusion between his views and those propounded by Nowell Smith[4] and Richard N. Bronaugh.[5] According to the latter philosophers, freedom is the absence of particular excuses. Nowell Smith states: ". . . in deciding whether an action was voluntary or not, we do not look for a positive ingredient, but rather for considerations that would preclude its being voluntary and thereby exonerate the agent" (*op. cit.*, p. 293). In like manner he claims: ". . . compulsions are not objects inside us; and we use the word 'compulsion', not because we have isolated and identified the object which caused [a person] to do what he did, but because we want to excuse him in the same sort of way that we excuse someone who is literally pushed. . . ." (*op. cit.*, p. 296). This particular defeasibility account of freedom has been justifiably criticized, but has been wrongly attributed to Austin by Haksar (*op. cit.*) and Robert Young.[6] In "A Plea for Excuses," Austin nowhere claims that the breakdowns in the machinery of action necessarily operate as excuses, although they frequently do. He nowhere affirms the view, attributed to him by Young (albeit with caveats), that ". . . the concept of freedom can be explained negatively by reference to the absence of particular excuses so that 'He did A freely' means (roughly anyway) 'His A'ing was not accidental, not a mistake, not done under duress and so on'" (*ibid.*, p. 81). Certainly, on Austin's view, the class of free acts includes actions satisfying the descriptions: "His A'ing was not accidental, not a mistake, not done under duress," and so on; however, the principle for inclusion in this class is *not* the absence of particular excusing conditions, but rather the absence of certain kinds of breakdown in the machinery of action. Austin also claims that various excuses "signalize" breakdowns, but he nowhere *defines* freedom in terms of absence of excuse. Young and others are right to point out that not all unfree acts excuse, but Austin can accept that, for not all breakdowns excuse.

---

4. *Ethics* (Harmondsworth: Pelican, 1954).
5. "Freedom as the Absence of an Excuse," *Ethics*, LXXIV (1963–64): 161–73.
6. *Freedom, Responsibility and God* (New York: Macmillan, 1975).

(iii) *Human Potential in Agency*

Austin's defeasibility conception of freedom serves admirably as the basis of the background theory. The idea that freedom connotes the absence of a wide variety of limitations in the practical process rather than the presence or absence of a relatively homogeneous type of item shows promise of permitting the accommodation of a wide range of endoxa. Although Austin's conception provides the bones of our theory, it does not provide the meat. There is not yet enough substance to govern the way coherence is to be achieved and to provide the rationale for the preservation of endoxa. There are all kinds of flaws in the practical process, not all of which bear on freedom. If those limitations providing excuses do not fix on the correct area, what kinds of limitations do?

To answer this question, we need to propose a hypothesis about the distinctive point of classifying a range of phenomena as freedom phenomena. It will be recalled that the formal property of freedom is defined by the point of classifying heterogeneous phenomena—with perhaps no material properties in common—in a specific way. This point is given by the value that freedom is perceived to possess. The remainder of this section is devoted to developing a hypothesis about the nature of this value, a hypothesis whose adequacy is determined by the requirements of an adequate coherence theory given above (chapter 2).

The hypothesis is:

> (T_1) The perceived value of freedom lies in the value of realizing the various aspects of individual human potential in agency, for the actualization of potential in this area contributes to individual flourishing.

(T_1) provides the basis of the claim that the formal property of freedom is constituted by those limitations in practical activity which impede development of individual potential in agency. Something is a *limitation* relative to some end, goal, value, or comparison class. Thus, the practical activity of a human being may be limited with respect to a value, such as justice or efficiency, with respect to a social or divine purpose, with respect to the practical activity of beings of superior intelligence, and so on. I shall develop the view that limitations related to the *free-*

dom of a given individual are relative to the potential of that individual in agency.

Individual human potential in agency has several aspects, some of which are more normative than others. As this work progresses, we shall see that notions of freedom, too, are more or less normative, according to their focus on the different aspects of potential in agency. In a relatively nonnormative sense of potential in agency the notion relates to capacity, in particular the capacity to bring about states of affairs. If alternatives are blocked, or opportunities are lacking, my capacities in this sense are limited. In this sense of potential, there is no suggestion that the agent has propensities or tendencies to bring about outcomes, nor that the capacities to bring them about are valuable. Even in this weak sense of potential, however, there is a perceived prima facie value in the expansion as opposed to the limitation of potential, for, ceteris paribus, expansion rather than limitation of options contributes to individual flourishing. For there is a value in deliberation among alternatives and the exercise of choice, as well as in the quality of the objects chosen, as J. S. Mill recognized. Nonetheless, the value of the expansion of an individual's capacity to bring about states of affairs is more or less easily overridden if the alternatives are evil, stultifying, or otherwise undesirable, or if the factors blocking off those alternatives are legitimate in various ways.

In another sense, "potential in agency" signifies the propensity or tendency to perform certain actions. The tendency or propensity of a thing is its likely behavior given opportunity and lack of constraint. The notion of potential in this sense does not presuppose assessment of particular propensities in terms of their conduciveness to the flourishing of the individuals possessing them. One can possess propensities inimical to flourishing. Nonetheless, there is a perceived prima facie value in providing opportunities and removing constraints on the realization of propensities, for one element of flourishing is the absence of excessive dissatisfaction or frustration, the absence of despair, impotent anger, and so forth. Again, however, this value is more or less easily overridden if the propensities are evil or do not conduce to flourishing in its more important aspects, or if the obstacles on their realization are legitimate or their removal illegitimate.

In the richest sense of potential in agency, that potential is not just one component or aspect of flourishing qua agent: it is synonymous with that flourishing. A person realizes his potential if and only if he flourishes or is "self-realized." This conception of potential presupposes a value-based selection of capacities and propensities to be realized by the flourishing agent.

We shall presently discuss problems concerning the nature of flourishing and the connection between flourishing and value. First, we should indicate how freedom bears on individual potential in agency. As we have seen, human potential in agency has various aspects, and, as will be revealed in more detail later, different conceptions of freedom bear on different aspects of potential in agency. Some conceptions of freedom—those which emphasize the absence of restrictions on alternatives—focus on limitations of potential as capacity. Others focus on potential as propensity or tendency. Thus, conceptions of freedom as the absence of obstacles to the realization of desired actions (as opposed to action in general) see unfreedom as a limitation not on capacity but rather on propensity. Finally, there are virtue-oriented conceptions of freedom for which the relevant notion of potential is the most highly normative—viz., self-realization or flourishing.

The claim that freedom is a value related to individual human potential in agency accounts for the valorization of freedom in some cultures and the comparative hostility accorded to the value in others. As Richard E. Flathman[7] points out, it is not self-evident that freedom has high value: for some societies, a preoccupation with individual potential militates against "extra- or supra-individual goods and ideals," such as the good of the collectivity, class, party, or, I may add, the wider ecology; or it conflicts with some putative divine will. Nonetheless, agreement about the nature of the value of freedom may survive disagreement about the weight to accord freedom when it conflicts with other values.

It is time to say more about the nature of the value of freedom. According to (T_1), the perceived value of freedom lies in the value of realizing the various aspects of individual human potential in agency, for the actualization of potential in this area contributes to human flourishing. The connection between flourishing of organisms and value, however, is problematic. Is

---

7. *The Philosophy and Politics of Freedom* (Chicago: University Press, 1987): 229–30.

there even a prima facie value to the flourishing of any given organism, for example, the AIDS virus? Nonetheless, in speaking of the perceived value of human freedom, this interesting and difficult problem need not bother us: those societies which value freedom highly perceive the flourishing of individual humans to be of extremely high value. From the truth of this perception, it does not follow, of course, that it is always wrong to interfere with or inhibit the flourishing of the individual (including its freedom) for the sake of societal goals.

There remain problems, however, with the nature of the connection between human flourishing and value. The basic worry may be expressed as follows. First, one cannot posit a value-free notion of flourishing if one is to erect on that foundation a system of value. On the other hand, if the notion is value-impregnated, the following dilemma arises. Either the founding of any value system on a conception of flourishing is circular, or conceptions of flourishing are too thin to provide an adequate foundation for any value system sufficiently rich to do justice to our moral practices and conceptions.

I shall grant that flourishing is a normative notion. There seems to be no nonnormative way of fixing on the characteristics that comprise flourishing, although some of the arguments for that claim are defective. For example, Bernard Williams[8] attacks attempts to found a conception of flourishing on a nonnormative notion of human essence. He wrongly identifies essential characteristics of humans with characteristics distinctive to humans, however, and the notion of flourishing with *maximizing* those characteristics. With these dubious assumptions, the attempted reductio of nonnormative notions of flourishing is all too easy to achieve:

> If one approached without preconceptions the question of finding characteristics which differentiate men from other animals, one could as well, on these principles, end up with a morality which exhorted men to spend as much time as possible in making fire; or developing peculiarly human physical characteristics; or having sexual intercourse without regard to season; or despoiling the environment and upsetting the balance of nature; or killing things for fun (*op. cit.*, p. 73).

8. *Morality: An Introduction to Ethics* (New York: Cambridge, 1972).

Focusing on distinctive characteristics that are also *sine qua non* characteristics may do greater justice to the efforts of founding conceptions of flourishing on essence. But what could those characteristics be? I can think of no better candidate than Aristotle's distinctively human rationality. A conception of rationality that is sufficiently rich to found a conception of flourishing must, however, include more than instrumental rationality but also, as Aristotle's does, rationality of ends. But any conception of rationality of ends must have normative elements built in.

Founding a conception of flourishing on a purely nonnormative notion of essence is problematic. Rather, one must accept at the outset that, fixing on the characteristics constitutive of flourishing, is a normative enterprise. Given this, our first task is to avoid the charge of circularity. The charge is avoided if the normative elements determining a conception of flourishing are thinner than the value system erected on that conception.

Let us now provide an outline of a conception that satisfies this condition. Individual flourishing is constituted by the satisfaction and development of those needs and capacities which, under good conditions, human beings characteristically desire to satisfy and develop, and whose development and satisfaction they enjoy under those conditions. The notion of good conditions is, of course, value-impregnated, but those values may be relatively austere as opposed to heavily ideological. Good conditions would be defined by, e.g., conditions conducive to absence of suicidal tendencies, chronic exhaustion, and lassitude; absence of chronic boredom, ennui, anxiety, loneliness, severe stress, feelings of worthlesssness; absence of brainwashing, terror, fear, coercion. Thus, the fact that sex is not desired under conditions of chronic fatigue, stress, or fears of dying agonizingly in childbirth will not militate against a claim that sex is a human need that humans characteristically desire to satisfy.

The norms defining good conditions are not necessarily derived from statistical norms. Even if every elm tree dies as a sapling of Dutch Elm disease, it does not follow that the flourishing elm tree has a brief life. Second, the norms defining good conditions define what is good or optimal for the *individual* and not necessarily the *normal* conditions of growth and development. In their normal undiseased, good environment, nearly all sugar maple seedlings die through lack of light: they grow to

Chapter 3 A Defeasibility Account of Freedom

mature specimens only if an older tree falls, allowing light to penetrate. We are tempted to say here that in their normal course of development most maples fail to realize their potential. Here, individual flourishing is attained not by development under good conditions simpliciter, but by development under good and optimal conditions for the *individual*. These conditions are not necessarily optimal for the species.

This fact raises the following problem. Given that optimal conditions for the flourishing of the individual are not necessarily coincident with conditions of development characteristic of the species, it is problematic to form a direct link between the flourishing human and the characteristic or nondefective features of human qua species. A worker bee who fails to work ceaselessly under all possible working conditions may be defective as a worker bee, but does it thereby fail to flourish? Could it not free ride and live longer? Though this failure of guaranteed coincidence is a serious problem for conceptions of ethics based on a linkage between characteristic features of human qua species and human flourishing, it need not concern us, however. For according to (T_1), the particular point of *freedom* is related to *individual* flourishing. Henceforth, therefore, I shall speak of the flourishing of human beings as individuals, while mindful of the fact that the determination of desirable social arrangements, and even of the individual virtues, depends crucially on whether there are perceived tensions between the flourishing of single individuals, all individuals equally, the elite, the group or species as a whole, the wider ecological community, and so on.

Finally, it should be said that a conception of flourishing related to good conditions for individual development need not yield answers about values appropriate to conditions of scarcity, great evil, extreme fear, and social disintegration. The values erected on a conception of flourishing are relative not only to species, but also to the conditions under which they find themselves—their nature, the possibilities of their amelioration, and the costs to individuals of that amelioration.

Having clarified our conception of flourishing, we turn to the dilemma outlined above. I claimed that our conception of flourishing will avoid the charge of circularity, for that conception is thinner than a value system based on it. Let us now defend this claim.

Once the needs and capacities whose satisfaction and development are constitutive of individual human flourishing are identified, a (partial) value system can be erected. Social arrangements and the acquisition and possession of individual character dispositions and individual states will be defended as valuable on the basis of the conception of flourishing. For example, the individual character trait of temperance may be recognized as a virtue, or the state of freedom as valuable, since they conduce to flourishing. Circularity is avoided, because, for example, it may be moot whether or not some individual states or traits perceived as valuable are in fact conducive to flourishing. Does a high degree of choice, for example, produce anomie, or militate against communitarian values that are arguably more important for individual flourishing? Emile Durkheim's claims that enhancement of choice by reducing social regulation and role differentiation produce distressing mental conditions—leading even to suicide—are empirical claims. There need be no analytical connection between flourishing, as I have understood it, and choice expansion.

Claims that certain dispositions of character are virtues will also be controversial, for it may be disputed whether their cultivation conduces to flourishing. Is justice a virtue? Chastity? Humility? Even more obviously, there is controversy about which social arrangements conduce to flourishing. On this view, it is not even analytic to say that justice is a virtue of social arrangements (as Nietzsche recognized). (I have assumed that justice is defined in terms of the justice phenomena as determined by the endoxa (suitably pruned and adjusted) rather than as *whatever* institutional arrangements of rights and duties are as a matter of fact conducive to human flourishing.) (See further above, chapter 2, section (ii).) For most, it is obvious that justice is a virtue; nonetheless, as the works of Nietzsche remind us, conceptions of value founded on flourishing need not assume that this connection is analytic. Since the truth of these claims depends on empirical assumptions tested by psychological and sociological theories, circularity is avoided.

The points made above are compatible with the view that our conception of flourishing is value-impregnated. Our conception of "good conditions" is informed by very basic notions of what is evil, or "beyond the pale." Thus, one cannot define flourishing simply in terms of "value-neutral" psychological or behavioral states, such as contentment or being well adjusted, since we might be contented in, and well adjusted to, evil societies.[9] Contentment in Nazi Germany would be regarded as culpable complacency, requiring such dispositions as closing one's eyes to the facts, insensitivity to the sufferings of others, extreme insularity, and so on. The conditions of Nazi Germany would not be regarded as good conditions for the development of capacities and states that human beings typically desire and enjoy. Admittedly, then, the notion of good conditions in terms of which flourishing is defined is not value-theory-independent, but this is not a flaw provided that the conceptions of value erected on that basis are richer than the admittedly theory-dependent basis itself. That is, the equilibrium attained is wide rather than narrow, since it partakes of, e.g., psychological and sociological theories going beyond those employed in the conception of "good conditions."

We turn now to the other horn of the dilemma, namely, the accusation of "thinness." It appears that the charge of circularity can be met only at the cost of inviting the former charge. It is claimed[10] that conceptions of flourishing (which underpin virtue ethics and also, on my account, the value of freedom) provide an inadequate basis for a system of rules that fully determine ethical options as either required, prohibited, or permissible but not required. This claim, I believe, is true, both because of imprecision in any favored account of flourishing and because no unique way to flourish can be recovered from an account of human nature. In this, Bernard Williams[11] is correct:

> Even if we leave the door open to a psychology that might go some way in the Aristotelian direction, it is hard to believe that an account of human nature—if it is not already an ethical theory itself—will adequately determine one kind of ethical life as against others. Aristotle saw a certain kind of ethical, cultural and indeed political life as a harmonious combination of human potentialities, recoverable from an absolute understanding of nature. We have no reason to believe in that (*ibid.*, p. 52).

9. See further Abraham Maslow, *Towards a Psychology of Being*, 2nd ed. (New York: Van Nostrand Reinhold, 1968): 5–8.
10. By, e.g., Robert B. Louden, "On Some Vices of Virtue Ethics," *American Philosophical Quarterly*, XXI (1984): 227–35.
11. *Ethics and the Limits of Philosophy* (London: Fontana Press, 1985).

The charge of underdetermination of prescriptions by an underlying conception of flourishing is true, but is it damning? Maybe one should rail not at conceptions of value based on flourishing but at rule-governed systems that attempt to cover every contingency by rule. Those areas of our lives on which values impinge are complex and prone to conflict—it is not surprising therefore that rules will not cover every contingency. Despair at this fact arises only because of a false equation of underdetermination by rule with irrationality. Where precise rules run out, standards of reasonableness can still apply, and both performing and avoiding an action can be judged reasonable. The fact that 'dirty' is a vague term when applied to shoes does not suggest that the masters of Auckland Grammar are irrational to punish the worst breaches of the rule against dirty shoes. Nor does it suggest that, in borderline cases, standards of rationality in enforcing the rule do not exist. The masters should show discretion and humanity: polite warnings and turning a blind eye are both reasonable options; dragging a boy out by the ear and caning him in the corridor for wearing slightly dusty shoes is unreasonable, callous, and cruel.

At the level of social organization, too, there may be several reasonable ways of doing things, none of which is clearly the best. Reasonable variation can occur in such matters as standards of hospitality, social distance, expression of emotion, the use of tact or confrontation. Pluralism, of course, should not be equated with conventionalism or relativism. A society whose standards of hospitality have become so exaggerated that the community impoverishes itself can rightly be censured by appeal to a system of values based on conceptions of flourishing. Again, the value of tact and discretion, as opposed to confrontation, may become so distorted that organizations are enmeshed in a web of deceit and self-deception so damaging to communication that it becomes impossible to secure (or revise) their goals. Conceptions of value founded on flourishing permit pluralism, but this is not to say that rational appraisal of actions cannot occur in the absence of precise rules.

The enriched Austinian picture of freedom developed in this chapter will enable us to satisfy the requirements of our background theory, for it will enable us to see the rationale of the extremely varied endoxa of freedom. The collocation of a heterogeneous range of phenomena as one and all *freedom* phenomena will be seen to have a distinctive point, viz., their perceived value as constitutive of one aspect of well-functioning human practical activity, viz., that which relates to *individual potential in agency.*

Flourishing humans are not mere receptacles of pleasure, not merely preference satisfiers, not merely cogs in efficient societal arrangements, not merely instruments of grand social or divine purposes, and not merely interacters within just social structures. They are also individuals with their own goals, their own projects, their own intentions to implement—some of which may be incompatible with efficiency, justice, their own want satisfaction and that of others, and the maximization of their own and overall pleasure. It is this latter, intention-directed component of flourishing to which the value of freedom relates.

It must not be thought that this view of freedom is committed to the controversial view that, assuming freedom really does have the value it is perceived to have, it must *always* have value. It is true that, on this conception, freedom is always partially constitutive of a valuable complex, viz., human flourishing. But even if human flourishing always has value and, indeed, always has intrinsic value, it does not follow that freedom itself would always have value. In some contexts, the combination of freedom with undesirable states of affairs may change the character of the freedom itself as valuable. To give an analogy, let us assume that every intrinsically valuable state of affairs includes experiences of pleasure. It does not follow that pleasure is always valuable. Indeed, taking pleasure from cruelty may not only lack *any* value, but may make that state of affairs worse than a state of affairs where no pleasure is taken from cruelty. This possibility is quite consistent with the (undoubtedly implausible) view, for example, that all intrinsically valuable states of affairs are ones involving the pleasurable exercise of virtue.

To conclude. We have claimed that the freedom phenomena are constituted by the absence of various flaws, breakdowns, and restrictions on human practical activity, namely, those which limit the individual potential of human beings as agents. Potential in agency has three aspects: capacity, propensity, and flourishing or self-realization in agency. All three aspects find a voice in views of freedom. Virtue therefore has importance, but this importance is limited by a major factor. In imperfect worlds, there will be conflicts between the attainment of virtue, the enhancement of capacity, and the realization of propensity. This conflict arises from the fact that the propensities and capacities which people actually possess may not be ones that would have been acquired under the "good conditions" in terms of which flourishing is defined. Second, the costs of changing those propensities and capacities into those constitutive of flourishing may be great; indeed, it may be impossible to make the change.[12] There are therefore problems in assessing freedom in imperfect worlds. These problems are considered in chapters 11 and 12. In chapter 11, I discuss the concept of interests—a concept which is crucial for assessing lack of freedom, and which provides a conception of relative flourishing in imperfect worlds. In chapter 12, I discuss the problem of conflicts of freedom.

---

12. Indeed, Aristotle believes that a life, once ingrained in vice, is virtually unsusceptible of redemption; *Nichomachean Ethics*, 1114a, 8–27.

CHAPTER 4

Limitations in Practical Activity

(i) *The Connection between Freedom and Practical Activity*

According to the background theory as so far developed, the formal property of freedom is the absence of certain types of limitations in human practical activity, namely, those which limit individual potential in agency. The intimate connection between freedom and practical activity has implications about the nature of the endoxa concerning freedom. The purpose of this chapter is to discuss these implications. In this section, I consider the consequences of the view that freedom is connected with individual potential in *practical activity* as opposed to other areas of human life that affect flourishing. The *nature* of practical activity also has implications about the types of limitations that might reasonably be expected to bear on an agent's freedom. Accordingly, in section (ii), I shall examine in more detail the nature of practical activity, with a view to classifying the types of limitation that beset it (section (iii)). When this is done, we will be in a position to discern the point of the vast array of endoxa and conceptions of freedom.

Although the nature of limitations restricting freedom cannot be fully determined until the endoxa are considered, the mere fact that freedom is the absence of certain limitations on *practical activity* has certain important implications about which agents can properly be said to be free, which obstacles properly limit freedom, and which states constitute states of freedom or unfreedom. First, freedom cannot be identified with mere want satisfaction, or even the absence of obstacles to want satisfaction; for not all objects of desire are objects of practical activity (whether of deliberation, intention, or merely attempt, depending on how sophisticated that activity is). It is not a limitation of my freedom that the world contains objects hated by me such as ants, fundamentalists, or indecent behavior. It could be a limitation of my freedom, however, if I am prevented from acting, e.g., from attempting to exterminate ants or convert people to a decent way of life. Nor does it enhance my freedom that mere idle wishes of mine be satisfied, e.g., my wish to *be* a millionaire (as opposed to *taking steps* to be a millionaire). Further, doing things by accident, such as finding buried treasure by accident, cannot be something I am free or unfree to do, although, of course, I could be unfree to look for buried treasure.

Second, not all barriers and obstacles limit freedom, since not all barriers are barriers to practical activity. Hence the existence of fences and barriers designed to prevent accidents *protects* us from accidents and does not limit our freedom in this regard. Since falling is not an object of practical activity, a high fence does not limit our freedom *tout court*, but it may limit our freedom to commit suicide.

Finally, a consequence of the view that freedom is the absence of certain limitations in practical activity is that only beings capable of intentional action are proper subjects of freedom. This claim is not as controversial as it looks, however. In particular, I shall presently argue, I have not committed myself to the espousal of "rationalist" conceptions of freedom, such as those advocated by W. E. Connolly[1] and Benn.[2] According to Connolly: "X acts freely in doing Z when (or to the extent that) he acts without constraint upon his unconstrained and reflective *choice* with respect to Z" (*op. cit.*, p. 157). He rejects definitions of freedom in terms of wants "because the notion of a choice embodies more fully a reflective or deliberative dimension" (*op. cit.*, p. 157).

Again, Benn supposes that ascriptions of freedom or unfreedom "presuppose an agent in a standard choice- or decision-situation" in which he possesses "goals forming an ordered preference set in the light of which he makes choices" and a set of beliefs about resources at his disposal, his opportunity costs, and the relation between these and the realization of his goals.[3]

---

1. *The Terms of Political Discourse* (Lexington, MA: Heath, 1974).
2. "Freedom, Autonomy and the Concept of a Person, "*Proceedings of the Aristotelean Society*, LXXVI (1975–76): 109–130.
3. "Freedom, Autonomy and the Concept of a Person," p. 111.

Chapter 4 Limitations In Practical Activity

Such "rationalist" conceptions of freedom have been criticized on the grounds that they render nonsensical the claims that closing the door on a baby about to crawl through, forcibly removing the china ornament from its grasp, or locking it in an attic, do not invade its freedom.[4] Furthermore, aligning myself with those who espouse such rationalist conceptions of freedom would defeat a major purpose of the background theory, which is to demonstrate the rationale of a wide variety of conceptions of freedom. I do not wish to rule out, *ab initio*, such obviously important conceptions as Bertrand Russell's[5] notion of freedom as "the absence of obstacles to the realization of desire" (*ibid.*, p. 231) or Hobbes's[6] notion: "A free man is he that, in those things which by his strength and wit he is able to do, is not hindered to do what he has a will to do" (*ibid.*, ch. 21). Russell's and Hobbes's conceptions presuppose that desiring or willing beings are either free or unfree; and a being can desire or will without possessing the degree of practical and epistemic rationality required by Connolly and Benn. Clearly, the thwarted baby has willed (tried) to grasp the china ornament, to go through the door, even if it can provide no reasons for doing so.

My view that freedom is defined by the absence of certain limitations in practical activity does not commit me to the rationalist conceptions of freedom mentioned above, for the following reasons. First, intentional action as defined by Anscombe does not require a "reflective or deliberative dimension." Clearly an action may be intentional in Anscombe's sense in the absence of deliberation. Activity in accordance with unreflective following of rules counts as intentional if reasons for the activity can be provided *ex post facto*.

More importantly, as Anscombe argues in "Under a Description,"[7] her account of intentional action does not require that reasons for the action be articulable by the agent. Although the concept of practical activity has its natural home when applied to agents able to engage the full panoply of Aristotelian practical reasoning, the concept is applicable, by appropriate extension,

---

4. See Colin Lankshear, *Freedom and Education* (Auckland: Milton Brookes, 1982), pp. 51–2.
5. "Freedom and Government," in Ruth Nanda Anshen, ed., *Freedom, Its Meaning* (London: Allen, 1942).
6. *Leviathan*, ch. 21.
7. *Noûs*, XIII (1979): 219–33.

to cases well beyond its natural home. To be sure, in the standard or paradigm case the question—"Why did someone do that?"—is answered by asking the agent what her reasons were, but the ability to answer such questions is not necessary for action to be intentional. As Anscombe claims, to ascribe intentional action to an agent it is necessary to know under what description an action is intentional; but to do that in turn it is not necessary that the agent have a "thought *about* a description" (*ibid.*, p. 221). Intentional action not only does not require a "deliberative dimension," it does not require a "reflective dimension." She asks us to consider the case of a bird landing on a twig covered with bird lime. We can say that the bird's action was intentional because we can know under what description it is intentional. It is intentional under the description, 'landing on the twig', but not intentional under another description, 'landing on the bird lime'. The justification of this claim would be that "the bird meant (wanted) to land on the twig [to get at the nearby seed] but not to land on the bird lime" (*ibid.*).

I shall follow Anscombe in assuming that practical activity terminating in intentional action can be undertaken by non-language-using beings. Hence the background theory has not ruled out the claims of "non-rationalist" conceptions of freedom.

(ii) *The Nature of Practical Activity*

We turn now to the characterization of the various stages in the process of practical activity. Once its nature is understood, we can consider the notion of limitations in that activity. As I have said, typically, practical activity is a process of focusing desires onto the world through intentional action. In its most complex manifestations, practical activity comprises several stages. Agents' desires provide the rationale for practical activity; their deliberations rank their desires in order of importance, indicate their means of fulfillment, and determine when, how, and in what order they are to be fulfilled; their deliberations terminate in judgments about the thing to do; their intentions set their minds to performing the appropriate actions now or in the future; finally, they try to perform the relevant actions, and, barring breakdowns, those actions are performed.

It is not to be assumed that all these stages are present as separate mental acts or stages in all cases of practical rational activity; still less do I wish to make causalist assumptions about the relationships between those links. Nonetheless, there are differences between them, differences that become important in distinguishing the various types of flaw to which practical activity is subject. I shall briefly describe each stage in turn.

(a) *Desires.*

I shall take the orthodox view that, in many cases at least, the motivating force for practical activity is a desire for some end. It seems unnecessary, however, to postulate desires for ends as explaining *all* practical processes. I see a stone in front of me, and I immediately set myself to kick it with my right foot. It is not necessarily the case that one of the desires I possess as I walk down the footpath is to kick stones, or to kick the first large stone I see, and so on. Nor does it seem necessary to postulate the onslaught of an episode of desiring to kick *this* stone, which antedates the formation of an intention to kick it.

What is a desire? Anscombe's view that the "primitive sign of wanting is trying to get"[8] applies to the kind of desires which often initiate practical activity. This view is compatible with the drawing of a distinction between what Harry Frankfurt[9] calls "effective" and "noneffective desires." An *effective* desire is a desire that "moves (or will or would move) a person all the way to action" (*ibid.*, p. 8). The force of the 'would' here is mysterious: perhaps Frankfurt means that effective desires are ones that the agent *attempts* to act on and would succeed in acting on if certain conditions (unspecified) are met. On the other hand perhaps, noneffective desires are desires that "merely incline" an agent to act (*ibid.*). The force of 'merely' is also mysterious: however, I shall understand the qualifications as follows. Either the agent does not attempt to act on the desire, or, if he does, the attempt would be unsuccessful even if the (unspecified) conditions alluded to above are met.

For our purposes, the problem is to distinguish noneffective desires from what Anscombe calls "idle wishes" (*op. cit.*,

---

8. *Intention*, p. 66.
9. "Freedom of the Will and the Concept of a Person," *The Journal of Philosophy*, LXVIII, I (January 14, 1971): 5–20.

pp. 66ff.). The making of this distinction is important in our understanding of freedom. As I claimed above, the presence of obstacles to the realization of idle wishes is not an impairment of an agent's freedom. The way I distinguish idle wishes from noneffective desires when there is no attempt to act in accordance with them is this. In the case of a *noneffective desire* to *j*, an agent would attempt to *j* or take steps necessary to *j*ing, if

(1) she had the requisite capacities, opportunities, and knowledge;
(2) there is no conflicting desire that rationalizes some action that precludes *j*ing.

Where there is an idle wish to *j*, *j*ing may not be a logically proper object of attempt, or, if it is, there would be no attempt to *j* or to take steps necessary to *j*ing even where (1) and (2) above obtain. An idle wish to be a millionaire is not a desire to *bring it about* that I be a millionaire at all: it is *merely* a wish that I *be* in a certain state, e.g., "Would that I were Richard Hadlee!"

(b) *Practical Judgments.*

I shall understand a practical judgment to be a judgment of the form *j*ing is the thing to do. Such judgments need not be of the form "*j*ing is the *best* thing to do all things considered" or "*j*ing is better in the circumstances than any other available alternative," or even "*j*ing is better in the circumstances than any available alternative I am aware of." Satisficing or "satisizing" agents may form judgments about satisfactoriness or adequacy while refraining from making *any* of the above kinds of judgments.

Judgments about the thing to do are to be distinguished from judgments about what is good and fitting. The agent may in a given circumstance believe that what is good or fitting is not to be done; since the doing of that thing requires, for example, heroic or saintly behavior that the agent is disinclined to perform. Nor are judgments about the thing to do to be identified with effective desires. First, an agent may act on a desire without forming *any* judgment about the thing to do; for example, a baby reaching for a bright object. Secondly, there is the possibility (discussed below) that an agent may act on a strong or salient desire in ways contrary to his judgment about the thing to do.

(c) Deliberation.

Practical judgments are often made after a process of deliberation which ranks desires in order of priority, and which determines when, how, and in what order they are to be fulfilled. I understand deliberation to be a process of working out the thing to do. In cases where the time to act on that judgment is now, the judgment about the thing to do standardly coincides with the agent's attempting to do the thing in question. In cases of lack of resolution, however, and possibly also weakness of will, the judgment about the thing to do need not even match an agent's intention, let alone an attempt. For example, I may after deliberation judge that the thing to do is to read certain important philosophy books soon, but I may never set myself to do those things, or even to form *plans* to do them.

Deliberation is a process of *working out* what to do, but not all intentional actions are preceded by such a working out. For example, a baker taking a cake out of the oven may simply unreflectively apply a rule: an individual possessing requisite skills need not deliberate in a context where she is using those skills in standard circumstances. Furthermore, there are spontaneous acts that do not even appear to be preceded by a judgment about the thing to do. For example, my spontaneous kicking of a stone on the footpath does not appear to be preceded by such a judgment, let alone by deliberation. Yet such an action may be intentional in Anscombe's sense.

(d) Forming Intentions.

I shall understand an agent's forming of an intention to j as an agent's setting himself or herself to j now or in the future. Intentions are not to be identified with practical judgments. I may judge $j$ing to be the thing to do without setting myself to j; furthermore, I may set myself to j without judging that $j$ing is the thing to do. (I may make *no* such judgment [as in idly kicking stones], or, [if a certain account of weakness of will is accepted] I may set myself to do something contrary to that judgment.)

It is sometimes believed that one does not form an intention to j unless one believes one is *going* to j. This appears not to be the case. I may believe that I will break down under torture, but not intend to break down. Indeed, I may intend not to break down.[10]

The point of setting myself not to break down, however, is to attempt to falsify my belief—an attempt that I may know has virtually no chance of success. This point raises the vexed question of whether one can intend the impossible. The torturer example alluded to above is described more fully by Anscombe as follows: "In some cases one can be as certain as possible that one will do something, and yet intend not to do it. . . . A man could be as certain as possible that he will break down under torture, and yet determined not to break down" (*ibid.*). Irving Thalberg[11] apparently takes Anscombe to be affirming that one can intend what one believes to be impossible, for he believes Stuart Hampshire[12] to hold the "contrary" view, which he later describes thus: "It would be self-contradictory to say 'I intend that to happen, but . . . I believe that it is impossible'."[13] I believe Thalberg to be wrong in describing Anscombe's and Hampshire's views as contraries: indeed, I believe both views to be true. Hampshire claims that (1) is self-contradictory:

(1) I intend x, but I believe x to be impossible.

Anscombe claims that (2) is possible:

(2) I intend x, but I am as certain as possible that I will not do x.

I shall argue that a belief in the self-contradictory nature of (1) is consistent with a belief in the possibility of (2).

One might hold with Hampshire that (1) is contradictory in the way that (3) below is contradictory:

(3) I believe x but I believe x is false.

That (3) is self-contradictory is, however, consistent with (4) below being possible.

(4) I believe x but I am as certain as possible that x is false.

I take (4) to be equivalent to:

---

10. See Anscombe, *Intention*, p. 93.
11. "Can One Intend the Impossible?" in his *Enigmas of Agency* (London: Allen and Unwin, 1972).
12. *Thought and Action* (London: Chatto and Windus, 1959).
13. *Ibid.*, p. 134; quoted in Thalberg, p. 105.

(5) I believe *x* despite the fact that all the best evidence in my possession suggests that *x* is false.

It is evident that (5) does not entail (3): hence, given the equivalence of (4) and (5), the self-contradictoriness of (3) does not entail the self-contradictoriness of (4). Furthermore, it seems evident that, though a belief of the type described by (5) may violate a norm of practical rationality, that belief is not self-contradictory. Similarly, I would claim, the self-contradictoriness of (1) does not entail the self-contradictoriness of (2). In (2), the agent is merely affirming that, although all the best evidence available to him suggests that he will not bring off the intended action, he is nonetheless committing himself to the attempt. This is presumably on the grounds that by making appropriate efforts he leaves open the possibility that the interplay of forces beyond his ken will enable him to perform the intended action. In short, the possibility of (2) does not entail the possibility of (1).

We have seen that intentions are not to be identified with beliefs about the thing to do, or with beliefs about what one is going to do. Nor are intentions to be identified with desires. One can desire something that one affirms to be impossible, but one cannot intend to do something that one sincerely affirms to be impossible (as opposed to being *extremely* unlikely).

It might be assumed that *all* intentional actions are preceded by the formation of intentions. If the formation of an intention is to be identified with the agent's setting herself to do or omit something, however, there are problems with this view. Consider a woman—aware of a snake in front of her—who omits to touch it. She can give reasons for not touching it without its being the case that, at some stage, she forms the intention not to touch it; for it is not always sensible to postulate a time at which such a "setting of herself" took place. This does not, of course, preclude the possibility that, with respect to some acts of omission, such a postulation is plausible. Imagine that someone offers the woman of our example $100 if she touches the snake within sixty seconds. The lookers-on await with bated breath. The woman contemplates the possibility of touching the snake, wanting the $100. Her distaste and fear of being bitten overtake that want, and she forms the intention not to touch the snake.

Nor does it appear that all intentional acts of commission are preceded by the formation of intentions. I have a desire, let us say, to talk about action theory to my colleague. To this end, I string together a set of hopefully coherent sentences. It is true that each sentence I utter is a way of fulfilling my desire, but false to say that each sentence is preceded by an episode of setting myself to utter it. Yet the utterance of each sentence is intentional: if my colleague were to interrupt at the end of each one and ask—"Why did you say that?"—I could give an answer (no matter how bad).[14]

Even in the case of fully deliberated actions, it seems unnecessary always to postulate episodes of forming intentions. A lengthy process of deliberation concerning my priorities for the morning terminates in the practical judgment that the thing to do here and now is to perform some particularly simple action (start reading the essay in front of me). I straightaway read the first sentence. It seems unnecessary to postulate the existence of an episode of setting myself to read the essay, which postdates the formation of the practical judgment.

(iii) *Limitations in Practical Activity*

This section presents a taxonomy of breakdowns, flaws, and restrictions[15] of various kinds in the various stages or aspects of practical activity as identified above, which various theorists have thought to be relevant to the freedom of agents. Chapter 5 contains a discussion of the controversies about the relevance to the freedom of agents of the various limitations, while chapters 7 to 10 present a detailed account of those limitations which our coherence theory deems to affect freedom.

Limitations may attach either to the *process* of acquiring desires, of deliberating, intending, and implementing intentions, or to the *objects* of those desires, deliberations, or intentions. I wish to allow for the possibility that the processes could be flawed without the objects being flawed, and vice versa.

Limitations in the *processes* by which desires, intentions, and so forth are realized in action are of two broad types.

    A(1) Limitations affecting the construction of reason-giving links in the process of forming practical judgments. This

---

14. This example was suggested to me by Ismay Barwell.
15. Henceforth to be called limitations.

classification embraces the flawed acquisition of desires, such as subliminal advertising and other forms of manipulation, ignorance of alternatives, interferences with the deliberative process, such as menticide.

A(2) Limitations in the process of converting judgments and intentions (however formed) into action. This process may be marred or inhibited by various flaws and breakdowns, such as anomie, akrasia, lack of resolve, lack of nerve. These might be regarded as failures in the executive aspect of practical activity.

The second broad area of limitation occurs in the *objects* of the various intentional states and processes characterizing practical activity.

Conceptions of freedom vary according to the type of objects which, if flawed or limited in certain ways, render agents unfree. I shall distinguish between the objects of desires, the objects of deliberation, and the objects of intention.

B(1) The objects of desires. Desires could be flawed not merely by being acquired in a flawed way, but by being desires for improper objects, e.g., desires for objects that are degrading, licentious, harmful to self-realization.

B(2) Objects of deliberation. In *practical* activity, the sorts of things an agent deliberates about are actions that it is possible for him to undertake. (The relevant notion of "possibility" is discussed in chapter 7, section (ii)). The characteristics which limit actions qua objects of *deliberation*—those which render them not proper objects of deliberation—are those which make it impossible for agents to undertake them. Let us call actions that are not proper objects of deliberation *unavailable*.

B(3) Objects of intention. At the level of forming an *intention* to perform an action, an action may be restricted in some way, even where at the level of deliberation it is not. A contrast must then be drawn between the unavailability of actions and the *ineligibility* of actions. For example, acceding to actions to which threats are attached, such as demands of the blackmailer, need not be limited at the level of deliberation. Where it is possible for one either to accede or to fail to accede to the demands, I may properly deliberate about whether or not I should do so. Qua object of intention, however, acceding to the demands is constrained by virtue of threatened sanctions on noncompliance.

According to the above account, there is a wide variety of flaws, limitations, and breakdowns that beset the various stages and aspects of the practical process in a way that limits potential in agency. These are flaws in the *formation* of attitudes, breakdowns in the *conversion* of attitudes into appropriate action, and flaws and limitations in the *objects* of desires, deliberation, and intentions. All these types of limitation have been thought by various theorists to restrict freedom, and, according to the background theory, they have a strong claim to be so regarded. Let us now determine if that claim can be substantiated by putting the background theory to the test. Can the theory satisfy the twin goals of accommodating a wide range of conflicting endoxa while at the same time demonstrating their reasonableness in the light of the perceived value of freedom hypothesized by that theory? To make this task manageable we shall investigate rival conceptions of freedom and the endoxa that support them.

PART III

Conceptions of Freedom

Chapter 5

Rival Conceptions of Freedom

(i) *Identification of Conceptions of Freedom*

As Rawls and Daniels emphasize, the process of attaining reflective equilibrium involves consideration of rival conceptions of the ideal under investigation. The "favored conception" emerges only ". . . after a person has weighed various proposed conceptions and he has either revised his judgments in accord with some of them or held fast to his initial convictions (and the corresponding conception)" (TJ, 48).

My view differs from Rawls's in that conceptions are not compared with the theorist's initial convictions, but with the endoxa. I shall argue that the endoxa lend support to a variety of incompatible conceptions. The task of the coherence theorist is not merely to resolve tensions in the endoxa and the conceptions supported by them, but to do this in a way that does justice to their good points, as revealed by the background theory. In this chapter, I consider a wide range of conceptions all supported by endoxa, and argue that those endoxa are all worthy of preservation. In chapter 6, I develop a conception that accommodates the endoxa, resolving the tensions between them.

The question first arises: What is to count as a conception of freedom? In my own theory, what counts as a conception of freedom is determined by the coherence theory itself. Only putative conceptions of freedom that have *no* support in either the background theory or the endoxa will fail to count as conceptions of freedom. This is a liberal enough criterion, clearly eliminating only obviously outrageous "conceptions," such as, e.g., freedom is having a purple bathroom suite. It is certainly more liberal than that implicit in the essential contestedness theory, and that adopted by Rawls himself, according to which a conception C of x is by definition any "interpretation" of a single agreed upon concept C of x (see chapter 1, section (i)). To adopt this criterion for demarcating the class of conceptions of x is both unnecessary and undesirable. It is undesirable, because there is no more reason to believe in the existence of agreement on a concept of freedom than in the existence of agreement on conceptions of freedom (see chapter 1). In the absence of agreement on the special value of freedom, why should agreement on a core concept be assumed? For such agreement presupposes at least an accord on a *broad* characterization of the point or value of freedom. Indeed, as was noted in the Introduction, there is not even agreement on the canonical form of freedom. It is not agreed, for example, whether the relation or property of freedom is triadic, dyadic, or monadic.

More seriously, as I suggested earlier, the assumption that there must be a core concept of freedom common to all contested conceptions misrepresents the nature of the disputes. Typically, protagonists accuse each other of espousing conceptions which are not conceptions of freedom at all, but which are rather conceptions of power, opportunity, will, self-realization, and so forth. To assume that there is a core concept of freedom common to all conceptions is to assume agreement on at least some essential characteristics of freedom. But, for example, those[1] who regard freedom as essentially "negative" will reject MacCallum's schema as too broad; those who believe that freedom is essentially self-realization will reject it as too narrow.

Furnishing a "core concept" of freedom common to rival conceptions is also unnecessary to our theory. No putative concep-

---

1. See, e.g., Parent, "Some Recent Work on the Concept of Liberty."

Chapter 5   Rival Conceptions of Freedom   63

tion supported by the endoxa will be ruled out in advance because it fails to be an "interpretation" of some putative core concept. Rather, any such conception will be considered in the light of our theory as a whole, after which it will be eliminated entirely, or its strengths accommodated in the *further development of the theory*.

(ii)   Core Disputes and Peripheral Disputes

There is a vast number of conceptions of freedom, and in consequence a considerable variety of dispute about the nature of freedom. To make discussion of these disputes manageable, I propose a distinction between core disputes and peripheral disputes—a distinction that has its basis in the background theory.
   Core disputes are of two major types.

   A. Disputes concerning the relevance of *types of limitation* identified above (chapter 4, section [ii]), to the freedom of agents.
   B. Disputes concerning the relevance of the *significance* of actions, to which those limitations are attached, to the freedom of agents.

Peripheral disputes are of two corresponding types.

   A. Disputes concerning the precise specification of the types of limitation deemed relevant to the freedom of agents.
   B. Disputes concerning the sense in which the significance of actions is relevant to the freedom of agents.

An example of the distinction between a peripheral and a core dispute is this. Some conceptions of freedom affirm, and some deny, that breakdowns and limitations in the deliberative process are relevant to the freedom of agents. This is a core dispute. Of those conceptions which affirm that breakdowns of that type do limit freedom, some affirm and some deny that only deliberate interferences with the deliberative process are relevant to the freedom of agents. This is a peripheral dispute. In the remainder of this chapter, I elaborate on the nature of disputes in the core area; in the next chapter, I achieve coherence in the core area.
   Conceptions of freedom vary according to different views

about the relevance of different types of limitation in the practical process to the freedom of agents. I will consider, first, conceptions focusing on limitations in the objects of the various stages of the practical process (e.g., the objects of desire, deliberation, intention); and, second, conceptions focusing on limitations in practical activity seen as a process.

Conceptions in the core area also differ on the relevance of the *significance* of actions to the freedom of agents. The debate between those who believe that an agent's freedom is dependent on the significance of actions (with respect to which practical activity suffers from limitations), and those who do not believe this, is taken up in section (vii).

In the remainder of this chapter, I show that a whole range of conflicting endoxa in the core area are worthy of preservation. The background theory shows that there are reasonable points of view on both sides of the various debates discussed. Chapter 6 is devoted to the task of cohering the endoxa in the core area.

(iii) *The Relevance of Limitations in the Object of Desire*

There is a dispute between those who believe that flaws in the object of desire limit freedom, and those who do not believe this. The root idea of the former position is that virtue is essential to freedom. Full virtue is seen as a disposition involving rationality of ends embraced by the agent, integration of desire with those rationally embraced ends, and authenticity (the ends embraced must in some sense be one's own). Since full virtue requires a disposition of *right* desire, virtue-oriented notions of freedom do not see freedom merely as an absence of obstacles to the realization of actual desire; for that suggests that all desires are on a par, whereas some are seen as a hindrance to freedom. This point has support in the endoxa:

E_1: He who is a slave to his passions (e.g., the compulsive gambler) is not free.

Again, the pursuit of noble ends may be impeded by craven or self-indulgent impulses, thus limiting one's potential in agency.

Perhaps the founding father of virtue-oriented conceptions of freedom is Plato, but such conceptions have also enjoyed a

Chapter 5   Rival Conceptions of Freedom

strong modern and contemporary following. For Dewey[2] freedom requires a disposition of right desire, namely, those informed by intelligence. Desires not themselves under the control of the agent's reason count as controlling the agent:

> . . . it is easy . . . to escape one form of external control only to find oneself in another and more dangerous form of external control. Impulses and desires that are not ordered by intelligence are under the control of accidental circumstances. It may be a loss rather than a gain to escape from the control of another person only to find one's conduct dictated by immediate whim and caprice; that is, at the mercy of impulses into whose formation intelligent judgment has not entered. A person whose conduct is controlled in this way has at most only the illusion of freedom. Actually he is directed by forces over which he has no command (*ibid.*, pp. 64–5).

The idea here is not simply that the "controlling" desires are obstacles to agents' capacities to act as such. More importantly, they are limitations to their realizing their potential in agency in another, more normative sense: they limit their self-realization. This idea also lies behind Charles Taylor's[3] claim that it makes a difference to my degree of freedom not only "whether one of my basic purposes is frustrated by my own desires, but also whether I have grievously misidentified this purpose" (*ibid.*, p. 192). Benjamin Gibbs[4] has a similar view. He describes "natural freedom" as "felicity," "the perfection of nature," and "freedom in its fullest, least qualified sense" (*ibid.*, p. 67). He continues: "If I possess good abilities and opportunities, but through some defect of character (servility, indolence, alcoholism, addiction to gambling, or whatever) lack the motivation to exploit them, then my condition falls short of perfect freedom" (*ibid.*, pp. 67–8).

Opponents of virtue-oriented notions of freedom form two major groups. First, there are those who claim that, though desire is relevant to freedom, the *quality* of desire is not; for

---

2. *Experience and Education* (New York: Collier, 1963).
3. "What's Wrong with Negative Liberty," in Alan Ryan, ed., *The Idea of Freedom* (New York: Oxford, 1979): 175–193.
4. "Taking Liberties with Freedom," in A. Phillips Griffiths, ed., *Of Liberty*, Royal Institute of Philosophy Lecture Series, 15 (1983): 61–72.

freedom just is, for example, the absence of obstacles to the realization of desire. Second, there are those for whom desire is completely irrelevant to freedom: freedom just is the absence of certain obstacles to action. On my view, there is a powerful case for accommodating all three conceptions of freedom, for each focuses on limitations on the different aspects of individual potential identified above, viz., capacity, propensity, and self-realization, as these relate to agency.

Nonetheless, Flathman (*op. cit.*, p. 102) offers an interesting argument suggesting that the endoxa relating freedom to virtue are not worthy of preservation, for the apparent rationale for preserving them rests on confusion. According to Flathman, virtue conceptions of freedom would make sense as conceptions of *freedom* only if flawed desires are literally obstacles to action. But as Flathman argues—correctly in my view—not all nonvirtuous desires are phobias, compulsions, and obsessions. As his discussion of akrasia indicates, some involve character defects that manifest a high degree of purposiveness on the part of the agent.

I believe, however, that Flathman's argument for excluding virtue conceptions of freedom fails. His argument is successful only on the assumption that the MacCallum model of freedom, as essentially involving a triadic relation between agents, obstacles, and actions, provides the correct rationale for collocating putative freedom phenomena as genuine freedom phenomena. This assumption, explicitly made by Flathman, is problematic. Where virtues of specific kinds are seen as having overriding importance for freedom, freedom is regarded as a monadic property of agents rather than as essentially a triadic relation. I shall discuss further the limitations of the MacCallum schema below: suffice it to say here that a superior rationale saves more endoxa, while both demonstrating their worthiness to be saved and maintaining coherence. It is my claim that the background theory outlined above offers that superior rationale. The connection between virtue and freedom is licensed not by the fact that nonvirtuous dispositions of desire limit an individual's *capacity* to perform actions, but rather that they limit the individual's potential qua agent in a more normative sense. In that sense, an agent's reaching her potential necessitates that the agent flourish. This requires not merely the absence of obstacles to action but the absence of defects of character related to agency. Of course, defense of a specific virtue conception of freedom requires establishing the precise connection between specific virtues and flourishing qua agent. Those virtues involved in autonomy and executive success are discussed in this work, since they are the most closely associated with agency; nonetheless, some of the more traditional virtues of character, such as temperance and courage, also arguably improve freedom by reducing deficiencies in agency. A disposition of temperance enhances agency because the agent is not debilitated by powerful temptations;[5] a courageous disposition enhances agency by encouraging correct assessment or risk, stiffening the resolve, and reducing debilitating fear.

Endoxa linking virtue and freedom are worthy of preservation. Precisely *how* they are to be accommodated so as to avoid tension with other endoxa, and accusations of confusing freedom with virtue or self-realization, is a topic of the next chapter.

(iv) *The Relevance of the Ineligibility of Options*

It will be recalled that limitations on a course of action are of two types:

(i) The limitations render it unavailable to an agent (i.e., not a proper object of deliberation). In this case the course of action is not an *option* for that agent.

(ii) The limitations render it ineligible to an agent. In this case, though the course of action is an option, it is costly or difficult to implement.

Many philosophers, for example C. W. Cassinelli,[6] Parent,[7] and Hillel Steiner,[8] believe that only the unavailability of courses of action curtails freedom. Hence, for them, only obstacles that render it impossible to perform or avoid action render one unfree. Most theorists, by contrast, believe that intimidation by

---

5. For arguments that virtue rather than enkrasia enhances flourishing, see Gregory W. Trianosky, "Rightly Ordered Appetites: How to Live Morally and Live Well," *American Philosophical Quarterly*, XXV (1988): 1–10.

6. *Free Activities and Interpersonal Relations* (The Hague: Nijhoff, 1966).

7. "Some Recent Work on the Concept of Liberty."

8. "Individual Liberty," *Proceedings of the Aristotelian Society*, LXXV (1975): 33–50.

threat that renders options ineligible, though still available, limits freedom.[9]

The endoxa offer support to both viewpoints. Consider the following:

E_2: "A person cannot be unfree to do something he actually does."[10]

E_3: In New Zealand, a person is not free to commit acts of murder.

E_4: The man who hands over his money, having yielded to credible threat at gun point, does not perform a free act.

E_5: To assert that "I freely did what I was not free to do" is paradoxical.

Parent agrees with Cassinelli that E_2 is "self evident" (*ibid.*). He also claims that E_2 supports our reluctance to say of a person who has broken the laws that he was unfree to do so. The reason for this reluctance is made explicit in E_5. Yet E_3 and E_4 are self-evident to most people. There is then a prima facie tension between the endoxa—a tension that reflects the conflict between, e.g., Parent's and Benn and Weinstein's conceptions of freedom.

The background theory allows us to discern strengths in both Parent's and Benn and Weinstein's conceptions of freedom. It is possible to see a role played by both availability and eligibility of action in an agent's freedom, for each focuses on different aspects of the practical process. In some sense, availability of options enhances our freedom no matter how ineligible: they are, after all, options, i.e., possible objects of choice. They are items about which we can deliberate and on which we can exercise our will. Thus, ineligibility of action does not limit potentiality in agency at the level of capacity, and, given that one can deliberate about anything that is in one's power to do, it does not limit deliberation.

The will or intention is also an aspect of the practical process, however, and it, too, can be restricted in operation. Parent[11] is admittedly right in drawing a *distinction* between factors that "undermine the will" to *j* and factors that prevent us from *j*ing.

---

9. See, e.g., Benn and W. L. Weinstein, "Freedom as the Non-Restriction of Options: A Rejoinder," *Mind*, LXXXIII (1974): 435–8.
10. Parent, "Some Recent Work on the Concept of Liberty," p. 160.
11. "Freedom as the Non-Restriction of Options," p. 433.

But this is hardly an argument for the claim that the former are irrelevant to freedom. The background theory supports those endoxa suggesting that ineligibility plays some role in freedom, for it limits potentiality in agency at the level of propensity. Agents who have or might have a propensity to hang on to their money are thwarted in that propensity by threats rendering that option ineligible. There are, of course, problems concerning what *kind* of "undermining of the will" limits freedom: for example, can offers limit freedom? Those problems are addressed in chapter 8.

(v) *The Relevance of Limitations in the Formation of Attitudes*[12]

Conceptions of freedom focusing on limitations in the *formation* of desires, practical judgments, and intentions are generally labeled conceptions of freedom as autonomy. Richer conceptions of autonomy include also virtue-oriented requirements for full freedom, and I shall follow this usage in later discussion. In the meantime, however, I shall discuss the issue of limitations in the formation, as opposed to the objects, of practical attitudes.

There is a dispute between those who believe that all conceptions of freedom as autonomy should be rejected, and those who favor a conception of this type. Some philosophers can make sense of the idea of "breakdowns" (such as conditioning, ignorance, extreme emotion) that rule out freedom at the stage of forming attitudes, analogous to those we rule out when speaking of freedom at the stage of *acting on* those attitudes. According to many, then, not only the determinants of agents' actions, but also the determinants of their desires and intentions to act are relevant to their freedom.

Thus Benn[13] recognizes that a threat is posed to freedom not only by coercers and impeders, but also, in a different way, by opinion manipulators of various sorts. He claims: "The problem posed by propagandists, advertisers and public relations experts is quite different. They aim not at overruling contrary intentions

---

12. For convenience, I use the term 'attitude' to include desires, practical judgments, and intentions.
13. "Freedom and Persuasion," *Australasian Journal of Philosophy*, XLVII (1967): 259–75.

by threats of coercion but, by persuasion, to create a willing—if possible an enthusiastic—accord. They seek to avoid or dissolve conflict, not to overrule it" (*ibid.*, p. 261). He states that a person's freedom has been infringed to the extent that some part of the deliberative process has been inhibited or some element of action put beyond the possibility of rational criticism (*ibid.*).

Other philosophers, by contrast, dismiss the language of freedom, in this context, as mere metaphor. Freedom for them has to do with the implementation of desires—how the desire comes about is irrelevant to the question of the *freedom* of agents. K. J. Scott, in "Conditioning and Freedom,"[14] suggests that determinants of desire, such as hidden persuasion, conditioning, and subliminal advertising, ought not to be seen as limiting a person's freedom. Scott claims that freedom is giving effect to "spontaneous desires": it is not concerned with the origin of those desires. Just as Steiner and others concentrate on only one aspect of potential in agency (viz., capacity), Scott, too, is narrowly focused on potential as propensity. The model he employs of unfreedom is the Hobbesian one of thwarted tendencies. As we have seen, however, there are richer notions of potential as self-realization, which in the area of freedom is generally labeled autonomy. Where a tendency is "other-directed," its realization is not a full manifestation of freedom.

The arguments against the view suggested by the background theory are less than convincing. All too often, philosophers point to the existence of distinctions, and then hand wave in the direction of "ordinary language," despite the conflicting endoxa. The mere existence of a distinction between the breakdowns on which Benn focuses and restraints on giving effect to our desires (however formed) is not sufficient to show that the former are irrelevant to the freedom of agents. In making out his case, Scott does not give an account of *why* one sort of breakdown should be seen as limiting freedom and the other as not. For example, Scott claims that conditioning, unlike restraints on giving effect to our spontaneous desires, does not give rise to feelings of frustration. This may be so, but is this a relevant difference? Since many philosophers[15] would deny that unfreedom

---

14. *Australasian Journal of Philosophy*, XXXVII (1959): 215–20.

15. See, e.g., Barry, *Political Argument* (London: Routledge and Kegan Paul, 1965): 139.

Chapter 5 Rival Conceptions of Freedom

is synonymous with the presence of frustration (for they reject the model of unfreedom as thwarted tendency), the relevance of the difference is problematic.

Different endoxa appear to support both Scott's views and the opposing viewpoint of Benn and others. Consider the following:

E_6: Those who can achieve their goals without interference are free.

E_7: The individuals in *Brave New World* are not free.

There is tension between E_6 and E_7 inasmuch as E_6 seems to imply that individuals in Brave New World—a society in which all can achieve their goals—are free. E_7, on the other hand, suggests that where one's goals have been determined by deliberate and planned interference with desires and the deliberative process, one is unfree even where there are no limitations on achieving goals. The point behind E_7 is this. As Benn indicates, someone who does not want you to do specific things can achieve his aim very effectively by reducing your motivation to do those things. According to Benn, he thereby reduces your freedom, not by interfering directly with your range of action but by interfering with various stages in the process of choosing to act.

In the next chapter, where coherence in the core area is achieved, the tension between the above endoxa will be removed in such a way that their point is preserved.

(vi) *The Relevance of Executive Failure*

Executive failure involves a mismatch between relevant practical attitudes (such as desire, practical judgment, and intention) and action. This mismatch may be of two broad types.

First, the practical process may not be completed: the agent is "paralyzed" in some way so that the practical process fails to go through the appropriate phases. Such "paralyses" can occur at various stages. In anomie, for example, the clashing desires of the agent are undisciplined and unordered: there is a failure to embark properly in a process of deliberation determining whether, when, and in what order desires are to be satisfied. At the other end of the practical process, there may be a last-second failure of nerve, where a proximate intention is not implemented,[16] or, more mysteriously, there are phenomena, such as "driver's yip" in golf, where the *attempt* to do something here and now fails to issue in action. In the other kind of mismatch, the practical process goes through its various phases, but somehow the action performed matches the wrong practical attitude. For example the action may match an intention, or a desire, but not the practical judgment about the thing to do. Weakness of will is arguably an executive failure of this kind.

The view that executive failure is a distinctive and interesting category of unfreedom enjoys a relatively low profile. For example, executive failure is sometimes amalgamated to heteronomy as a species of irrationality or inauthenticity in the practical process. I shall argue in chapter 10 that the defects of disposition or character which characterize executive failure are of quite a different type: involving a failure of "courage" in the face of indeterminacies of reason.

For others, executive failure limits freedom only insofar as it is construed on the model of obstacle to action. For example, weakness of will is sometimes assumed to be a species of compulsion. In this case, weakness of will would render actions unavailable due to internal preventing impediments. Most accounts of weakness of will reject this idea, however, in which case its relation to loss of freedom becomes more problematical. According to Young,[17] weakness of will limits freedom (or autonomy) in a dispositional sense. It is not the case that an episode of weakness renders a particular action unavailable: rather, its effect on a person's self-directedness is more or less pervasive depending on "the seriousness of the actions it affects, and on the range of such actions" (*ibid.*, p. 62). Young does not develop his own view that weakness of will is a defect of disposition or even character, but his insight, I believe, is correct, and will be developed in chapter 10 on the model of regular cowardice.

The germ of the idea of executive failure as a manifestation of cowardice of a sort is indeed to be found in Scott's views. Despite his belief that conditioning does not limit freedom, he

---

16. See Colin McGinn, *The Character of Mind* (New York: Oxford Press, 1982): ". . . you may intend to put a question to the distinguished speaker, but lose your nerve (will) at the last minute, though the intention may survive" (p. 95).

17. *Personal Autonomy: Beyond Negative and Positive Liberty* (Beckenham: Croom Helm, 1986): 57f.

clearly believes that courage in the face of threat enhances freedom:

> E_8: "The people who are especially resistant to threats have the widest freedom, though they may have to suffer for it, heroes, criminals, saints" (*op. cit.*, p. 218).

The intuition behind E_8 supports the view that all kinds of executive failure, leading to mismatch between espoused principle and action (or more broadly, a relevant practical attitude and action), constitute limitations in agency which restrict freedom. I myself shall develop the view that there are a number of defects of executive cowardice analogous to that of which Scott speaks, all of which limit freedom.

(vii) *The Relevance of Restraints on Insignificant Courses of Action*

Many philosophers consider that the existence of certain types of restraint rendering courses of action unavailable or ineligible is *sufficient* to limit freedom. If these limitations occur, then, according to these philosophers, freedom is curtailed whether or not the courses of action are in any way significant to the agent (e.g., are desired or chosen options). Others, by contrast, consider that only restraints on significant courses of action limit freedom.

We might illustrate this dispute by contrasting Joel Feinberg's[18] and V.D.P. Dryer's[19] conceptions of freedom. Feinberg dubs his analysis of freedom as the "breathing-space" model. For him, freedom is "room to manoeuvre" (*op. cit.*, p. 6). Since merely possible options have a way of *becoming* significant (viz., chosen options), Feinberg claims, obstacles on possible options limit freedom. For Feinberg, then, freedom is not just the absence of obstacles to the implementation of a choice that has been made, but the absence of obstacles on options that might be chosen in the future. J. P. Day,[20] too, supports this view of freedom, citing the following endoxon:

---

18. *Social Philosophy* (Englewood Cliffs, N.J.: Prentice Hall, 1973).
19. "Freedom," *The Canadian Journal of Economics and Political Science*, XXX (1964): 444–8.
20. J. P. Day, "On Liberty and the Real Will," *Philosophy*, XLV (1970): 177–92.

E_9: "[A person is] unfree when he is restrained from doing anything that it is in his power to do, regardless of whether he wants to do it or not" (*ibid.*, p. 179).

Dryer, on the other hand, understands freedom to be a matter of there not being restrictions (of a certain kind) on pursuing *chosen* options. In support of this view he claims that the freedom of a prisoner who prefers not to leave jail "can no more be said to be impaired than is that of someone who would not choose to throw himself off a cliff and is protected by a high fence from going over the edge" (*op. cit.*, p. 445). This view flies in the face of the extremely well entrenched endoxon:

E_{10}: Those in prison are not free regardless of their desires, goals, or choices;

but appears to be supported by

E_6: Those who can achieve their goals without interference are free.

Other philosophers, too, opposing the "breathing space" model, support E_6. Thus, for Russell: "Freedom in general may be defined as the absence of obstacles to the realization of desires" (*op. cit.*, p. 231). Robert A. Dahl[21] defines freedom in a similar manner: "The 'freedom' of an individual is 'the opportunity to achieve his goals without external restraints'" (*ibid.*, p. 27). As the above endoxa suggest, both Feinberg's conception of freedom and Dahl's have merit. Feinberg has a point in claiming that statements like the following are paradoxical:

(S) *A* is totally free when all his options are closed except the only thing he wants to do, viz., stay within the confines of a prison cell.

(S') *A* is totally unfree when he suffers no restriction on any options except one, and that is the only one he wants to realize, viz., be incarcerated in a prison cell.

On the other hand, Dahl and Charles E. Lindblom[22] seem correct in focusing on a weakness in the "breathing space" model of freedom. If one's freedom is *simply* a matter of the absence of restrictions on courses of action, then an individual

---

21. *A Preface to Democratic Theory* (Chicago: University Press, 1956).
22. *Politics, Economics and Welfare* (New York: Harper, 1963).

Chapter 5 Rival Conceptions of Freedom

having a thousand options open to him is necessarily freer than the individual having only ten. Dahl and Lindblom rebut this idea by appealing to the following endoxon:

E_{11}: If the first individual feels adequate opportunity to achieve his goals among the ten choices he has, whereas the second feels frustrated because the thousand choices he has are trivial, then the second individual is not necessarily freer than the first (*ibid.*, p. 31).

In the next chapter, I will resolve the tensions revealed in the endoxa by developing a conception of freedom that accommodates the points made both by Feinberg and by Dahl and Lindblom.

CHAPTER 6

Coherence in the Core Area

(i) *Introduction*

In the previous chapter, I considered a wide range and variety of endoxa and conceptions of freedom, thereby satisfying desideratum (b) of an adequate coherence theory (see above, p. 27). Two major conclusions emerged from the discussion.

First, although the conceptions considered appeared to focus on important aspects of individual potential in the practical process and should not be dismissed as confusing freedom with other values, they were found wanting with respect to desideratum (d). They all ignored important endoxa. Second, the endoxa considered are worthy of preservation: the background theory provides a rationale for their inclusion in a fully developed theory of freedom. Despite their heterogeneity, the material properties picked out by the endoxa can be understood as forming a genuine collocation, because they can each be reasonably understood as satisfying, in appropriate contexts, the formal property of freedom, viz., the absence of limitations (of various kinds) on the realization of individual human potential (in its various aspects) in the different stages and aspects of practical activity. Although the endoxa are reasonable, however, they appear to conflict in serious ways. My task is to accommodate all the endoxa while resolving the tensions between them, thereby satisfying desiderata (a) and (d).

It may be thought that MacCallum has provided the materials for accommodating all the endoxa with his schema of freedom as a triadic relation, presented in his important paper "Negative and Positive Freedom." Here, he argues persuasively that the debate between those espousing "negative" versus "positive" conceptions of freedom can be defused by a recognition of the credentials of both. Both can be understood as conforming to his schema of freedom as a relation between agents, obstacles, and actions. Although MacCallum's theoretical apparatus aids an understanding of the nature of peripheral disputes, e.g., what kinds of obstacles or action are freedom-limiting obstacles, it does not greatly assist us in the core area. It does not get to grips with disputes about which general types of relation affect freedom, for his model is essentially a narrow "obstacles to action" model. Even the notion of a person "being free *simpliciter*" is understood as elliptical for sets of statements identifying the presence or absence of specific restrictions and so forth on specific actions, usually those judged to be important (*op. cit.*, p. 329).

But flaws in the objects of desire, flaws of character, flaws in reason-giving links in practical reasoning and in the executive phase of practical activity should not necessarily be understood on the model of obstacles to "actions," mental or otherwise. For example, I do not understand weakness of will as an obstacle (such as the onslaught of an irresistible desire) to the implementation of an action (see chapter 10, section (ii)). Furthermore, MacCallum's formula allows of only one way of recognizing the role played by the degree of significance of action in the assessment of freedom, namely, the range of actions one is properly free or unfree to perform includes only important actions. That approach is unsatisfactory, since not only is it necessary to select an arbitrary cutoff point between important and unimportant actions, but also one cannot claim that the *more* significant are the actions one is unfree to perform, the less free one is *simpliciter*. This way of understanding the role played by significance of action is not available to MacCallum, for one cannot say that the degree of a person's freedom *simpliciter*—that is, the degree of a person's freedom from obstacles *to* perform a set of actions—is a function of the degree of significance of those actions. In the next section, I present a broader theoretical apparatus than MacCallum's for accommodating the endoxa in the core area.

(ii) *The Concept of Overall Freedom*

In this section, I develop a concept of freedom that achieves coherence in the core area. In doing this, I attempt to do justice to all the endoxa E_1–E_{11} that, to varying degrees, lend support to a variety of rival conceptions of freedom. The tensions between E_1–E_{11} require that they be "pruned and adjusted" so that the modified judgments are co-assertible, and the point of the original judgments is as far as possible preserved. I believe that there is a theoretical framework permitting the resolution of tensions in the endoxa. This framework is provided by an explication of what I have elsewhere called *overall freedom*.[1]

The concept of "overall freedom" assumes that it makes sense to form "on balance" judgments about the extent of an agent's freedom with respect to a large class of actions. It is, however, broader than MacCallum's "freedom *simpliciter*," since it allows that several types of relation between an agent and actions that that agent is properly said to be free to perform or omit may affect the extent of her overall freedom. This feature is central to the resolution of those tensions revealed in the previous chapter.

The conceptions of freedom discussed in the previous chapter suggest that limitations in the practical process affect overall freedom in two major ways.

(a) The degree to which various aspects and stages of the practical process are relevantly flawed or limited.
(b) The degree of significance of the actions with respect to which the practical process is (to a given degree) flawed or limited.

We first discuss (a), before turning our attention to (b). In section (iii), I defend the view that our concept of overall freedom accommodates all the endoxa in the core area in a coherent way.

Previous discussion suggests that the *endoxa* support the view that a variety of types of breakdown or flaw affect overall freedom. These are:

(1) Certain sorts[2] of unavailability of actions to an agent.

---

1. "The Concept of Overall Freedom," *Australasian Journal of Philosophy*, LVII (1979): 337–49.
2. The qualifications 'certain' and 'certain sorts' indicate that not *all* restrictions, unavailabilities, etc., are relevant to the *freedom* of agents. Just which restrictions and so forth are so relevant will be discussed in later chapters in connection with disputes in the peripheral area.

Chapter 6 Coherence in the Core Area

(2) Certain sorts of ineligibility to the agent of available actions.

(3) Certain limitations in the formation and nature of an agent's desires and other practical attitudes toward the performance of actions.

(4) Certain limitations in the conversion of an agent's desires and other practical attitudes to the execution of actions.

Each of these relations is given detailed discussion in chapters 7–10.

On the view proposed, the degree of one's overall freedom with respect to a given set of actions is not simply a matter of the degree of one's freedom to perform each member of that set. Obstacles on performance is only one freedom-limiting relation besetting practical activity. The endoxa not only recognize others, but can also be rendered consistent by being recast in the following propositions.

P_1: An agent is the freer overall, ceteris paribus, the fewer options are unavailable due to freedom-limiting factors.

P_2: An agent is the freer overall, ceteris paribus, the less are his available options rendered ineligible, due to freedom-limiting factors.

P_3: An agent is the freer overall, ceteris paribus, the less limited (in a freedom-limiting way) is the formation and nature of his attitudes toward the performance of actions.

P_4: An agent is the freer overall, ceteris paribus, the less limited (in a freedom-limiting way) is the conversion of practical attitudes to the execution of actions.

I turn now to the role played by the significance of actions in the assessment of overall freedom. There are a number of ways in which this role has been recognized. First, some have been tempted to believe, like MacCallum and Taylor, that the question of freedom arises *only* with respect to significant actions. Taylor claims, for example, that the installation of a set of traffic lights is not an infringement of freedom at all despite the fact that crossing against the lights is a prohibition backed by the coercive apparatus of the law. Of this example he claims: "It is not just a matter of our having made a trade-off, and considered that a small loss of liberty was worth fewer traffic accidents, or less danger for the children; we are reluctant to speak here of a loss of liberty at all. . . ." (*op. cit.*, p. 182). Taylor concludes that, where external obstacles on the performance of action affect freedom, it is "the absence of external obstacles to *significant action*" which limits freedom.

It is true that the level of freedom of an individual is improved rather than worsened, ceteris paribus, where the agent becomes free with respect to more rather than less significant actions. To accommodate this truth, however, it is unnecessary to exclude from the realm of freedom altogether actions deemed relatively insignificant on the basis of some ideal-regarding notion of significance. Who are the 'we' who are so reluctant to speak of freedom where so-called insignificant actions are involved? Commuters may not *complain* of loss of freedom since traffic regulations are regarded as a fact of life, but, nonetheless, ease of access to work is a significant issue for many people. It is true also that freedom is a value, but, again, to preserve this truth it is unnecessary to exclude from the realm of freedom relatively valueless freedoms. For the value of freedom is connected not merely with the value of *actions* agents are free or unfree to perform, but with all kinds of valuable aspects of the practical process.

On an alternative view, freedom is diminished when and only when the agent is subject to freedom-limiting obstacles on the realization or implementation of her wants, intentions, or will. This view, exemplified by Russell's conception of freedom as the absence of obstacles to the realization of desire, is frequently criticized on the grounds that it leads to paradox. It has been suggested that, according to conceptions of this type, there are two ways to maximize freedom—eliminate obstacles to the realization of desire, and eliminate those desires themselves. A being who desires nothing is, accordingly, maximally free.

On our preferred view, the role played by the significance of action in the extent of an agent's overall freedom is described in the following proposition.

> P_5: An agent is the freer overall, ceteris paribus, the less significant are the actions with respect to which practical activity is limited in the ways described in P_1–P_4.

In the next section, I defend the view that P_5 is superior to alternative views in accommodating the endoxa.

(iii) Accommodating the Endoxa in the Core Area

The task of this chapter is to accommodate the endoxa in the core area in a way that satisfies the requirements of our coherence theory. In this section, I consider the endoxa, addressing the following questions: Have the endoxa been accommodated, and have they been accommodated in a way that avoids tension with other endoxa? In section (iv), I consider broader requirements of coherence; specifically, Is the concept of overall freedom itself sound?

First, I consider the above questions in relation to those endoxa supporting virtue-oriented conceptions of freedom. They focus primarily on flaws in the objects of desire, but it will not be immediately obvious how those endoxa are to be accommodated. The reason for this is the complexity of their relation to freedom. Let us illustrate with the endoxon:

E_1: Persons who are "slaves" to their passions, e.g., compulsive gamblers, are not free.

First, flawed desires could be seen as obstacles to action: an obsessive desire may literally be an internal impediment rendering the avoidance of gambling either unavailable or extremely difficult. That is, flawed desire may be seen as limiting freedom under the aspect of availability or eligibility of action. Second, a flawed desire could be seen as limiting freedom because it is not merely a powerful but also an *alien* force. The passion for gambling, for example, may be seen as an alien desire because the agent does not identify with it, or it impedes instrumental rationality (see further, chapter 9).

Being a "slave" to one's passions, however, does not seem to capture the whole truth about flawed desires limiting freedom. Consider the following endoxon:

E_{12}: An all-consuming desire to complete a great work of art does not limit an agent's freedom, even though it renders the option of wasting time very difficult to entertain.

We are reluctant to say that an obsessive passion directed at noble ends limits freedom. As we have seen, for many philosophers, including Taylor, flawed desires may limit freedom, not because their obsessive or powerful nature renders them an "alien" force or limits the availability or eligibility of alternatives, but because they are vicious or otherwise in error. The idea that dispositions of flawed desire limit freedom because they are vicious could be accommodated by employing virtue-oriented notions of rationality and authenticity in describing the various aspects of autonomy. Thus, rationality is demonstrated not merely in instrumental rationality but also in the kinds of ends pursued by the agent. Authenticity of desire is not mere nonvicariousness of desire, or identification with desire, but nonvicarious identification with those desires arising from, or compatible with, relevantly virtuous dispositions (see further below, chapter 9).

There is also another way of accommodating the apparently competing endoxa E_1 and E_{12} available to me. I have recognized that freedom is affected by the significance of actions with respect to which one is free or unfree in various respects, and I shall interpret the notion of significance in a way that does justice not only to want-oriented notions of freedom, but also to virtue-oriented notions of freedom (see below, chapter 11).

I believe that my theory can accommodate virtue-oriented conceptions of freedom. But does this accommodation avoid tensions with other endoxa? It will be objected that virtue-oriented conceptions are incompatible with endoxa supporting P_1 and P_2—viz., endoxa supporting conceptions of freedom as absence of obstacles to action. This objection rests on the idea that virtue-oriented conceptions of freedom are necessarily committed to the equation of free action with virtuous action. Such an equation would indeed be incompatible with P_1 and P_2, but virtue conceptions of freedom are not necessarily committed to that equation. They need be committed only to the idea that it enhances an individual's potential qua agent, and thus his freedom, to cultivate and possess virtuous *dispositions*. This does not entail that freedom is manifested only when virtuous *acts* are performed. It may be that a disposition of temperance enhances agency because the agent is not debilitated by powerful temptations; nonetheless, my consuming six chocolate eclairs in one sitting on one occasion may cause indigestion and add fractionally to my weight, while doing nothing to limit my capacities or potential as an agent at that time or in the future. More generally, real nonidealized human agents with virtuous dispositions may perform wrong acts on occasion, and not all of

Chapter 6   Coherence in the Core Area

these limit freedom. Indeed, the fact that an individual's freedom may actually be curtailed by her performance of right acts makes it even clearer that the connection between virtue and freedom is at the level of disposition and not act. Although acquiring a courageous disposition may remove limitations in an individual's potential qua agent and thus enhance that agent's freedom (e.g., it reduces paralyzing fear), not all courageous *acts* improve freedom. Becoming a brain-damaged vegetable in the course of a courageous action on the battlefield hardly enhances agency: it terminates agency and therefore freedom altogether!

Hence, virtue conceptions of freedom need not equate freedom and virtuous action. Indeed, they need not even *equate* freedom with acquisition and possession of virtuous dispositions. Recognition of this reduces tension among the endoxa and defuses unfair criticism of virtue conceptions. It would be a crass error to assume that philosophers such as Taylor and Benjamin Gibbs claim that virtue is synonymous with freedom, as if a virtuous slave or a virtuous prison inmate is free. Nor does Gibbs claim, *pace* Anthony Flew,[3] that freedom involves *making* people do what is good; that freedom requires compulsion, indoctrination, and brainwashing. It is claimed merely that virtue is a *necessary* condition for *perfect* freedom—a view compatible with the idea that, in certain imperfect worlds (e.g., where people are ingrained in vice), maximal freedom in those worlds (which is not perfect freedom) may not involve possession of virtue. Gibbs's view does not eliminate as irrelevant other dimensions of freedom, and can be accommodated within the framework of my coherence theory, as we shall see.

By making a place for virtue-oriented conceptions of freedom, therefore, I have not confused freedom and self-realization. The point of the endoxon, emphasised by Raz, can be preserved:

E_{13}: "The autonomous person is the one who makes his own life and he may choose the path of self-realization or reject it."[4]

E_{13} is rendered plausible by Raz's understanding of self-realization as consisting in "the development to their full extent

---

3. See his critique of Gibbs's *Freedom and Liberation* (London: Sussex UP, 1976), in "Freedom Is Slavery: A Slogan for Our New Philosopher Kings," in Griffiths, ed., pp. 45–59; and Gibbs's reply in "Taking Liberties with Freedom," pp. 70–1.
4. *The Morality of Freedom* (New York: Oxford, 1986), p. 375.

of all, or almost all the valuable capacities a person possesses" (*ibid.*), and autonomy as a distinct but complex ideal concerned basically with *how* one becomes more or less self-realized in that sense.

Given that understanding of "self-realization" and "autonomy," E_{13} can be saved in my theory. For me, too, self-realization in Raz's rather narrow sense is neither necessary nor sufficient for full freedom. It is not necessary, because not all valuable capacities are connected with the enhancement of individual potential in agency. It is not sufficient, since the realization of potential in agency involves not merely the *nature* of agency-related capacities but also the manner of their acquisition. That is, the free agent not only is relevantly self-realized in Raz's sense, but has also in some sense chosen the path of self-realization.

In accommodating the endoxa, the second area of concern is the tension between those endoxa which apparently deny and those which affirm that ineligibility of action limits freedom. How can P_2 be compatible with E_2 and E_5—judgments that suggest that freedom is not affected by the degree of eligibility of actions? P_2 is compatible with E_2 and E_5, provided the latter are correctly interpreted. The sense in which E_2 is true is the sense in which freedom is a degree concept: "A person cannot be unfree to do something he actually does" means "A person cannot be *totally* unfree in doing something he actually does." This is compatible with P_4, however, according to which people are *to a degree* unfree in doing the things they actually do, in those circumstances where they have to overcome restraints rendering actions ineligible, such as certain types of obstacle and sanction. In the sense of freedom where "freedom" is not a degree concept (as in "One is unfree to move a pawn backward in chess"), E_2 is clearly false: one can be unfree to move a pawn backward in chess and still move the pawn backward.[5]

The third major area of conflict of endoxa in the core area is that between those suggesting that the significance of actions to an agent plays a role in the determination of overall freedom, and those suggesting otherwise. I shall defend my view that P_5 accommodates the endoxa in this area, and is superior to alternative views in resolving the tensions between the endoxa.

---

5. For more on this notion of freedom and its connection with the unavailability of courses of action, see ch. 7, sec. (iii).

Chapter 6 Coherence in the Core Area

Adopting "Russellian" conceptions of freedom as the absence of obstacles to chosen, desired, or otherwise significant options is not the way to accommodate them. From the point of view of a coherence theory, such conceptions contain a serious flaw. True, they accommodate the endoxa E_6 and E_{11}, but they ignore totally the important endoxon highlighted by Day:

> E_9: "[A person is] unfree when he is restrained from doing anything that it is in his power to do, regardless of whether he wants to do it or not" (*op. cit.*).

This is the truth behind the "breathing space" model of freedom favored by Feinberg. But how can one both recognize that truth, and do justice to the idea that the extent of freedom is *somehow* affected by the significance of the actions with respect to which agents are free or unfree in various respects? We have done this by recognizing two separate categories of influence on overall freedom:

(a) The degree to which various aspects and stages of the practical process are relevantly flawed or limited (by, e.g., the presence of restraints on the performance of actions).

(b) The degree of significance of the actions with respect to which the practical process is (to a given degree) flawed or limited.

The first aspect, (a), salvages E_9, whereas the second aspect, (b), saves E_{11}. E_{11} is preserved in the idea that, for a given degree of flaw or limitation, an agent is the freer overall, the less significant is the action with which the flaw or limitation is associated.

It might be thought that our way of reconciling E_9 and E_{11} has not saved the following endoxon appealed to by Dryer:

> E_{14}: The person who is protected by a high fence from going over the edge of the cliff has not had his freedom impaired by the existence of the fence.

Does not E_{14} suggest that Dryer is correct in his claim that the freedom of a prisoner who prefers not to leave jail is more impaired than that of a nonsuicidal person protected from going over the edge of the cliff? This inference from E_{14} is fallacious, however. The truth captured by E_{14} is not that the question of freedom arises only when an option is chosen. Rather, the question of freedom arises only where there is a genuine action in the offing (as opposed to an accident) (see above, chapter 4). Specifically, the fence does not impair one's freedom with respect to *falling* off the edge, but that is perfectly consistent with the claim that the fence impairs one's freedom to commit suicide (whether or not one has chosen to).

This same point facilitates understanding of Mill's infamous example of the man who is restrained from crossing the bridge: agreed, the man does not want to fall into the water; and, agreed, the man who restrains the would-be crosser does not restrict his freedom with respect to that state of affairs. The reason this is so, however, is not because freedom is "getting what one wants," as Mill claims, but because one is neither free nor unfree with respect to *falling* off the bridge. All this is quite compatible with the fact that the man's freedom is restricted with respect to *crossing* the bridge.

I believe that P_1–P_5 not only accommodate the wide variety of endoxa in the core area considered in chapter 5, but accommodate them in a way that resolves tensions between them. The question arises, however, whether those tensions have themselves been resolved in a coherent way: specifically, is the concept of overall freedom itself sound? This is the topic of the next section.

(iv) *The Soundness of the Concept of Overall Freedom*

Feinberg argues that we cannot assess the extent of what he calls an individual's "on balance" freedom, or compare the extent of an individual's on balance freedom with that of another, since the same individual is free to perform different sets of actions at different times, and different individuals are free to perform different sets of actions. He claims:

> The difficulty in striking . . . totals of 'on balance freedom' derives from the fact that the relation among the various 'areas' in which people are said to be free is not so much like the relation between the height, breadth, and depth of a physical object as it is like the relation between the gasoline economy, styling, and comfort of an automobile. Height times breadth times depth equals

Chapter 6 Coherence in the Core Area

volume, a dimension compounded coherently out of the others; freedom of expression times freedom of movement yields nothing comparable (*op. cit.*, p. 19).

It should be noted that Feinberg does commit himself to accepting the legitimacy of a very limited comparison, viz., one person A is freer on balance than another person B, when A is free to do all the things that B is free to do, as well as other things that B is not free to do.

I agree with Feinberg that no one has developed or even can develop a dimensional account of overall freedom in the precise mathematical sense of "dimension." This claim is not to the point, however. The point is we do sensibly make judgments, like "The economic sector is freer now under 'Rogernomics' than it was under Prime Minister Muldoon," without the need for mathematical dimensions of freedom. What is needed is a conceptual basis for these judgments, and this does not require the production of mathematical dimensions.

It is instructive here to compare Jeremy Bentham's "hedonic calculus." This calculus has been much maligned for its spurious mathematization of so-called quanta of pleasure and pain. But Bentham's conceptualization of features of episodes of pleasure and pain—such as intensity, duration, fecundity, purity—provide a sharper understanding of the conceptual basis of such obviously sensible judgments as "Body surfing gives me more pleasure than table-tennis," or "Tom will derive more pleasure from his recorder than Eric from his Easter egg." In brief, the concept of overall freedom elucidates *the basis* of ordinal comparisons about the extent of overall freedom. I do not intend to produce, by means of multiplicative dimensions, a method of attaching numerical values to the extent of agents' overall freedom. Although I shall sometimes refer to availability, eligibility, autonomy, and so forth as dimensions of freedom, I do this only for terminological convenience. Indeed, I do not even mean to suggest that each "dimension" is composed of one factor. I shall claim, for example, that degree of availability is a function of both number and variety of options, and that degree of autonomy is a function of degree of rationality and authenticity of attitudes toward actions. One can be almost indefinitely fine-grained about freedom factors: rationality, for example, is an extremely complex quality, itself composed of several aspects.

Although it is wrong to imagine that the concept of overall freedom involves a commitment to dimensions of freedom in a strict sense, it is nonetheless inherently pluralistic. As we saw in chapter 2, embracing pluralism is a technique that allows one to preserve a range of apparently incompatible endoxa. One might regard the loss of simplicity as a sacrifice not worth making, however, for the sorts of reasons outlined by Flathman. Speaking of conceptions such as Steiner's and Parent's, he says:

> . . . the severe schematic quality of this view is at least initially attractive because its steadfast dismissal of the subjective elements of freedom holds out the promise that the theorist of *freedom* can stay out of the philosophical quagmire that is the theory of desires and other motives to and reasons for action. Its lean conception of agency and action permits a stripped-down and manageable theory of freedom (*op. cit.*, p. 31).

The point of sacrificing simplicity, however, is to do justice to the complexity of the data. Admittedly, simplicity and elegance are regarded as virtues in physical theory, but doing justice to the data is a higher virtue. It may be argued that rationality is a higher virtue still, but are "severity," "manageability," and so forth virtues of rationality? Notions like "severe" and "stripped-down" denote merely aesthetic values contrasting with "baroque," "complex," "ornamental"; and the denoted values are controversial ones at that. "Unmanageable" is a different idea, since it connotes disorder and incoherence. The respect in which pluralism betokens disorder is the proneness to conflict within and between the various elements of the pluralistic conception. Certainly pluralistic conceptions of freedom allow the possibility of conflict within areas or aspects of freedom, but does this pose problems of rationality? This is an important issue deserving a chapter in its own right (see chapter 12).

In Part II, I have endeavored to achieve coherence in the core area. In the next five chapters of part III, I shall examine, in turn, the relationships described by P_1–P_5. The aim is to determine the nature of those factors constituting unfreedom, thereby achieving coherence in the peripheral areas. The freedom phenomena will have been described in a way that saves the endoxa.

PART IV

The Freedom Phenomena

CHAPTER 7

Unavailability of Actions

(i) Restraints

The topic of this and the next chapter is the contribution made to an agent's unfreedom by *restraints on her actions* (whether or not these actions are wanted, deliberated, intended, or tried).

Restraints are of two broad kinds: those which render actions unavailable, and those which render them ineligible. This chapter is concerned with the former kind, but for the sake of clarity it will first be necessary to discuss the notion of a restraint in general. Attention is then turned toward the following problems:

(a) What counts as an *available* course of action?
(b) What types of restraints rendering actions unavailable limit the *freedom* of agents?
(c) How is the degree of (freedom-limiting) unavailability of actions to be understood?

One of the difficulties of providing an acceptable definition of a restraint is the immense range of dispute about which restraints limit freedom. My aim here is simply to provide an analytical structure within which such disputes can be discussed (see section (iv) of this chapter and chapter 8, section (ii)). With this in mind, I aim for a definition that is sufficiently broad to accommodate the most liberal conceptions of restraints on action that limit freedom.

A *restraint on action* is defined as anything that

(i) makes it impossible for an agent to do or avoid something;
(ii) makes it more difficult for an agent to complete successfully or to avoid the action to which the restraint is attached than would be the case if the restraint were absent;
(iii) raises the prospects of costs to be incurred subsequent to the completion or avoidance of the action to which the restraint is attached—costs that are (prospectively) greater than would be the case if the restraint were absent.

Restraints can be classified according to several principles of division. Firstly, those which form the topic of this chapter render actions unavailable. These are of type (i) above, and can be distinguished from those which render actions ineligible (those of types (ii) and (iii)).

Second, restraints of types (i) and (ii) may be labeled impediments, while those of type (iii) are deterrents and inducements. An impediment, unlike a deterrent or inducement, intervenes between the attempt and the performance, sometimes preventing the successful completion of the latter. Thus, a high wall is an impediment to my entering private property, and may act as a deterrent to making the attempt. The existence of a landing tax is an impediment to immigrating (because one cannot immigrate without paying it), but is a deterrent, and not an impediment, to emigrating (because it is incurred only after one has emigrated).

The brief characterization of a deterrent given here obscures difficulties that will be dealt with in chapter 8, section (iii).

Finally, Feinberg suggests two principles that feature importantly in controversies about the nature of freedom (*op. cit.*, p. 12). One yields a negative-positive dichotomy, the other an external-internal dichotomy. A *positive* restraint is the presence of something. A *negative* restraint is the absence of something. An external restraint is understood by Feinberg as one that comes from outside a person's body-cum-mind. All other restraints are *internal*. Feinberg gives the following examples to illustrate his categories. Internal positive restraints, e.g., headaches, obsessive thoughts, compulsive desires. Internal negative restraints, e.g., ignorance, weakness, deficiencies in talent or skill. External positive restraints, e.g., barred windows, locked doors, pointed bayonets. External negative restraints, e.g., lack of money, lack of transport, lack of weapons.

(ii) *Availability of Actions*

The notion of an available action was introduced in the background theory. Here it was claimed that an *option*, i.e., a course of action available to an agent, includes any course of action that is a proper object of deliberation in practical activity. Unavailable actions are excluded from deliberation, since they are subject to restraints rendering them impossible in a sense to be elucidated.

I do not mean to suggest that actions are available or unavailable only to agents capable of deliberation. On the assumption that leaving the closet is impossible for the closet child, leaving that closet is an improper object of deliberation for that child; and this remains true whether or not the child is capable of deliberating. Hence, one can properly say of agents incapable of deliberating that actions are available or unavailable to them.

In connecting the relevant sense of possibility with that of being a proper object of deliberation in *practical* reasoning, Aristotle notes: ". . . nobody deliberates about things which are invariable or about things which he cannot do himself."[1] I shall not dwell on the notion of invariability, for the interesting notion as far as political and social freedom is concerned is person-relative impossibility. One problem about invariability, relevant to freedom, should be mentioned, however. One form of "invariability" is that of deontic impossibility, where such an impossibility is any that does not permit the inference from "necessary not-p to not-p." As Benn and Weinstein[2] note: ". . . there is a rule-derived sense in which a person is unfree to do anything forbidden by a rule (i.e. not 'praetermitted') irrespective of any sanction, as one is unfree to move a pawn back-

---

1. *Nicomachean Ethics*, 1140a24–b12.
2. "Being Free to Act and Being a Free Man," *Mind*, LXXX (1971).

wards in chess. If A has undertaken to have dinner with B this evening, A is not free to accept another invitation. He has already limited the alternatives he is *entitled* to choose among" (*ibid.*, p. 207).

One way to accommodate the "rule-derived" sense of freedom in our model is to extend the notion of impossibility to include deontic impossibilities. Thus, rules that "limit the alternatives one is *entitled* to choose among" render actions deontically impossible (relative to contexts, such as playing a game of chess), and are therefore restraints rendering actions unavailable.

I turn now to person-relative impossibility. We might say that an action is unavailable to an agent in this second sense to which Aristotle alludes, if and only if that agent himself cannot bring it about that he perform that action. Several points need to be made to clarify this notion.

First, it is not sufficient to be able to bring something about that one has the ability to do the thing, in the sense of "is good enough to do it." Consider Bjorn Borg's ability to beat Chris Lewis at Wimbledon 1981. Where this means that Bjorn Borg was good enough to beat Lewis at Wimbledon in 1981, this ability exists whether or not Lewis is eliminated by a third party, or in which part of the draw Lewis is placed. Assume that Lewis is eliminated in the first round. As of then, Borg cannot bring it about that he beat Lewis at Wimbledon 1981. Borg cannot reason practically about beating Lewis once the latter is eliminated, since he cannot initiate a course of action that will lead to this. He can, of course, indulge in theoretical reasoning about how he would have beaten Lewis had he played him (in this sense one can even "deliberate" about the past). Hence, even though Borg has the ability to beat Lewis at Wimbledon 1981 (and this ability remains when Lewis is eliminated), beating Lewis at Wimbledon 1981 is not *available* to Borg once Lewis is eliminated.

Second, one can bring something about even when one does *not* have the ability to do the thing, in the sense of "is not good enough to do the thing." For example, due to my present state of unfitness, I do not now have the ability to swim twelve lengths of the pool, yet I now have the ability to initiate a course of action that will, in due course, lead to my swimming twelve lengths should I desire to do so and have the opportunity to do so. Thus, swimming twelve lengths of the pool is an available course of action, because I can deliberate about it and initiate a (regrettably protracted) course of action to bring it about. What is unavailable right now is my swimming twelve lengths of the baths *right now*, or a baby's swimming twelve lengths *now or in the future*. (The baby cannot initiate now a course of action to bring it about.) At some time, however, swimming twelve lengths *will* become available to a one-month-old future swimming champion.

Thirdly, a person can bring about something herself even though she cannot bring it about unaided. If P can bring it about that she φs provided Q cooperates, and P can bring about Q's cooperation, then P can bring it about that she φs. On the other hand, the fact that I would be a millionaire if a number of possibilities, each realizable by human agency, obtained (e.g., people's generosity miraculously all converged on *me*) is not sufficient for becoming a millionaire to be something I can bring about, and to be an available option for me. If, however, I can *get* people to contribute sufficiently lavishly, then the option is available.

In general, being able to bring about φ is not consistent with φing only as a result of accident or luck (e.g., coming across buried treasure by accident), or φing as a result of physical compulsion. φing as a result of unintentional, or even intentional, action does not entail being able to bring about φ. (My digging the garden is an intentional action; I come across unknown treasure (accidentally) as a result of that digging, but I am not able to bring it about that I came across that treasure.) On my account, φing is available to me only if my practical activity can be instrumental in my φing (i.e., my φing can be the result of my deliberating, intending, or trying to φ).

Fourthly, a person can bring about something himself, even though on a given occasion he fails due to the intervention of "untoward" events. A precise definition of an untoward event cannot be given, but the general idea can be illustrated by way of example. We might say that would-be escapees from Colditz can bring about an escape by tunneling even if *on each attempt* the tunnel has been discovered by "unlucky chance." One would not say, however, that escape by tunneling is possible, if, for example, it can only take place under the noses of the guards, if construction difficulties render the collapse of tunnels inevitable, and so on.

Fifthly, and finally, a person is not necessarily deemed able to bring about something if she can do so only by dint of "unnatural" effort. Again, no definition of "unnatural" can be given, but the idea is that any agent is not deemed able to bring about something if, for example, she can do so only after a lifetime of unrelenting effort. The vagueness in this has the consequence that it is not always easy, or even plausible, to distinguish restraints that render actions unavailable from those which merely render them ineligible. The difference between "extremely difficult for P to φ" and "impossible for P to φ" is not and should not be regarded as precisely determinate. For example, is it impossible or merely extremely difficult for an unintelligent man, completely unversed in the art of escape, to overcome the obstacles presented by high walls, Alsatian dogs, vigilant guards, and barbed wire? From the fact, however, that the application of a distinction in certain areas is uncertain, arbitrary, or indeterminate, it does not follow that there is no distinction to be drawn.

It is admitted, then, that restraints that prevent an agent from performing an action are not always clearly distinguishable from those which merely render that performance extremely difficult. It does not follow from this, however, that severe *deterrents* can render actions unavailable. The deterrent itself does not *prevent* an agent performing an action under sanction (although extreme fear, caused by knowledge of the deterrent, may constitute an internal preventing impediment to that performance). Certainly the sanctions may be so severe that only saints or heroes would intend to perform those actions in the face of them, but the existence of those sanctions does not exclude them from deliberation. That is, deliberations about such actions would not be out of order. In their "Being Free to Act and Being a Free Man," Benn and Weinstein claim that someone who denies that several penal sanctions make an action *unavailable* to any reasonably prudent man must assume that "the man who submits to the law does so as freely, no more, no less, than the man who deliberately defies it" (*ibid.*, p. 207). This does not follow. For there are dimensions of freedom other than that of availability of actions on which to compare their respective freedom. In particular, it is important to hold firm to the distinction between availability and eligibility of actions.

Parent is clearly correct in distinguishing factors that prevent agents from doing things from those which merely undermine the will. Where he is wrong is in assuming that the latter cannot restrict freedom. Furthermore, the unavailable and the ineligible limit practical rational activity in different aspects: the former is a limitation in the objects of potential deliberation, the latter a limitation in the objects of potential intention.

(iii) *Unavailable Actions That Limit Freedom*

An *unavailable* action is any action that is not available. The question arises: Which kinds of restraints, rendering actions unavailable, limit the *freedom* of agents? Answers to this question provide a rich source of controversy. As we saw in the introduction to this work, many philosophers recognize some sort of distinction between freedom and ability: for them, only a subclass of unavailable actions limit freedom. For example, according to Bernard Gert,[3] a cripple is free to dance, despite his inability to do so, as long as no one is hindering him from dancing. Dancing for Gert, then, is an unavailable course of action that does not render the cripple unfree.

Disagreement centers on the question where to draw the line between mere inability and inability that is also a lack of freedom. One may think that, in the context of social and political freedom, inabilities arising from factors outside the realm of human agency, and unremovable by human agency, do not constitute lacks of freedom. But, alas, even on this point there is not unanimity. In "Some Recent Work on the Concept of Liberty," where Parent examines "recent work on the concept of social and political freedom," he claims: ". . . it is not at all clear why natural events like snowstorms should be excluded from the class of external impediments capable of infringing upon one's freedom" (p. 149); his sole argument for this claim being an appeal to ordinary usage: "Is not the assertion 'the blizzard rendered X unfree to continue his travels' perfectly intelligible?" (p. 159).

The relationship between inabilities suffered by persons and human agency may be more or less close, and conceptions of freedom differ about how close it has to be in order for freedom to be limited. At one extreme is the view that there need be no connection between inabilities rendering one unfree and human

---

3. "Coercion and Freedom," in Roland J. Pennock and John W. Chapman, eds., *Coercion* (Nomos XIV) (Chicago: Aldine Atherton, 1972), pp. 30–48.

agency. This position is occupied by Parent. At the other extreme is Scott's[4] position. According to him: "We are neither free nor unfree to do things we are unable to do . . . [except] where the inability is the result of a conscious human intention to render us unfree" (*ibid.*, p. 182).

In between these extremes, there is a variety of relations between the existence of inabilities or obstacles held to limit freedom and human agency. The following is a sample.

(i) "I am normally said to be free to the degree to which no human being interferes with my activity."[5]

Here the relation of unfreedom is a relation of interference by one human agent with the activity of another: it is not necessary that the interference be made with the intention of restricting freedom.

(ii) "If I can't act in a specific way, I am unfree to do so only if a specific actor has performed an action which is a sufficient condition for my inability."[6]

An action can be a sufficient condition for an inability without its constituting an *interference*.

(iii) ". . . to suggest that freedom is at stake is to invite the question of what person or what social system are deliberately impeding someone's attempts to lead a happy life."[7]

Here it is recognized that exploitative social arrangements, as well as relations between individual actors, can deprive of freedom.

(iv) In his "second thoughts" on "Two Concepts of Liberty," Berlin affirms that relations of unfreedom can exist which in no way are traceable to human contrivance. For him, a state of unfreedom may embrace ". . . the closing of doors or the failure to open them, as a result intended or unintended of alterable human practices" (*op. cit.*, p. xi).

4. "Liberty, Licence and Not Being Free," *Political Studies*, IV (1956): 176–85.
5. Isaiah Berlin, "Two Concepts of Liberty," in *Four Essays on Liberty*, p. 122.
6. Felix Oppenheim, *Dimensions of Freedom* (New York: St. Martin's, 1961), p. 69.
7. Alan Ryan, "Freedom," *Philosophy*, XL (1965): 93–112, p. 110.

Chapter 7 Unavailability of Actions 97

Berlin's suggestion that relations of unfreedom may exist which are not imposed by human agency resembles the view of Raphael: "And we may speak of freedom from want, or of freeing mankind from the scourge of cancer, when we mean that the impediments to which we refer, although, not imposed by human action, are capable (we hope) of being removed by human action" (*op. cit.*, p. 115). Finally, J. R. Lucas strikes a strange intermediate position in *The Principles of Politics*,[8] where he claims that an important area of freedom is freedom from the "pressures of factual circumstances": "freedom from pressures, freedom from pain, from hunger, from ill-health, from fear, from want, from arbitrary arrest, from public opinion" (*ibid.*, p. 145). Yet no less than two pages further on, he contrasts lack of money with lack of freedom, saying that "Poverty can be an evil, and great poverty is a great evil: but it is a different evil from lack of freedom" (*ibid.*, p. 147). It is quite unclear on what grounds Lucas distinguishes inabilities due to lack of money from inabilities due to want, ill-health, fear, and so on.

Given the wealth of disagreement in this area, it is of no avail to claim that the endoxa alone clearly support or undermine one or other conception. We need to look at the requirements of the coherence theory as a whole to determine how the endoxa should be cohered. In the determination of the freedom phenomena, a wide range of endoxa should be saved, provided they can be cohered in a way that determines their worthiness to be preserved. Since the endoxa do not clearly support a narrow conception of freedom, there is a presumption, then, in favor of a wider conception that allows for the inclusion of a wide range of freedom-limiting restraints. But can the rationale for a wider conception be demonstrated?

I believe that it can. The narrower conceptions are right in focusing on the fact that freedom is a normative notion: delimiting the class of limitations on action must be based on the normative point of freedom. I suggest, however, that this point, as outlined in the background theory, demonstrates the rationale of saving a wide range of endoxa, and that the narrower conceptions have misidentified that point.

First, the narrower conceptions correctly appreciate the connection between freedom and agency, but make that connection in the wrong way. The point of freedom is the enhancement of

---

8. New York: Oxford, 1966.

an individual's potential in agency, which restraints limit, ceteris paribus. Its point does not lie in the assignment of causal or moral responsibility for the imposition or removal of these restraints, although, as apologists for narrow conceptions point out, we are often most interested in, e.g., restraints imposed by contrivance. Such interests, however, relate to the feasibility of, and responsibility for, the enhancement of freedom and the assignment of blame for its restriction. The *existence* of freedom is a different matter.[9]

Second, some narrow conceptions are right to focus on the fact that freedom is connected with normality. In particular, I have suggested, the standards of freedom are derived from normal human development in agency as this relates to individual potential. Thus, Berlin is correct to say that the inabilities "to fly like an eagle or swim like a whale"[10] are not limitations on human freedom. He is right though, not because unfreedom does not include inability, but because those types of ability are not within the range of *human* potentiality.

Some who embrace narrow conceptions of freedom, however, have not correctly characterized the connection between freedom and normality. One important account is that of Benn and Weinstein. In their "Being Free to Act and Being a Free Man," they claim that there is a background of "normal conditions of actions" that define the range of initial alternatives open to one. Alternatives are said to be restricted in such a way as to reduce one's *choice* only if they are restricted relative to those initial alternatives. For example, charging 62 cents as the price of a dozen eggs will not be understood as limiting a pauper's freedom as long as ". . . the general framework of property rela-

---

9. This point is neglected by David Miller in "'Constraints on Freedom," *Ethics*, XCIV (1983): 66–86. In defending his claim that "we use the notion of freedom . . . in the subclass of cases where the presence of an obstacle can be attributed to the action of another human being or beings" (p. 68), he confuses the point of *having* freedom with the issue of justification for the "continued presence" of obstacles. If the point of freedom were indeed to raise such issues of *justification*, then the *human* origin of obstacles could possibly be relevant (but in making out this claim, Miller confuses justification for origin with justification for continued presence). The same error, I believe, is made by Benn and Weinstein in "Being Free to Act and Being a Free Man," p. 199: ". . . an onus of justification" for the presence of freedom-limiting conditions is confused with "the reasons for saying a person is not free in respect of . . . an action."

10. Quoted from Helvetius, in "Two Concepts of Freedom," p. 122, n.2.

Chapter 7 Unavailability of Actions

tions is taken to define the normal conditions of action, and therefore the initial opportunities and alternatives available, just as the laws of mechanics determine the conditions under which we can fly."[11] They continue, however, ". . . it is a well established move in radical argument to call into question the hitherto given initial conditions, like property institutions, by arguing that they *do* close alternatives otherwise available . . ." (*ibid.*, p. 202).

In my view, however, there are considerable costs to this approach, for a judgment concerning the freedom of an agent is dependent on a prior judgment on whether closures of options are just. As Benn and Weinstein suggest, just social arrangements are held to be part of the *normal* background conditions of choice. So, presumably, just imprisonment does not limit the freedom of prisoners. A deeper objection appeals to the difference between the point or value of freedom and that of justice. On my view, the point of freedom is the value of the absence of limitations inhibiting individuals' potential in their practical rational activity. On many views of the point of justice, however, it is the value of regulating the *relationship* between individuals whose interests conflict but who nonetheless should be treated as Kantian ends-in-themselves. Even if one wishes to make the controversial claim that the free human being possessed the *virtue* of justice (because that virtue, among others, is deemed to enhance potential in agency), it does not follow that obstacles to action limit freedom only if they are unjust *obstacles*. Obstacles, just or unjust, limit potential in agency. Nor would it follow that freedom is equated with just *action*. Being just on an occasion may cost you your life and thereby terminate your freedom.

Accordingly, it is far better to keep the values of freedom and justice distinct. Far better to say that any system of property, whether private or collective, just or unjust, limits the freedom of *some* agents with respect to some actions. For a system of property just is a system of legal relationships to resources which protect property holders by coercive means. Hence, in a system of private property, the person who lacks money to obtain a dozen eggs is not suffering from a mere physical inability to obtain those eggs: rather, if he attempts to obtain them without paying, he is liable to be forcibly prevented or subjected to

11. "Being Free to Act and Being a Free Man," pp. 201–2.

legal process.[12] In a system of collective ownership, the person who wants to destroy or dismantle a communally owned bicycle, or use it at a prohibited time, is again not suffering from a mere physical incapacity with respect to those actions. The existence of legal and physical restraints inherent in *any* property system, just or unjust, should be regarded as restrictive of freedom. Whether those restraints are just or not is a separate matter.

On my view, then, a restraint limits an agent's freedom, ceteris paribus, if it *restricts* the potential of that agent's practical activity, whether justly or unjustly, legitimately or illegitimately. It is important to realize that the issue of what restraints are freedom-limiting should be kept quite distinct from the issues of which freedoms enhance the *net* amount of overall freedom of that agent or other agents, or which freedoms enhance values other than freedom. From the fact that freedom has value, it does not follow that concern should be expressed or even felt for each of the myriad of actions specific agents are unfree to perform. Certainly, the everyday doings of people whose paths never cross constantly close off options. For example, people legitimately park in vacant lots, preventing me from parking there. It may seem odd to suggest that the presence of those cars constitutes freedom-limiting restraints, when we see no (net) value in removing them in order to expedite my shopping duties. This oddness may result, however, from confusing the view that freedom is a value with the clearly false propositions that for any agent P, and any action φ, there is some net value in P's being free to φ;[13] and for any agent P and any action φ that P is currently unfree to perform, there is a *net* value in P's being *rendered* free to φ.

(iv) *The Degree of Unavailability*

It is obvious that the degree to which courses of action are unavailable is at least partly a function of the number of actions unavailable. As is well known, however, there is a problem in counting alternative actions. In an oft-cited passage, Berlin claims that ". . . the method of counting these [alternatives] can

---

12. I am indebted to Jeremy Waldron for this point.
13. Indeed, there may be no value *at all* in P's being free to φ (see above, pp. 55–6).

Chapter 7 Unavailability of Actions

never be more than impressionistic. Possibilities of action are not discrete entities like apples, which can be exhaustively enumerated. . . ." (*op. cit.*, p. 130, fn.). In his *Dimensions of Freedom*, Oppenheim also notes the problem: "In most cases, it is simply not feasible to count actions, let alone potential actions or kinds of actions" (*op. cit.*, p. 195).

The practical problem is deciding whether to count similar act types as one alternative or several. It seems clear that, if one act type is available to an agent, but another act type is unavailable, they should be counted as two, no matter how similar. Assume that a dictator obsessed by a hatred of daffodils has banned the painting of houses daffodil yellow, but not lemon. In this case, painting one's house daffodil yellow and painting one's house lemon should count as two actions even though their similarity suggests their subsumption under one alternative (e.g., painting one's house yellow).

Unfortunately, however, the counting of different act types as distinct alternatives when one and the same action is available under one description, but not available under another, is threatened by paradox. In his "Freedoms and Utilities in the Distribution of Health Care," Peter Singer[14] claims that "expanding" a person's options to *sell* as well as to give blood might actually constitute a diminution of freedom, since the option of giving something that cannot be bought would become unavailable, and this freedom is incompatible with the freedom to sell.

Gerald Dworkin[15] regards this claim as paradoxical, giving the following example:

> Suppose in a certain prison mail could go out only after being read by a censor. New regulations allow prisoners a choice of sending their mail out in the accustomed fashion or unread by a censor. Surely we would regard this as an expansion of freedom. Yet, a Singerian argument could be constructed to show that whereas previously a prisoner could send a letter knowing it would be read by a censor, now the nature of the prisoner's letter is altered. The recipient of the letter is not guaran-

14. In *Markets and Morals*, G. Dworkin, G. Bermant, and P. Brown, eds. (New York: Washington Hemisphere, 1977), p. 163–6.
15. "Is More Choice Better than Less?" in *Midwest Studies in Philosophy*, VII, Peter A. French, Theodore E. Uehling Jr., Howard K. Wettstein, eds. (Minneapolis: Minnesota UP, 1982), pp. 47–61, here p. 53.

teed to have had the letter read by other than the writer of the letter. Of course the example is silly because we can think of no reason to want to be assured of this fact. But this seems to show that it is the alteration of the nature of the gift and not the effect on freedom that is crucial (*ibid.*, p. 53).

Despite the appeal of this example, it is crucial to be able to regard one act as available under one description and not available under another, and crucial for this feature to affect an agent's overall freedom. A starving peasant who sold his labor to Jones on Monday may be free under the description "selling his labor to *Jones*" but not free under the description "selling his labor"; for he may be compelled to sell his labor, but not compelled to sell it to Jones. How then do we avoid the paradox highlighted by Dworkin? The solution is to maintain the Singerian position but to resist the paradox by the following move. The new regulation in Dworkin's example "expands options" in an intuitive sense because the option added is highly significant to the prisoners, whereas the option subtracted is ludicrously lacking in significance. In this sense, whether or not a factor genuinely expands or limits options depends not only on the number of alternatives, but also on their significance. Thus, Singer's position is neither confused nor necessarily false: he is correct if he can show that the freedom to sell blood is less significant than the freedom to give blood that cannot be bought.

In the above, I considered the problem of individuation where actions are available under one description but not under another. In cases where sufficiently similar actions are all available, or are all unavailable, subsumption under one description is justified on the assumption that they are sufficiently similar. No hard and fast rules can be offered for what counts as sufficiently similar; and the motivation to provide such rules is in any case reduced by the fact that the degree of availability of courses of action is a function of variety as well as of number. Consider the following sets of act types:

A: Playing hockey for team *A*; playing hockey for team *B*.
B: Playing hockey; playing squash.

A pupil for whom only the alternatives specified in *A* are available on a sports afternoon enjoys less variety of alternatives than the pupil who can play hockey or squash. Thus, even if alternatives are specified in such a way that freedom-limiting obstacles leave agents with the same number of alternatives, the agent enjoying the greater variety has the greater freedom with respect to availability of alternatives.

I shall not canvass any particular method of assessing variety of alternatives. Any such method, however, should preserve judgments, such as "Set B above specifies a greater variety of alternatives than set A," and

E_{15}: "If I am free to be a pitcher or a poet, I am freer than if my options are being a pitcher or a shortstop."[16]

I shall merely point out that there are difficulties in preserving judgments such as E_{15}, if the subject of freedom is considered the final arbiter of degree of difference between alternatives. For example, Crocker proposes the following criterion: ". . . we might take as definitive the degree of difference the individual would judge there to be between two alternatives if he or she had tried both of them" (ibid., pp. 55–6). One can imagine a top professional baseball player, a natural shortstop but forced to pitch, and a hater of poetry, who regards the second pair of alternatives specified in E_{15} as more diverse than the first pair. The obvious reply is that the judger is confusing degree of significance-to-him of alternatives, with degree of difference between alternatives. It is natural for the agent himself to be the final arbiter of his own preferences between pairs of alternatives, but the notion of degree of difference between alternatives seems to be an objective notion. Indeed, Crocker's motivation for regarding the agent as the ultimate judge of degree of *difference* is misguided. He claims: "Since we are concerned about the value of freedom for the individual, the appropriate measure of degree of difference is, for the most part, the individual's own" (ibid., p. 55). The *degree* of availability of alternatives in terms of number and variety, however, is not conceptually linked with the significance of those alternatives to the individual. Although in standard cases an individual's interests may lie in having a greater rather than lesser variety of alternatives, this is not necessarily true of individuals with specialized interests.

16. Lawrence Crocker, *Positive Liberty: An Essay in Normative Political Philosophy* (The Hague: Nijhoff, 1980), p. 55.

CHAPTER 8

Ineligibility of Actions

(i) *Ineligibility*

To claim of an action that it is to a degree ineligible presupposes its availability. For an ineligible action is not excluded from deliberation: even where penalties attached to its performance are severe, it is a possible terminus of the practical process.

I earlier described actions as being ineligible to the extent that restraints attached to the performance of actions render them difficult or costly to perform. More specifically, I shall say that a restraint R renders an action A (to a degree) ineligible, if and only if R makes A more difficult or costly (relative to not performing A) than would be the case were R not present. According to this definition, R can render an action ineligible even though R improves the total choice situation for P relative to that existing before R obtained. It follows that any manipulation of the costs and benefits facing P renders certain actions (to a degree) ineligible for P. This consequence of the definition does not matter for my purposes, for the burden of my analysis lies in answering the question: Which restraints rendering actions ineligible limit the *freedom* of agents?

(ii) *The Nature of Threats and Offers*

The ultimate purpose of the next two sections is to examine the question of the effect on freedom of threats and offers. I shall suggest that the current thinking on this issue is radically misguided. To show this, I first need to discuss the distinction between threats and offers, and my opposition to current analyses.

In his article "Coercive Offers," Robert Stevens[1] argues against the account of threats and offers proposed by Steiner

---

1. *Australasian Journal of Philosophy*, LXVI (1988): 83–95.

Chapter 8 Ineligibility of Actions

(*op. cit.*), claiming that it is vulnerable to counterexample. I shall suggest that Stevens's own account is also susceptible to counterexample. More importantly, I shall claim, this susceptibility, shared by Steiner and Stevens, is symptomatic of a radical mistake made by both Stevens and those whom he criticizes. The current thinking on the nature of threats and offers shares a common presupposition which I shall question.

Threats and offers are currently distinguished by focusing on the proposee's preference schedule, relative to a baseline of what Steiner calls a concept of "normalcy"—a baseline from which threats and offers are deemed to be specific kinds of departure. Authors differ on the details of this basic idea, however. For Steiner, the standard of normalcy is "the course of events which would confront the recipient of the intervention were the intervention not to occur" (*op. cit.*, p. 39). An intervention is an *offer* relative to this norm, if and only if "the compliance-consequence represents a situation which is preferred [by the recipient] to the norm while the noncompliance-consequence represents a situation on the norm, no more or less preferred than it because identical to it" (*op. cit.*, p. 39). An intervention is a *threat* relative to this norm, if and only if "the compliance-consequence represents a situation which is less preferred than the norm . . . but the noncompliance-consequence represents a situation which is still less preferred . . ." (*op. cit.*, p. 39).

In disagreeing with Steiner's account, Stevens offers the following counterexample:

> Suppose P offers Q a handful of beans for her cow. It is likely that P prefers her cow to a handful of beans (unless they are magic beans). If so, the desirability to Q of noncompliance with P's offer . . . is greater than the desirability to Q of compliance with P's offer (*op. cit.*, p. 84).

Stevens's account of offers is as follows.

P's proposal to Q that Q do A is an offer if and only if the desirability to Q of Q's doing A relative to what it would have been if P made no proposal is increased, and the desirability to Q of Q's doing not A relative to what it would have been if P made no proposal is unchanged; or the desirability to Q of Q's not doing A relative to what it would have been if P made no proposal is increased, and the desirability to Q of Q's doing A

relative to what it would have been if *P* made no proposal is unchanged (*op. cit.*, p. 85).

This account accommodates the cow for beans case, in that *Q* presumably prefers giving away her cow in exchange for beans to giving away her cow simpliciter. Stevens's account, too, is vulnerable to counterexample. Assume that I have a number of garden gnomes in my garage which I cannot sell. I offer *Q* a dozen of my choicest gnomes for her cow. *Q*, though, hates garden gnomes and does not want the bother of getting rid of them. *Q* prefers giving away her cow simpliciter to giving away her cow in exchange for gnomes. The desirability to *Q* of giving away her cow relative to what it would have been had there been no proposal is decreased, and the desirability to *Q* of not giving away her cow relative to what it would have been had there been no proposal is unchanged. So, on Stevens's account, the proposal of gnomes for cow is not an offer. Yet surely my proposal, though unfortunate and perhaps even misguided, is still an offer?

I shall claim that both Steiner and Stevens make the same radical mistake. Stevens follows a long line of accounts that distinguish threats and offers by focusing on their effect on the preferences of the proposee. In short, they treat threats and offers as perlocutionary acts. A treatment of threats and offers as illocutionary acts would lead to quite different results. The reason the gnome lover's proposal is an offer despite the preferences of the gnome hater has to do with the conventions surrounding the making of offers and the context surrounding the proposal.

More specifically, the fact that the proposal is an offer has nothing to do with the preferences of the person to whom the offer is directed: preferences that determine the perlocutionary effect of the offer but not the nature of the proposal as an offer. The proposal to exchange gnomes for the cow is an offer, given the following:

> (i) the proposal falls within the accepted range of locutions conventionally assigned to the making of offers: paradigmatically the uttering of the words: "Would you care for my gnomes in exchange for your cow?" rather than, e.g., a locution designed for insulting: "If you don't prefer my gnomes to your miserable beast, you're even more of an idiot than I thought."

Chapter 8 Ineligibility of Actions

These conventions are designed for:

(a) Securing a certain uptake (viz., "... bringing about the understanding of the meaning and of the force of the locution,"[2] even though that uptake may not be secured on a given occasion (the offeree did not hear, for example).

(b) Taking effect in a certain way (whereby "... in consequence of the performance of this [illocutionary] act, such and such a future event, *if* it happens, will be *in order*, and such-and-such other events, *if* they happen, will not be in order").[3] For example, rolling up one's sleeves may be in order as a consequence of the slight to one's animal and one's intelligence, but definitely not in order as a consequence of the offer of exchange.

(c) Inviting further acts that are responses or sequels (in the case of offers, acceptance or rejection by the offeree, and if there is acceptance, the offerer's honoring his offer).[4]

(ii) The procedure for making an offer is invoked in appropriate circumstances: in a context where an exchange of cows for gnomes can be made. If there are no gnomes to exchange, if the context is a play, or a joke on a desert island, there is no genuine offer.

(iii) The proposal is designed for use by persons having certain intentions, expectations, and hopes:[5] e.g., the hope or expectation that the offeree will perceive the offer as a benefit, and the intention not to harm the offeree by the offer. Consequently, if the proposer believes the gnomes are filled with explosives and hopes to maim the proposee, the offer will be, to use Austin's words, "unhappy" (though Austin did not believe the performance to be "void" in these circumstances).[6]

---

2. See Austin, *How to Do Things with Words*, J. O. Urmson, ed. (New York: Oxford, 1962), p. 166.
3. Austin, "Performative-Constative," in John Searle, ed., *The Philosophy of Language* (New York: Oxford, 1971), pp. 13–22, p. 14.
4. Austin, *How to Do Things with Words*, p. 116.
5. See Austin, *How to Do Things with Words*, p. 39.
6. See further, Austin, "Performative Utterances," in *Philosophical Papers*, pp. 233–52, esp. p. 239.

I have denied that Stevens's account provides a necessary condition of offers. The root problem is his failure to appreciate the conventional aspects—illocutionary force—of offers. The same problem underlies the failure of his account to provide a sufficient condition of offers. Consider his following example:

> Highwayman P wants money. So P points a gun at traveller Q's head and says to Q 'I am going to kill you.' Some time later P still holding the gun at Q's head says to Q 'Your money or your life.' Preferring to keep her life to keeping her money Q gives P her money (*op. cit.*, p. 93).

It is a consequence of Stevens's view that this is an offer, and he accepts this consequence. Yet, surely, it has all the conventional force of a threat.

It may be argued that the problem lies in the standard of normalcy that Stevens has proposed. Perhaps the pre-offer situation that is the baseline for comparison should be prior to the context of the coercive setup within which the so-called offer is made. This suggestion does not help in the case of other counterexamples, however, which reinforce my claim that the real problem lies in the failure to appreciate that offers and threats should be understood as illocutionary acts. Consider again the standard highway robber's proposal: "Your money or your life!" Imagine that I, the proposee, am suicidal. Being of a cowardly disposition, I have failed to take my own life by the traditional methods. The highway robber provides me with just the situation I crave. By refusing to yield, I am able to end my miserable existence, and on a high note: my fantasies of dying while resisting the forces of evil are splendidly realized. Yet, surely, despite my bizarre preferences, the proposal is a threat.[7] The problem with Stevens's account is not that he fixes on the wrong baseline for comparison of preferences, but that he focuses on the preferences of the proposee at all. The reason the highway robber makes a threat is that the proposal has the illocutionary force of a threat. "Your money or your life" is text-book threatening language designed to invite the responses and sequels appropriate to threats; the context is appropriate to the issuing of gen-

---

7. It should be acknowledged that there is a sense of 'making a threat' where this is a perlocutionary act: X threatens Y only if Y is actually threatened by the threat. In this respect 'threaten' shares the ambiguity of 'warn'.

uine threats—one of attempted armed robbery; the robber has the appropriate expectations and intentions: his aims are not ones of the benevolent mercy killer, but are those of the traditional highway robber. In no way does the proposal have the illocutionary force of an offer. Yet on Stevens's account, the highwayman's proposal to me that I hand over my money is an offer. It is an offer, since one of the sufficient conditions for offers is satisfied: the desirability to me of my not handing over the money relative to what it would have been if the highwayman had made no proposal is increased, and the desirability to me of handing over my money relative to what it would have been if the highwayman had made no proposal is unchanged.

Although Stevens's account provides neither necessary nor sufficient conditions for proposals being offers, accounts such as his (and those he criticizes) are right to focus on the important distinction between the point of threats and offers: the point that distinguishes their illocutionary force. Threats are designed to limit options, whereas offers are designed to expand them. But Stevens's account, like those he criticizes, interprets this idea in terms of perlocutionary effect on the individual proposee, instead of the illocutionary force of the proposal. Whether or not a proposal is an offer does not depend on whether or not *in fact* the proposal expands options. It depends on whether the context is one in which it has the illocutionary force of an offer—on whether or not it is a conventionally recognized, context-sensitive, signal for option-expansion.

(iii) Do Threats and Offers Limit Freedom?

Whether or not threats and offers limit freedom depends on their perlocutionary effects. Because threats and offers have been standardly analyzed in terms of their perlocutionary effects, there has been a tendency to believe that getting straight on the distinction between threats and offers will answer the question about their relationship to freedom. Since the nature of threats and offers depends on their illocutionary force, however, and not on their perlocutionary effects, this belief is mistaken.

Threats and offers have many perlocutionary effects, not all of which determine their effect on freedom. As the background theory suggests, the relevant perlocutionary effects are whether or not the threat or offer limits the individual's potential in agency. There are two areas that are relevant: limitation of *autonomy*, and limitation of *options*. Both threats and offers may limit autonomy by subverting the deliberative process through debilitating fear or irresistible temptation. Since this chapter is concerned with eligibility of options, the autonomy factor will be deferred until chapter 9.

Consider first, threats. I shall argue that though threats paradigmatically limit options and therefore freedom, not all threats do, since threats are not defined in terms of their perlocutionary effects. First, however, we must consider an argument of Steiner's suggesting that *no* threats limit freedom. His argument is based on a similarity between threats and offers. People can be brought to do things that they otherwise would not do by both threats and offers, since both operate by manipulating the relative desirability of compliance and noncompliance. It is not necessarily the case that the difference in desirability between compliance and noncompliance is greater where the intervention is a threat as opposed to an offer: furthermore, both threats and offers can be so irresistible that reasonable people cannot be expected not to comply. Steiner concludes that "it is not necessarily true that offers are more resistible or exert less influence than threats" (*op. cit.*, p. 40). From this conclusion,[8] he draws the inference that, since there is no difference between the way in which threats and offers affect the practical deliberations of their recipients, no such difference can "constitute a reason for asserting that threats, but not offers, diminish personal liberty" (*op. cit.*, p. 43). He concludes that neither threats nor offers limit freedom.

This conclusion is at odds with the endoxa, e.g.,

E_4: The man who hands over his money, having yielded to credible threat at gun point, does not perform a free act.

E_{16}: The professional tennis player who accepts the promoter's offer of $50,000 merely to appear in a tournament in which he otherwise would not have appeared performs a free act, even though he could not be reasonably expected to turn down the offer.

The background theory not only demonstrates that the en-

---

8. For a fuller statement of this point, see Robert Nozick, "Coercion," in W. G. Runciman and Quentin Skinner, eds., *Philosophy, Politics and Society* (Fourth Series) (New York: Blackwell, 1972), pp. 101–135, esp. p. 129.

doxa can be saved, and their worthiness of preservation, but also what is wrong with Steiner's argument. The question the argument raises is: Why should the perlocutionary effect of relative degree of influence of a proposal determine a proposee's freedom? Surely a piece of advice may be so timely and apt that any reasonable person would be expected to go along with it. Admittedly, a threat may similarly powerfully influence a reasonable person, but surely the advice and the threat are not in the same boat as far as freedom is concerned. Why is this? According to the background theory, freedom is affected only where influence is seen as a *limitation* on the practical process.

A typical mistake (to be discussed more fully in the next chapter) has manifested itself in Steiner's argument. The mistake is a confusion between the material and the formal properties of freedom. Certainly, a frequent concomitant of freedom-limiting factors is relative irresistibility of influence on an agent's practical deliberations. This material property does not constitute a freedom-limiting factor, however, unless it is also true that it constitutes some kind of infelicity or untoward factor, viz., a flaw, limitation, or breakdown in the practical process. The advice does not limit agency: it enhances it.

The reason proposals manipulating costs and benefits restrict freedom as far as eligibility is concerned is that some *limit* options, whereas others expand them. According to Benn and Weinstein,[9] for example, threats standardly constitute limitations on options, whereas offers do not. This is the reason that threats, but not offers, standardly limit freedom. Although threats paradigmatically limit freedom by limiting options, not all proposals having the illocutionary force of threats do so. An example is the threat to the suicidal person discussed in the previous section.

Let us now turn our attention to the even more controversial area of offers. It may be thought that some offers limit freedom since they actually limit options. The problem is that whether or not an offer is regarded as a *limitation* depends on what counts as the "choice situation." An offer to beat a slave less if he works harder[10] constitutes an expansion of options relative to

---

9. "Being Free to Act and Being a Free Man," p. 201.
10. See the discussion in Virginia Held, "Coercion and Coercive Officers," in Pennock and Chapman, eds., pp. 49–62.

the current level of beating but does not constitute an expansion of options relative to the "norm," viz., a state of nonbeating. Hence, it may be asked: Should not the offer be seen as a "limitation" because it is a limitation relative to the relevant norm? More specifically, David Zimmerman[11] holds the view that the "offer" is coercive—being a limitation of freedom—because it is a limitation on options in the following sense. The slave owner prevents the slave from acting on his own or with the help of others to procure an *alternative* proposal situation that is strongly preferred to the actual one (*ibid.*, p. 133).

In order to answer this challenge, we must be clearer about the notion of a limitation of options. On our view, a restraint R that renders an action A_i ineligible is held to *limit* P's options with respect to A_i, if and only if for some pair of alternatives $(A_i \ldots A_j)$, where P must choose either A_i or A_j, R produces more restraint[12] attached to P's performance of A_i and A_j taken together than that which prevailed before R came into being. This view is distinct from the view that R limits options, if and only if for some large set of actions $A_i \ldots A_m$, R produces more restraint attached to P's performance of those actions taken together than would have been the case without R. The much criticized view that "that ill deserves the name of confinement which hedges us in only from bogs and precipices"[13] looks quite reasonable on the latter account of what counts as a limitation of options, provided it is assumed that the absence of the putative confinement would sufficiently increase the probability of falling into bogs and over the precipices. On my view, then, to claim that R limits freedom *with respect to the eligibility of P's performance of A_i* does presuppose comparison with other actions, but the relevant comparison class is that action that P must perform if she does not perform A_i: it is not some larger set of actions. The larger set is relevant only *a propos P's overall* freedom with respect to eligibility. An important caveat must be made. Whether or not a cost/benefit manipulation limits options *from the standpoint of ineligibility* does not depend on the preferences of the proposee, even though there is, as we have already noted, a richer sense of limiting options where the degree of

---

11. "Coercive Wage Offers," *Philosophy and Public Affairs*, X (1981): 121–45.
12. The notion of *degree* of restraint is discussed below, section (iv).
13. John Locke, *The Second Treatise on Civil Government*, para. 57.

limitation is a function of both degree of restraint and degree of significance of alternatives.

We can now reply to the views of Zimmerman, Virginia Held, and others. In assessing whether or not an agent is unfree in a certain respect, it is essential to specify the action with respect to which he is unfree, and the particular restraint that renders the agent unfree in that respect. My point is that, although Zimmerman correctly focuses on an area of unfreedom, viz., the action of attaining the strongly preferred proposal situation, the restraint that prevents or hinders the slave from attaining that goal is *not* the making of the offer to beat the slave less if he works harder. It is a quite different restraint or set of restraints: it is the restraints that prevent or hinder the slave from leading a life free of beatings. The offer itself is not a limitation with respect to the slave's options of not working harder or working harder. Similarly, the issuing of a threat, such as "Your money or your life," may enhance your options, where it involves the cancellation of a previous credible threat, "Your money, or the lives (after protracted torture) of all your children." But, of course, this does not alter the fact that the issuing of either threat involves a reduction of overall freedom relative to the tranquil situation that obtained before the robber impinged on your life.

(iv) *Degree of Ineligibility*

In this section, the types of restraints rendering P's performance of A ineligible are conceptualized in such a way that, for any such restraint R, one can conceive of R rendering A ineligible *to a certain degree*. In this respect, such restraints differ from those rendering actions unavailable. The latter do not admit of degree, for they cause the performance of actions to be impossible, and impossibility does not admit of degree. By contrast, restraints rendering actions ineligible cause their performance to be (in a certain degree) difficult or costly.

My preferred interpretation of degree of ineligibility of actions requires that the contribution made by impediments be treated separately from that made by deterrents. In broad outline, the degree of ineligibility caused by R on P's performance of A, where R is an *impediment*, is the least cost that P would incur while overcoming R in a performance of A.

There are three ways of *overcoming* R in order successfully to perform A in the face of R.

1. *Remove* or partially remove the restraint. This means destroying the restraint in whole, or in part, or effecting its total or partial disappearance.
2. *Bypass* the restraint. Here, one does not render the restraint absent, but renders it inoperative on one's performance or avoidance of A. Its restraining force on one is nullified.
3. *Endure* the restraint. Here, the restraint is both present and operative. One simply performs the restrained action in spite of its restraining force. One thereby incurs the cost of the restraint as it operates on one.

When there is more than one possible way of performing A with more than one corresponding cost, one measures whichever cost of performance is the smallest. Let me illustrate these three ways of performing A with some examples.

1. Let action A be stealing fruit from an orchard.
   Let restraint R be the high wall.
   R is removed by breaking down the wall.
   R is bypassed by going round the wall.
   R is endured by climbing the wall.
2. Let A be obtaining a fur coat.
   Let R be the monetary cost of fur coats.
   R is removed by bringing it about that fur coats are free, or partially removed by bringing down the cost.
   R is bypassed by stealing a coat, making a coat, having a coat given to one.
   R is endured (incurred) by paying the monetary cost of a coat.
3. Let A be avoiding imprisonment.
   Let R be being forced at bayonet point by guards.
   R is removed by disarming the guards.
   R is bypassed by running away.
   R is endured by standing firm.
4. Let A be attacking one's enemy.
   Let R be a lack of sophisticated weaponry.
   R is removed by obtaining sophisticated weaponry.
   R is endured by attacking without sophisticated weaponry.

Chapter 8 Ineligibility of Actions

It must be emphasized that the cost that measures the degree of ineligibility of actions does not measure the extent to which one is frustrated in being restrained from doing those actions. Rather, it is the cost one would bear in overcoming those restraints. The degree of ineligibility imposed by a high wall, for example, is not determined by the extent to which one longs for the fruit frustratingly out of reach. Rather, it is the cost (in terms of, e.g., fear, scraped knees, broken limbs) in overcoming that particular barrier.

A consequence of this analysis is that the degree of ineligibility of actions is not a function of opportunity costs. In pursuing actions, one foregoes others; the value of the actions foregone is the opportunity cost of the action pursued. One might think, therefore, that the higher the value of the actions foregone the more ineligible is the action pursued. The degree of ineligibility of actions, however, does not depend on the extent to which the agent values actions pursued or foregone. It is restraints (impediments and deterrents) that render actions ineligible, and the degree of ineligibility (in the case of impediments) is the cost of overcoming them. The value of actions to which restraints are attached is a quite separate freedom-affecting factor.

The analysis of the degree of ineligibility caused by deterrents poses problems. In the previous chapter, I understood a deterrent to be a restraint that raises the prospect of costs incurred on completion of actions. This characterization is, however, consistent with several ways of understanding the degree of ineligibility imposed by deterrents.

(i) One view assesses degree of ineligibility caused by deterrents in the same way as that caused by impediments: one simply considers the least cost that would be suffered by P in overcoming R in a performance of A. For example, one might *remove* a threat by silencing the threatening agent (e.g., by killing him), or by effecting the withdrawal of the threat (e.g., by making a counterthreat). Alternatively, one may *bypass* the threat by rendering it pointless or, finally, one may *endure* the threat (e.g., one makes oneself invulnerable to it) by performing the action and risking the implementation of the threat. Some philosophers appear to accept the view that it is the costs of acting in the face of deterrents—especially, for example, punishment—which limit an agent's freedom. For example,

Oppenheim claims: "Any 'punishment', however trivial, limits the victim's freedom to do—or most precisely—to have done what he is being punished for" (*op. cit.*, p. 76). This view, however, carries the controversial implication—which Oppenheim accepts—that, with respect to *eligibility* of actions, a person is quite free despite *threat* of punishment, as long as she is not punished (*op. cit.*, p. 80).

(ii) A second view would understand degree of ineligibility imposed by a deterrent as the least cost that P anticipates may be incurred by him while overcoming R in a performance of A, multiplied by the subjective probability of that cost's occurring.

This second view saves the well-entrenched endoxon:

E_{17}: Legal sanctions that are standardly enforced limit the freedom of those who perform the sanctioned actions and are not caught.

The second view appears, however, to neglect another important endoxon:

E_{18}: Laws with associated sanctions restrict an agent's freedom even if she is ignorant of the law.

Surely, a deterrent limits freedom even if it is not anticipated; and, surely, the matter is even worse if an entire populace were deliberately kept in ignorance of draconian sanctions.

(iii) A third view, which saves E_{18}, understands the degree of ineligibility of A resulting from R as the least cost an agent may incur while overcoming R in performing A, multiplied by the objective probability of R's occurring.

View (iii) indeed accommodates both E_{17} and E_{18}, but runs counter to

E_{19}: Anticipated punishment limits one's freedom inasmuch as it constitutes a threat that *inhibits* agents performing actions.

E_{19} has the support of Scott, for whom deterrents limit freedom in proportion to their efficacy in inhibiting an agent from performing the sanctioned action:

E_8: "The people who are especially resistant to threats have the widest freedom, though they may have to suffer for it, heroes, criminals, saints" (*op. cit.*, p. 218).

Chapter 8 Ineligibility of Actions

This view suggests a fourth way of conceptualizing degree of ineligibility.

(iv) The degree of ineligibility of A resulting from R is the cost, caused by R, incurred by the agent in overcoming his reluctance to perform A in the face of R.

Our coherence theory demands that, where possible, the endoxa are saved; but can this be done, given the apparent tensions between them? On my view, E_8 and E_{19} can be accommodated by the aspect of freedom that I have termed autonomy: the deterrent *effect* of R on an agent's psyche concerns not so much the eligibility of A, but the reason-giving links in P's practical reasoning, which culminates in a decision by P to perform or omit A. As far as eligibility is concerned, the background theory supports view (ii), for according to that view deterrents limit freedom inasmuch as they constitute limitations on an agent's practical activity. Sanctions on A of which the agent is unaware neither render A unavailable[14] nor affect the formation of intentions regarding the performance of A. Can view (ii) be adopted while preserving E_{18}, however? The answer is "yes." Sanctions of which agents are unaware restrict their freedom by rendering unavailable actions other than A. If an agent is subject to sanctions of which she had been unaware, then the action of (intentionally) avoiding the pains of, e.g., fines or imprisonment has been rendered unavailable by the existence of the internal restraint of ignorance.

---

14. Except perhaps in the "rule-governed" sense of freedom discussed in ch. 7.

CHAPTER 9

Heteronomy

(i) *The Nature of Heteronomy*

The aspect of unfreedom as heteronomy comprises two major components. The first consists of limitations in the *nature* of those mental states which can be broadly termed attitudes to action (whether pro, anti, or indifferent). These states include desires, practical judgments, and intentions. The second consists in limitations in the *origin* and formation of those states. Here, limitations denoted by 'heteronomy' occur in the processes of acquiring desires and beliefs, linking these in deliberation (where this occurs), and forming practical judgments and intentions (whether or not these are the termination of a prior process of deliberation).

I distinguish the flaws characterizing heteronomy in this sense from executive failures (see chapter 10). The latter are breakdowns in the conversion of reason-giving links into action. Among these types of flaws, I shall include anomie (where reason-giving links do not terminate in a judgment about the thing to do), and weakness of will and lack of resolve (where judgments about the thing to do do not result in appropriate action).

What types of limitations in the practical process are denoted by 'heteronomy'? As the etymology of 'heteronomy' suggests, limitations constituting heteronomy fall into two broad categories: those which render the nature and formation of practical attitudes (a) non-law-governed or irrational, and (b) inauthentic.[1] Notions of rationality and authenticity can be relatively austere, or relatively virtue-oriented. I have argued that virtues related to agency have a strong claim to be incorporated in notions of freedom. Given this, rationality will be understood not merely as instrumental rationality but as demonstrated also

---

1. See R. M. Hare, "Chairman's Remarks," in S. C. Brown, ed., *Philosophers Discuss Education* (New York: Macmillan, 1975), pp. 36–7.

Chapter 9   Heteronomy

in the kinds of ends pursued by the agent. 'Authentic' basically means nonalien, but this, too, can be interpreted more or less austerely. A rich virtue-oriented notion of authenticity contrasts "alien self" with the self who is self-realized in her role as agent. The authentic self in this sense embraces, nonvicariously, ends that are conducive to flourishing qua agent, possesses desires that are integrated with those ends, and identifies with those desires and ends. A virtue-oriented notion of authenticity will not therefore follow the common, more austere understandings of the notion as simply a contrast to vicariousness or nonidentification.

Before moving on to a more detailed discussion of rationality and authenticity, a general difficulty with conceptions of freedom as autonomy must be noted. A problem in making sense of heteronomy is the separation of determinants of desires, practical judgments, and intentions in general from determinants of heteronomous or freedom-limiting ones. In particular, one has to grapple with the hard determinists' claim that none of our actions is ever free, since wants to perform those actions are one and all determined by factors other than an individual's own agency. It is not part of my intention to discuss the metaphysical problem of free will and determinism. Given this, I have two options. The first is to claim that the problem raised by the hard determinist is irrelevant to the issue of social or political freedom because *no* determinants of wants (not even, e.g., subliminal advertising or "brainwashing") impair an agent's (political or social) freedom. The other option is to claim that, whether or not the hard determinist is correct, only *certain* determinants of wants can legitimately be regarded as limiting social and political freedom. This is the option I have adopted. The materials for defending it are contained in the background theory, viz., the view that *at least* in the context of social and political freedom, it is "unfreedom" which wears the trousers, since it signals the presence of a limitation in human practical rational activity qua human practical rational activity. Not all possible determinants of that activity can determine it as unfree, but rather only that subclass that constitutes limitations. Although it is contingently possible that all members of a class contain limitations (e.g., all motor vehicles ever assembled in New Zealand), it is not the case that all members of a class K can be called limited qua K's and yet it be metaphysically or logically impossible for them to be otherwise.

I allow for the possibility that all members of a class *K* may be limited *simpliciter*, or limited relative to items that are not *K*. For example, it may be held that all phenomena are limited *simpliciter* because they are limited or imperfect relative to Platonic Forms. Similarly, it may be held that all *human* actions are flawed relative to those of God or the angels, because causally determined. But it cannot be that all *human* actions are limited qua termini of *human* practical rational processes, when it is logically or metaphysically impossible for them to be otherwise.

(ii) *Rationality*

The tradition that puts rationality at the heart of autonomy has often been ignored by those who regard authenticity as sufficient for autonomy. For example, Crocker claims: "I understand an autonomous decision to be a decision which is genuinely the agent's own decision. It is not made or forced upon the agent by anyone else" (*op. cit.*, p. 36). Our methodology demands, however, that both traditions be accommodated, if possible, within a coherent view. I claim this can be done, but first it should be noted that philosophers vary on how stringently to interpret the rationality requirement for autonomy. For Kant, the autonomous agent not only engages in reasoning but such reasoning must conform to standards of correctness. These standards are enshrined in the universal law. Certainly, the autonomous agent must *voluntarily* align his will with the law—for Kant, autonomy requires authenticity. If his maxims do not *accord* with that law, however, they cannot be autonomous.

The Kantian notion of freedom is in many aspects taken over by several British philosophers of education, but not all interpret rationality so stringently. R. F. Dearden,[2] like Kant, sees autonomy as an ideal attained only when the process of choice is governed by laws of reason whose validity is independent of the desires, aims, or inclinations of the agent. Unlike Kant, however, he does not equate autonomous action with morally good action:

> . . . Kant wished to define autonomy in terms of acting on self-legislated moral laws, but surely a criminal could present a fine example of autonomy in action. However,

---

2. "Autonomy and Education," in R. F. Dearden, P. H. Hirst, and R. S. Peters, eds., *Education and the Development of Reason* (New York: Routledge and Kegan Paul).

what could much more plausibly be suggested is that autonomy is intimately connected with the action of *reason*, even if not with actual truth or with morality (*ibid.*, p. 456).

The background theory suggests that the appropriate conception of rationality for autonomy is a developmental one, centered on a conception of *human* flourishing, as opposed to some "ideal" rationality. Neither Kant nor Dearden quite fit this conception: Kant because his conception is not human centered; Dearden because his view of rationality is insufficiently linked to a conception of the kinds of ends that would be pursued by a flourishing human being.

What counts as goodness in human rationality cannot be determined merely by the statistical norms prevailing at a time. For, as I said in chapter 3, statistical norms need not determine potential. If most humans commit elementary fallacies, it could be because they are not trained under good conditions; they are not taught to reason well from primary school onward. It does not follow that we should allow our standards of goodness in *human* reasoning to accommodate such fallacies. On the other hand, if most human beings are not maximizers but are "satisficers," it may indicate (but not demonstrate) that maximizing notions of rationality do not provide adequate models of goodness in *human* rational processes. Some of us may have a potential to maximize in the sense of capacity or even propensity—but it does not follow that it is conducive to the realization of our potential in the sense of "conducive to our flourishing." What counts as goodness in reasoning in that sense is naturally controversial: should we accept a maximizing model, or should we allow that it is rational knowingly to choose alternatives that are adequate but known to be inferior?[3] The important point, however, is that what counts as goodness in human rationality is not determined by statistical preponderance but must be set against a background of a conception of human flourishing or success as a human being qua agent.

Such a conception is no simple one, however, even with

---

3. For a defense of the view that the flourishing human has a satisficing temperament in this sense, rather than a maximizing or optimizing temperament, see Michael Slote, "Moderation, Rationality, and Virtue," in Sterling M. McMurrin, ed., *The Tanner Lectures on Human Values*, VII (New York: Cambridge, 1986), pp. 53–99.

respect to rationality. Rational processes relative to goals of survival will not be coextensive with rationality relative to humans functioning in their intellectual capacities as truth seekers and good arguers. Flourishing humans are more than mere survivors. The fact that humans who regularly affirm the consequent, while airing their prejudices among like-minded bigots, survive quite well does not suggest that affirming the consequent is not a flaw of rationality. On the other hand, if it turns out that maximizing agents are exhausted, discontented, frustrated, and perfectionists impossible to live with, then perhaps the model is more suited to the gods than to humans.

What should be the standards of rationality for human beings in their diverse activities and roles is a vast and difficult topic outside the scope of this book. One further point related to freedom must, however, be reemphasized. I have said that standards of rationality appropriate to human freedom are those appropriate to the flourishing of humans in their various stages of development and "denouement." Standards of rationality appropriate to the freedom of infants, children, and the senile are those appropriate to those *phases* of human development and demise! As I emphasized earlier, this point ensures that I do not align myself with those holding "rationalist" conceptions of freedom according to which young children are not subjects of freedom. That is, I do not hold that freedom necessarily involves mastery of standards of rationality in its higher aspects. I do not, for example, insist that the free agent is a fully deliberative reflective agent (see chapter 4).

The view that conditions for autonomy, such as rationality, admit of degree has been subjected to a criticism taking the form of a dilemma. Either autonomy becomes a "vague, developmental property" that people instantiate to varying degrees, or autonomy is a threshold concept. If the first alternative is the case, an important moral value is undermined, viz., the requirement that autonomy be a property that is respected equally in one's treatment of individual persons. If the second alternative is the case, it becomes essential to specify the precise degree of rationality required for autonomy.[4] This task is impossible of fulfillment, however.

My reply to the dilemma is to attack the first horn, and main-

---

4. See John Christman, "Constructing the Inner Citadel: Recent Work on the Concept of Autonomy," *Ethics*, XCIX (1988): 109–24.

tain the view that autonomy is a developmental concept admitting of degree. I shall also concede that the fact that autonomy is a degree concept would license differing treatments of individuals in respect of their freedom. The moral requirement of according *equal respect* to all autonomous agents, however, does not entail a requirement of *equal treatment* in respect of freedom. There is a well-known distinction in writings on equality between equal respect and equal treatment. According equal respect may actually require unequal treatment in proportion to differing merits,[5] degrees of competence, and degrees of potentiality and capacity. It is indeed true that "the 'sliding scale' conception of autonomy" may "allow differing degrees of paternalistic intervention according to the level of competence a person displays in decision making" (*op. cit*, p. 116); but, *pace* Christman, such differences would not necessarily violate the principle of equal respect. Whether or not they do so depends on the context and nature of the differing treatments and on the reasons for those differences. We should treat children and adults with "equal respect" because they have equal worth in Gregory Vlastos's sense, but does this imply that, if adults should not be subjected to compulsory education, children should not be as well?

(iii) *Authenticity: Nonvicariousness*

The requirement of authenticity divides into two. First, there is the requirement of nonvicariousness: the reasoning process of the autonomous agent must not be determined by certain influences emanating from outside the body-cum-mind. Second, there is a requirement that might be termed non-innerdirectedness. Inauthenticity is often understood as the determination of reasoning processes by certain "alien" influences from within the body-cum-mind. In this section, I consider various forms of vicarious determination.

First, however, some general remarks are in order. The major difficulty in accommodating the endoxa relating to heteronomy as inauthenticity is the fact that writers do not fully appreciate

---

5. See Gregory Vlastos for the distinction between worth and merit which underlies the distinction drawn here; "Justice and Equality," in Richard B. Brandt, ed., *Social Justice* (Englewood Cliffs, N.J.: Prentice Hall, 1962), pp. 31–72.

that heteronomy involves a *limitation* in practical activity. This mistake is manifested in claims that qualities such as relative immunity from influence, nonimpulsiveness, identification with desires, and so on are essential to, or sufficient for, autonomy. These are all material properties of autonomy on which autonomy is supervenient, however, and any attempt to *define* autonomy in terms of them is doomed to failure. For not all items falling within various categories of material properties will be deemed, in various contexts, limitations in practical activity; and not all relevant limitations will be included within the various categories of material properties that the imagination of a single theorist can dream up.

The critical thrust of my discussion of autonomy as authenticity will be to remedy this defect with respect to a number of characteristics thought to constitute autonomy. For example, a feature of autonomy often emphasized is the *independence* of an agent's desires and practical judgments. 'Independent' does not here mean "nonconformist," "original," or "novel": it means "not directed by others." *Independence* of an agent's wants in its normal sense of relative immunity from influence is an important material property of autonomy, but not a defining property since nonindependence is not necessarily a limitation. For this reason Christian Bay[6] is wrong to think that autonomy is necessarily impaired when wants are changed or created as the result of what he calls "manipulation," characterized by him as the "instilling of wants which the subject would not otherwise have, and the significant alteration of priority amongst wants" (*ibid.*, p. 17). Surely appropriate nonindependence—"manipulation" in Bay's sense—enhances autonomy in a person who has been left in peace to develop attitudes based on ignorance and inappropriate emotion.

A search for a precise definition giving necessary and sufficient conditions for vicarious influence that *limits* practical activity is misguided, for the notion is context-dependent, open-ended, and complex. It is better to indicate how the concept is applied in various contexts where one draws the contrast between vicarious influence that limits practical activity and that which does not. I shall briefly discuss manipulation (as opposed to influence in general), persuasion (as opposed to advice), and indoctrination (as opposed to teaching in general).

6. *The Structure of Freedom* (Stanford: University Press, 1970).

Manipulation

Manipulation is defined by Oppenheim as the attempt at influence in which the influencer ensures that the influenced is unaware of the attempt (*op. cit.*, p. 27). The flaw at issue here is influence involving *deception*. Oppenheim's definition admits of several interpretations. One may not be aware that one is being influenced at all. One may be aware that *influence* is taking place, but be unaware that it contains elements of deception, i.e., manipulation. One may be aware that manipulation is taking place, but be unaware of its precise content.

The broadest interpretation may be illustrated by an example of Oppenheim's: the mother who purposely creates in her child a sense of dependency to satisfy her own possessive needs, and without revealing her motives to the child. In the case of subliminal advertising, one may be aware of influence, but not of manipulation. An example of the third type of manipulation is censorship: the selection and control of information such that the attempt at influence involves deception. One may be perfectly aware that censorship is being practised; the point is that one is unaware of the precise nature of selection in given cases or at given times.

Persuasion

Since I am talking about determinants of wants and not restraints on action, I am not concerned with usages like "we persuaded him to talk by using the thumbscrews." The features of persuasion that make it a determinant of heteronomous wants are best described in contrast with the notion of advice. In the words of R. M. Hare,[7] "advice is always addressed to a man *qua* rational being, whereas persuasion may be addressed to him *qua* affected by passions" (*ibid.*, p. 5). Although the intention behind the giving of advice is standardly the attempt to modify behavior and attitudes, the giver of advice also intends that the influencee should understand the reasonableness of the advice. On the other hand, persuasion is simply the modification of attitudes by various means, and the attempt to persuade is simply the attempt to modify attitudes. Hence, according to Hare, advice may be described as "silly" or "sensible"

---

7. "Freedom of the Will," in *Essays on the Moral Concepts* (New York: Macmillan, 1972), pp. 1–12.

while attempted persuasion is merely "effective" or "ineffective."[8] Persuasion makes the formation of practical judgments heteronomous because, in contrast to advice, it is part of the concept of persuasion that judgments instilled by the various methods of persuasion limit practical activity in a certain respect. In the words of Benjamin Barber,[9] forms of persuasion are "directed towards the reactive rather than the conscious person and designed to restrict rather than enlarge conscious deliberation" (*ibid.*, p. 66). Advice, by contrast—even advice which turns out to be poor—is designed to enlarge deliberation.

Forms of persuasion are multifarious—examples include repetition of slogans as in propaganda, and the association of commodities with ideas having powerful emotive content, as in advertising. The psychological technique known as behavior modification is also a form of persuasion. It is not classical conditioning, as the subject is induced to alter his behavior consciously for the purpose of rewards. Nor is the procedure *simply* inducement (a restraint on action) as the eventual aim is to cause the modified behaviors to persist in the absence of reward. If the "problem child" is to cooperate with the teacher in the absence of specific rewards, it would seem that a change in attitude toward cooperative behaviors is necessary. Although behavior modification programs involve some kind of deliberative behavior on the part of the subject, he is treated basically as a reactive rather than a deliberative being. The attempt to change wants is not primarily based on appeal to reason and knowledge.

Indoctrination

Finally, I shall contrast indoctrination with teaching in general.

It is argued by some that indoctrination is a species of teaching. According to Paul H. Hirst:[10] "In so far . . . as indoctrina-

---

8. This is not incompatible with Hare's remark that "advising" is not to be analyzed as "trying to persuade." Two points are involved in Hare's remark. First, advising, unlike persuading, is an illocutionary act. Second, even if advising is associated with the perlocutionary act of attempting to modify wants, advising itself cannot properly be described as the attempt to persuade.
9. *Superman and Common Men: Freedom, Anarchy and the Revolution* (New York: Penguin, 1974).
10. "What Is Teaching?" in Peters, ed., *The Philosophy of Education* (New York: Oxford, 1973).

tion and other activities involve the intention to bring about learning of some kind, they involve teaching and in so far as they are themselves processes for bringing about learning of certain kinds they are themselves forms of teaching" (*ibid.*, p. 175). If this is correct, then our concern is to distinguish indoctrination from other forms of teaching.

The distinction can be drawn formally in the same way as that between persuasion and advice. It is part of the concept of indoctrination (as opposed to teaching that is not indoctrination) that indoctrinated wants are flawed in ways that render them heteronomous in certain respects. This does not entail, of course, that indoctrination may not enhance freedom *in other respects* (indeed, many believe this to be the case); nor does it entail that indoctrination is a bad thing, all things considered.

This distinction does not get us very far in understanding the nature of indoctrination. To do this, we need first of all to take account of the endoxa. The tensions between these are exhibited in three major types of contested conceptions of indoctrination: conceptions that variously define indoctrination in terms of (a) a characteristic method, (b) a characteristic content, and (c) a characteristic aim.

I shall argue that none of these conceptions gives the complete picture. The reason is that each lights on an important material property common to many instances of indoctrination, and elevates that property to the status of a formal property. Of course, it may be claimed that there is controversy concerning the formal property of indoctrination, and I shall not dispute this. Our coherentist methodology provides a method for resolving such disputes, however. An adequate characterization of the formal property must do justice to the endoxa, namely, that indoctrination has *something* to do with certain aims, methods, and contents of teaching.

I shall first indicate the defects of defining indoctrination in terms of its material properties, before presenting my own account. Indoctrination should not be defined in terms of the utilization of specific methods, since, as John Wilson[11] points out, the methods deemed "unacceptable" in some contexts (e.g., hypnotic persuasion) would not count as indoctrination in other contexts (e.g., in the inculcation of multiplication tables). In the

---

11. "Education and Indoctrination," in T.H.B. Hollins, ed., *Aims in Education* (Manchester: University Press, 1964), pp. 24–46, esp. pp. 26–7.

latter kinds of contexts, the use of such methods is regarded as implanting belief in an efficient manner as opposed to one that harms or restricts potential.

Nor can indoctrination be identified with teaching having a specific content. According to Wilson, the test of indoctrination "consists of the *content* of what we teach" (*ibid.*, p. 35): specifically, to indoctrinate is to "teach as certain subjects where there is no real certainty" (*ibid.*, p. 33). A teacher could teach the uncertain as if it were certain, however, and yet make a complete hash of it: the students, fired with critical zeal, scour non-recommended literature and provide excellent arguments against the doctrines taught.

Thirdly, some have defined indoctrination in terms of characteristic aims. According to Hare:[12]

> . . . indoctrination only begins when we are trying to stop the growth in our children of the capacity to think for themselves about moral questions. If all the time we are influencing them, we are saying to ourselves, "Perhaps in the end they will decide that the best way to live is quite different from what I'm teaching them; and they will have a perfect right to decide that", then we are not to be accused of indoctrinating (*ibid.*, p. 52).

According to J. P. White,[13] the characteristic aim that defines indoctrination is "the intention of the indoctrinator to fix pupils' beliefs so that they are unshakable" (*ibid.*, p. 182).

The fact that the teacher has the above aims is neither necessary nor sufficient for indoctrination. It is not sufficient for the kinds of reasons presented above: a teacher may have indoctrinating *aims* without its being the case that any pupil's belief has been formed in a limited way. Nor is it necessary: a teacher may be the unwitting dupe of higher authorities, and have completely mistaken beliefs about the methods employed and the content taught. Despite the integrity of the teacher, the use of certain methods and content may in certain contexts count as indoctrination.

It remains for me to give an account of the formal property of indoctrination in a way that does justice to the endoxa. I suggest

---

12. "Adolescents into Adults," in T.H.B. Hollins, ed., pp. 47–70.

13. "Indoctrination," in Peters, ed., *The Concept of Education* (New York: Routledge and Kegan Paul, 1967), pp. 177–91.

that the point of classifying a range of phenomena as *indoctrination* is to draw attention to a type of teaching that results in limitations in the formation of judgments and wants. The relevant limitations are:

(i) impairments of the pupils' ability and motivation to appraise the influences working on them;
(ii) impairments of their ability to appraise those influences with adequate knowledge and reason;
(iii) impairments of their ability and motivation to form their wants and practical judgments on the basis of that knowledge.

For example, a pupil may possess a considerable amount of accurate information about a person or race which demonstrates that her hatred of that person or race is baseless. Nonetheless, emotions or other factors induced by the teacher prevent or hinder her from utilizing that information to found her practical judgments.

The type of teaching that results in those limitations characteristically, but not necessarily, possesses the material properties mentioned: it is characteristically informed by an interest in inculcating relatively unshakable beliefs in controversial or uncertain doctrines, theories, or facts, and it characteristically inculcates these beliefs by the use of methods that short-circuit the rational critical processes. The empirical manifestations of teaching that serve the point of implanting judgments in a limited way are too numerous to enumerate or even classify; and no such classification will provide necessary or sufficient conditions for indoctrination.

(iv) *Authenticity: Non-Inner-Directedness*

It is frequently pointed out that for autonomous choice to be genuinely *autos* it is not sufficient that it be merely nonvicarious in certain ways. In this section, I discuss the conditions under which the formation of a want is heteronomous qua innerdirected. I shall mean by an inner-directed heteronomous influence any relevant inauthentic influence from within the body-cum-mind. Although inner-directed inauthenticity has several forms, the structure of such inauthenticity is basically the same: the process of forming judgments about the thing to do is limited insofar as it is inappropriately determined by relatively inauthentic desires.

Two types of inner-directed inauthenticity have been identified by philosophers. Attitudes are deemed to be inauthentic when they (1) stem from or belong to the self as "reactor" (as opposed to the self as 'actor'); or (2) are desires with which the agent does not identify.

I shall discuss each of these notions of inauthenticity. It will be argued that, though each of these features constitutes an important *material* property frequently associated with heteronomy, none constitutes its formal property; none is *definitive* of autonomy in the relevant sense.

I turn now to the first conception of authenticity identified above, which Barber regards as the most important aspect of freedom in general. His "intentionalist" model of freedom distinguishes between the self as reactor and the self as actor: the self as reactor reacts impulsively to influences, whether inner or outer. The acceptance of "a massive bribe in the face of abject poverty" may be an intentional act in the Anscombian sense: the agent can cite reasons for such acceptance *ex post facto*. Yet, for Barber, such an "intention" is one in which genuine autonomous choice has been precluded "in favour of an immediate gratification of the drive for security unmediated by any form of intentionality" (*op cit.*, p. 65). For a choice to be autonomous in this sense, it must stem from the self as actor, i.e., the agent must "take an attitude towards it," "appropriate it as his own aim," and it must be preceded by self-conscious reflection.

For the condition of nonimpulsiveness to be satisfied it is not necessary that the conditions of rationality and nonvicariousness be satisfied. Indeed, as Barber points out, it is at least theoretically possible that "coercive influences" can enhance nonimpulsive choice: ". . . no intentionalist would want to contend that all forms of persuasion . . . aim at the crippling of the conscious self" (*op. cit.*, p. 71). This point raises the general problem that enhancing certain aspects of freedom may militate against other aspects: this problem is taken up in chapter 12.

The problem of distinguishing "inner-directed" influences that limit freedom from those that do not parallels the problem of distinguishing freedom-limiting from other outer-directed influences. The making of this distinction presupposes once again the idea of a limitation in the process of practical rational activity relative to individual potential in agency. For example,

Chapter 9   Heteronomy

impulsiveness may not be a limitation in this respect, and may be quite appropriate in certain contexts. Consider the busy career woman with plenty of money who hates shopping. Most of her consumer decisions may well be based on impulse. She sees a dress, likes it, and straightaway buys it. There is minimal deliberation, and minimal basis for selection. Yet, in this context, her impulsiveness cannot be described as a limitation, and this is especially true if her decision procedure—namely, not to engage in full-blooded "shopping around"—is itself deliberated.

A similar point applies to impulsive wants based on emotion such as love or anger. The less extreme are those emotions, and/or the more appropriate are they to their objects, the less inclined we are to say that wants based on them are heteronomous. For example, a spontaneous reaction of righteous anger over injustice will be contrasted with a reaction of ungovernable rage occasioned by a trifling slight. Wants emanating from virtuous dispositions, e.g., *appropriate* anger, need not be calculated and deliberated: indeed, as Aristotle emphasizes, it is the mark of virtuous desire that it is a cultivated and relatively fixed *habit* of right desire, leading to spontaneous and uncalculated actions of, e.g., loyalty in standard circumstances. In short, though heteronomy is frequently constituted by impulsiveness, an important material property of heteronomy, impulsiveness is neither essential to, nor sufficient for, heteronomy.

Much modern writing on autonomy understands an inauthentic want as one with which the agent does not identify. The notion of nonidentification, in turn, is cashed out in terms of Frankfurt's distinction between first-order and second-order desires (*op. cit.*). But there have been various ways of employing this distinction in the elucidation of the notion of nonidentification. For Frankfurt, one does not identify with a first-order desire (a desire to act) if one has a second-order desire not to have that desire at all; or, where the desire is "effective" (i.e., "moves the agent all the way to action"), one has a second-order desire that the desire not be effective.

According to Taylor, I do not identify with a first-order desire if I feel that the desire is not "truly mine": that is, ". . . I feel that I should be better off without it, that I don't lose anything in getting rid of it, I remain quite complete without it" (*op. cit.*, p. 188). More specifically, desires with which one does not identify are not merely ones that one prefers not to have but one judges best not to have as a result of evaluation about the kind of person one wants to be. I shall call this kind of phenomenon nonidentification, to be contrasted with mere failure to identify. Failure to identify may involve either nonidentification or the failure to possess any kind of second-order desire toward a first-order desire.

Many philosophers have made the notion of identification central to their account of freedom. For Frankfurt,[14] identification seems to be necessary for freedom, whereas "legitimacy" of the *origins* of one's desires is not necessary. It is necessary since freedom entails taking responsibility for the "springs of one's actions," and taking responsibility itself entails identification. He claims: ". . . to the extent that a person identifies himself with the springs of his actions, he takes responsibility for them; moreover, the questions of how the actions and his identifications with their springs are caused is irrelevant to the questions of whether he performs the actions freely or is morally responsible for performing them" (*ibid.*, p. 121).

The claim that identification with desires rather than their causal origin is crucial for freedom is problematic. Some philosophers[15] have focused on the possibility that higher-order desires might be conditioned and be more "alien" than the lower order desires with which one does not identify. How then can those higher-order desires be autonomous?

This point raises the following general problem. For the identification theorist, higher-order desires confer autonomy on lower-order desires. But what of the autonomy of the higher-order desires themselves? As has been pointed out by Marilyn Friedman (*op. cit.*), there are several possibilities. First, autonomy may be conferred on the higher-order desires by a similar process of identification: a third-order level of desire is required, thereby precipitating a regress problem. Second, autonomy is conferred by a process different from that of identification, but this solution, of course, threatens the "autonomy" of the identification account of autonomy. Third, the notion of identification could be rendered more sophisticated, so that the problem of the nonautonomous second-order desire is met. This is Gerald

---

14. "Three Concepts of Free Action," *The Aristotelian Society*, Supp. Vol. XLIX (1975): 113–25.
15. See, e.g., Marilyn Friedman, "Autonomy and the Split-Level Self," *Southern Journal of Philosophy*, XXIV (1986): 19–35; and Christman, "Autonomy: A Defense of the Split-Level Self," *Southern Journal of Philosophy*, XXV (1987): 281–93.

Dworkin's solution to the problem, a solution defended by Christman.[16] According to Gerald Dworkin,[17] there is a condition of adequacy on identification: identification confers autonomy only if it is "procedurally independent." That is, such identification must not have been "influenced in ways that make the process of identification in some way alien to the individual" (*ibid.*, p. 212).

The addition of this condition of adequacy does not solve our problem, however. Consider the woman whose second-order desire to be a "good" housewife is caused, and at least in part maintained, through her past and ongoing exploitation. Yet the process by which she *identifies* with that desire satisfies the procedural independence condition. Having critically examined much feminist literature, and finding its basic philosophical assumptions suspect, she comes to the conclusion that, for the sake of family values she holds dear, she ought to continue to be a "good" housewife. Yet because of the "alien" origin of the second-order desire itself, we may be reluctant to claim it is autonomous.

This kind of example also casts doubt on Young's[18] "revision" of Gerald Dworkin's account. According to Young, autonomy of desire involves identification after scrutiny of one's motivations, including scrutiny of the motivation to scrutinize and subsequently to endorse. It may be that all these underlying motivations, even when brought into the open and scrutinized, are so powerful, however, that they infect the process of scrutiny itself. The "vantage point" from which one views motivations may be in thrall to the very oppressive forces that determine the underlying motivations.

Perhaps, then, the second possible solution to the problem of conferring autonomy on higher-order desires should be explored. Autonomy is conferred by a process different from that of identification. This is a solution favored by Friedman, who rejects the hierarchical analysis of autonomy conferral, but maintains its root idea, viz., autonomy is essentially a matter of *integration* of desire. In this process, higher-order desires are not privileged: lower-order desires, "longings, urges, fears, anxieties

---

16. In "Autonomy: A Defense of the Split-Level Self."
17. "The Concept of Autonomy," in Rudolf Haller, ed., *Science and Ethics* (Amsterdam: Rodopi, 1981), pp. 203–13.
18. "Compatibilism and Conditioning," *Noûs*, XIII (1979): 361–78.

and so forth," can provide "touchstones of a sort for the assessment of the adequacy of one's principles" (*op. cit.*, p. 31).

As Christman[19] points out, however, the integration view cannot provide a full account of autonomy. Is it not possible that the exploited and demeaned woman has so internalized both first-order and second-order desires that there is no dissonance between them? Furthermore, the process of internalization could itself be the result of repressive external influence.

What has been said so far may suggest that autonomy *consists* in the fact that the origin of desires, whether first- or second-order, whether scrutinized or not, is "nonalien." The difficulty of spelling out the precise conditions for "nonalien" origin suggests, however, that this view, too, misses the mark. The origin of the desires of a woman with severely limited horizons, for example, may owe little to exploitation, repression, manipulation, and other standard "alien" influences. And yet those desires may be severely restricted by the narrow environment in which she finds herself. She may have had parents neglectful of her intellectual development, or have been brought up in conditions of poverty, ignorance, prejudice, vice, and a host of environmental circumstances that limit and distort her attitudes and aspirations, and her views about her roles.

Analyses that elevate factors such as identification, integration, and "independence" of origin of desires as definitive of autonomy all commit two related errors. The first is the failure to recognize that autonomy is a defeasible concept connoting the absence of a variety of nonenumerable limitations in not only the origin but also the nature of practical attitudes. The problem is not the vagueness of concepts such as identification, and the need to precisify them; the problem is the attempt to give a full account of autonomy in terms of one of these conditions.

The second error is the failure to recognize that factors such as nonidentification, nonintegration, etc., are material properties of autonomy that constitute *limitations* on flourishing in agency only in certain contexts. For the anorexic who experiences the healthy appetite as opposed to the obsessive desire for slimness as a fetter, "liberation" is obtained not by eliminating the desire with which she does not identify, but by eliminating the nontemperate second-order desire for slimness. Non-

---

19. "Autonomy: A Defense of the Split-Level Self," p. 287.

identification here is a sign of hope for recovery to healthy agency rather than constitutive of heteronomy. Similarly, the failure of the demeaned woman to integrate her desire to be a "good housewife" with her lower-order desires to escape her situation—desires marked by "urges and longings"—is not in that context a limitation. Rather, in that kind of context, it would be integration that is the limitation.

All this is not to deny that nonidentification with motivating desires is, in important contexts, an important limitation that reduces autonomy. Both the endoxa and my background theory show this. Desires with which one does not identify limit potential as propensity. Frankfurt's account of freedom builds on the basic idea of free action as willing action:[20] one is free to the extent that one's propensities in action are not restricted. This basic idea is made more sophisticated by the notion that one's propensities can be limited not just by physical barriers but also by desires with which one does not identify. The kind of endoxa relied upon here are such as the following:

E_{20}: A smoker who does not want to have the desire to smoke in a sense smokes unwillingly; his first-order desire, being a fetter to willing action, limits his freedom.

To build a theory of autonomy on this kind of example, however, is to commit the sin against which Wittgenstein warns: it is to focus on one kind of example. In another sense of potential in agency where realizing potential entails flourishing, motivating desires with which the agent does not identify are not necessarily fetters to that potential. As we have seen, flourishing in agency may be best served by the retention of certain healthy desires with which one does not identify, and by the elimination of warped, confused, or obsessive second-order desires that are the true "fetters." As long as wants coinciding with what one *takes* to be important fail to coincide with what is conducive to flourishing, any attempt to give a *complete* account of autonomy in terms of identification or integration will fail.

---

20. See further Don Locke,"Three Concepts of Free Action," in *The Aristotelian Society*, Supp. Vol. XLIX (1975): 95–112.

CHAPTER 10

Executive Failure

(i) *What Is Executive Failure?*

Like heteronomy, unfreedom as executive failure focuses on failures and limitations in practical activity viewed as a process. Heteronomy consists of limitations in the reason-giving links that terminate in desires, practical judgments, and intentions. These involve irrationality and inauthenticity. Executive failures are failures leading to a mismatch between desires, practical judgments, and intentions—whether autonomous or heteronomous—and action. This mismatch is of two types. First, there are failures to *complete* the practical process properly by going through the appropriate stages. For example, in anomie, desires are not ranked, so no practical judgments about which desires to satisfy when are formed. In lack of resolve, desires may be ordered, but the deliberative process is not completed, so no action plan is formed. The second kind of mismatch occurs where the practical process is completed, but is completed in a way that involves a mismatch between the action performed, and some relevant intentional state which the agent is in. The nature of this mismatch in weakness of will is highly controversial, and will be singled out for attention in section (ii).

It may be thought that executive failure, like heteronomy, concerns limitations in the reason-giving links in the practical process, and that the limitations here concern either irrationality or inauthenticity. On my view, however, the limitations are quite different in kind. They are weaknesses of character not reducible either to bouts of irrationality, involving fallacies of reasoning or lack of knowledge, or to episodes of inauthentic "takeovers" of the "will." In the next section, I discuss the most paradoxical form of executive failure, viz., weakness of will. I there claim that weakness of will is not a bout of *irrational* takeover or bypassing of the will. In section (iii), I develop the idea of executive failure as weakness of character, and generalize the account to include a range of executive failures.

(ii) Weakness of Will

In his "A Paradox of Desire," Stephen Schiffer[1] criticizes the orthodox view that weakness of will is acting against one's all-things-considered judgments about what one ought to do. He supplies some alleged counterexamples, including the following: "There are smokers who with an enviable lack of perturbation will acknowledge that, for the obvious reasons, they ought not to smoke, that smoking is quite an irrational thing for them to do; but while they think of themselves as being irrational, they do not think of themselves as being weak willed, it not being their will to stop smoking" (ibid., p. 201). Schiffer's point highlights the depth of disagreement about the proper analysis of weakness of will. One can take it as agreed merely that weakness of will is acting in some sense against one's will. The identification of one's will with one's better judgment, however, is a problematical further step.

The orthodox identification of weakness of will with acting against one's better judgment has led to another orthodoxy: weakness of will is in some sense a manifestation of irrationality. Specifically, it involves an irrational bypassing of an all-things-considered judgment about what is best.

In Michael Bratman's[2] and Donald Davidson's[3] accounts, the putative irrationality lies in the reasoning to a practical conclusion (understood in different ways). In Hare's,[4] Gary Watson's,[5] and Pears's[6] accounts, the irrationality is an executive irrationality: a rebellious desire (i.e., a desire not in line with one's all-things-considered best judgment) "takes over" the will. This takeover may be seen as compulsive (Hare and Watson) or as noncompulsive (Pears).

1. *American Philosophy Quarterly*, XIII (1976): 159–203.
2. "Practical Reasoning and Weakness of the Will," *Noûs*, XIII (1979): 153–71.
3. "How Is Weakness of the Will Possible?" in Feinberg, ed., *Moral Concepts* (New York: Oxford, 1970), pp. 93–113.
4. *Freedom and Reason* (New York: Oxford, 1963), ch. 5, pp. 67–85.
5. "Skepticism about Weakness of Will," *Philosophical Review*, LXXXVI (1977): 316–39.
6. *Motivated Irrationality* (New York: Oxford, 1984).

I shall challenge the orthodox view that weakness of will should be understood as an irrational bypassing of an all-things-considered judgment about the thing to do. On that view, as Davidson rightly points out, the weak-willed sees herself as doing something "essentially surd" (*op cit.*, p. 113). Weakness of will is, however, a common phenomenon, so common, in fact, that there must at least be a presumption against its mysteriousness, absurdity, and irrationality. Any account of the phenomenology of weakness of will is obviously contested: nonetheless, a plausible account that satisfies the above presumption must be welcomed. My aim is to offer such an account.

My strategy is to offer, first, an alternative account of the phenomenology of weakness of will. I discuss familiar examples of weakness of will, such as Davidson's toothbrusher example, and offer an alternative description of what is going on. Instead of thinking of the phenomenon as a form of irrationality in which the agent sees himself as absurdly bypassing a clear-cut evaluative judgment, I suggest instead that he finds himself in a bind. Specifically, he is beset by dilemmas, being disposed to accept, on rational grounds, two conflicting all-things-considered judgments about the thing to do.

Secondly, I offer an analysis of weakness of will as a certain kind of response to the dilemmas of practical rationality outlined. The analysis satisfies two desiderata. First, it satisfies the presumption mentioned above: weakness of will is neither absurd nor irrational. Second, despite rejection of the orthodox view, it adheres to two central notions in the idea of weakness of will. First, it is in some sense action against one's "will," understood as a perceived requirement endorsed by the agent herself. Second, it is in some sense a *weak* response to a conundrum: it involves taking the "line of least resistance"; taking "the soft option."

The sense in which weakness of will is weakly acting against a perceived requirement is explicated in a way that defends my view that such action is not an irrational bypassing of a single all-things-considered judgment about the thing to do.

The orthodox view of the phenomenology of weakness of will is well expressed in the following claim made by Christopher Peacocke:[7] "The *akrates* is irrational because although he inten-

---

7. "Intention and Akrasia," in Bruce Vermazen and Merril B. Hintikka, eds., *Essays on Davidson Actions and Events* (New York: Oxford, 1985), pp. 51–73.

tionally does something for which he has some reason, there is a wider set of reasons he has relative to which he does not judge what he does to be rational" (*ibid.*, p. 52). Here, Peacocke supposes that the akrates acts against an alternative judged to be *superior* on the basis of a set of reasons that is wider than the set on which he acts. I question Peacocke's assertion by offering two types of example. I think that my account of these examples provides a fruitful understanding of a highly problematic phenomenon. To the extent that they are generalizable, they lend plausibility to the view that weakness of will is a certain type of response to dilemmas of practical reason, rather than an absurd, irrational bypassing of a single all-things-considered judgment about the thing to do.

The examples are of two types. In the first type (type A), the weak-willed agent is disposed to accept on rational grounds two candidates for an all-things-considered best judgment, both of which are based on the same set of reasons. In this type, the agent desires what Philipp Pettit and Geoffrey Brennan[8] call "vaguely defined gestalts," i.e., goods whose utility to the agent is not a linear function of the individual utilities of the acts contributing to those goods. I describe two kinds of case, the simple and the complex: discussion of the latter is intended to show that type A examples are far more pervasive than might be supposed. In the second type of example (type B), the weak-willed agent is disposed to accept on rational grounds two candidates for an all-things-considered best judgment, one of which embraces a narrower set of reasons than the other, but in which the sets of reasons are not "all of a piece," in a sense to be explained. In both types of example, the weak-willed agent acts against an alternative *not* judged as superior on the basis of a set of reasons that is wider than the one acted on, and hence does not do something clearly irrational in the way Peacocke suggests.

In both kinds of example, I present the weak-willed agent as afflicted by a dilemma of practical rationality analogous to standard accounts of moral dilemmas.[9] The agent is disposed to accept that

---

8. "Restrictive Consequentialism," *Australasian Journal of Philosophy*, LXIV (1986): 438–55.
9. See Earl Conee, "Against Moral Dilemmas," *The Philosophical Review*, XCI (1982): pp. 89–97.

(1) All things considered, the best thing to do is φ.
(2) All things considered, the best thing to do is not-φ.

Given the truth of Davidson's principle of practical rationality which he calls the principle of continence—viz., ". . . perform the action judged best on the basis of all available relevant reasons" (*op. cit.*, p. 12), then the agent is beset by a dilemma[10] analogous to standard accounts of moral dilemmas, viz., there are situations in which agents have (i) an all-things-considered duty to φ and (ii) an all-things-considered duty to not-φ.[11]

Type A Examples

The first type of example that presents problems for Peacocke's view is analogous to a group of paradoxes that arise out of the fact that ". . . group utilities are not always simply a linear function of individual utilities—i.e. . . . the collective utility of a group of actions may be greater or less than the sum of utilities of the individual actions comprising the group."[12] I believe that weak-willed agents are frequently faced by structurally similar paradoxes. A set of acts $A_1 \ldots A_n$ performed by the agent, *each* of which maximizes agent-utility taken in isolation, may not collectively maximize agent utility. The utility of the agent is maximized only if she fails to perform an appropriate sized subset of $A_1 \ldots A_n$. In more detail, the marginal contribution of *each* act to the production of a good may be sufficiently insignificant to be outweighed by the costs of that act. Hence, it seems best not to perform *any* such acts. The utility of the good foregone if *no* such acts are performed is, however, greater than the sum of utilities of the individual acts; indeed, it is best to perform as many acts as are required to secure the good.

(i) *Simple Cases*

Consider, for example, the "vaguely defined gestalt" of sound teeth. The contribution of *each* act of brushing one's teeth to

---

10. I owe to Richard Sylvan the idea that the examples to be presented should be described in terms of dilemmas.

11. I do not wish to make the assumption that agglomeration is a permissible move in the description of dilemmas. See further Bernard Williams, "Ethical Consistency," in his *Problems of the Self* (New York: Cambridge, 1973), pp. 166–86, esp. pp. 179–81.

12. Harry S. Silverstein, "Utilitarianism and Group Co-ordination," *Noûs*, XIII (1979): 33560, esp. p. 336.

sound teeth may be outweighed by the costs of the inconvenience of getting fresh water, etc. Yet if the teeth are never brushed, the good of dental health, which outweighs the combined costs of inconvenience, will be foregone. Or consider the case of the non-party-goer. This person considers on each occasion when an opportunity presents itself to go to a party that the cost of the taxi fares makes going to *this* party not worth the effort. Yet, let us assume, the agent recognizes that a life of total nonattendance of parties is an impoverished life. The utility of attending a given sufficient number of parties is not reducible to the sum of utilities of attending those individual parties.

In these kinds of cases, the agent is disposed to accept on rational grounds two all-things-considered best judgments, for example:

J_1: It is best for me not to clean my teeth now.
J_2: It is best for me to clean my teeth sometimes, and now is an appropriate time for me to clean my teeth.

Taking the "soft option"—acting against J_2—is generally weak-willed despite the espousal of J_1. The basis for a judgment of weakness of will is discussed below. Even though, I shall argue, acting against J_2 is weak-willed, it is unclear that, given J_1, such action is irrational. For given Davidson's principle of continence, I suggest, the agent is faced with the following dilemma. He ought to clean his teeth now; he ought not to clean his teeth now.

(ii) *Complex Cases*

Cases of weakness of will that involve the pursuit of goods whose utility is not a linear function of the utilities of individual actions may seem relatively rare. This is not so, however; there are many cases susceptible to a more complex treatment. In the complex case it is granted that the good *directly* aimed at by the agent is not a "vaguely defined gestalt" such as sound teeth, party-going. Nonetheless, in the complex case, a further good desired by the agent, viz., motivational integrity, is a vaguely defined gestalt, and is a good whose pursuit creates dilemmas for the agent.

Consider, for example, Davidson's weak-willed toothbrusher:

> I have just relaxed in bed after a hard day when it occurs to me that I have not brushed my teeth. Concern

for my health bids me rise and brush; sensual indulgence suggests I forget my teeth for once. I weigh the alternatives in the light of the reasons: on the one hand, my teeth are strong, and at my age decay is slow. It won't matter much if I don't brush them. On the other hand, if I get up, it will spoil my calm and may result in a bad night's sleep. Everything considered I judge I would do better to stay in bed. Yet my feeling that I ought to brush my teeth is too strong for me: wearily I leave my bed and brush my teeth. My act is clearly intentional, although against my better judgement, and so is incontinent" (*op. cit.*, pp. 101–2).

This case does not *seem* to involve a dilemma. Either the agent thinks that the stresses of resisting the desire to get up on that occasion outweigh the benefits of lying in bed on that occasion, or he does not. If he does, then getting up is perfectly rational; there is no weakness of will. If he does not, getting up is straightforwardly irrational in some way. Either way, there is no good involved whose utility is not a linear function of the utilities of individual actions.

I believe, however, that the toothbrusher case, and others, can be understood as involving such a good, and understood, therefore, as a type A example. In order to sustain this claim, I need to introduce a distinction, due to Watson,[13] between evaluative and nonevaluative reasons for action: an *evaluative* reason for action pertains to the evaluation of the object of a desire, whereas a nonevaluative reason for action pertains to the suffering of the agent caused by nonsatisfaction of desire. In the words of Watson:

> . . . any desire may provide the basis for a reason insofar as non-satisfaction of the desire causes suffering and hinders the pursuit of ends of the agent. But it is important to realize that the reason generated in this way by a desire is a reason for *getting rid* of the desire, and one may get rid of a desire either by satisfying it or by eliminating it in some other manner. . . . Hence this kind of reason differs importantly from the reasons based upon the evaluation of the activities or states of affairs in question. For in the former case, attaining the object of

---

13. "Free Agency," *The Journal of Philosophy*, LXXII, 8 (April 24, 1975): 205–20.

desire is simply a means of eliminating discomfort or agitation, whereas in the latter case that attainment is the end itself (*ibid.*, p. 210–1).

Watson gives several examples of dissonance between these two sorts of reason:

> Consider the case of a woman who has a sudden urge to drown her bawling child in the bath; or the case of a squash player who while suffering an ignominious defeat, desires to smash his opponent in the face with the racquet. It is just false that the mother values her child's being drowned or that the opponent values the injury and suffering of his opponent. But they desire these things nonetheless. It is not that they assign to these actions an initial value which is then outweighed by other considerations. *These activities are not even represented by a positive entry, however small, on the initial "desirability matrix"* (*ibid.*, p. 210; italics added).

Nor is it to be assumed that such dissonance occurs only in the case of impulses, as Watson points out. Habituated or acculturated desires may present the same problem. Davidson's example of the toothbrusher is of a person who does not value more his teeth being brushed than his remaining in bed. Indeed, it is possible that he does not value *at all* his teeth being brushed *on that occasion*. Nonetheless, he has a reason for brushing his teeth, viz., the agitation he experiences as a result of the nonfulfillment of a habituated desire.

Armed with the distinction between evaluative and nonevaluative reasons for action, I can now outline in more detail the view that Davidson's weak-willed toothbrusher is faced with a dilemma. For reasons given below, the toothbrusher is disposed to accept:

J_3: It is best for me to get up and brush my teeth now.
J_4: It is best for me habitually to resist the temptation to get up and brush my teeth when I have forgotten to do so, and *now* is an appropriate time not to get up.

The weak-willed toothbrusher acts against J_4, but it is unclear that such action is irrational, given J_3. My claim is that J_3 and J_4 are formed on the basis of the same set of reasons and are rationally formed. J_4 is rationally formed on the basis of the following considerations.

(i) The toothbrusher values most highly a state in which evaluative reasons for action prevail over nonevaluative reasons. That is, he values most highly a state of affairs in which desires that provide merely nonevaluative reasons for action are extinguished or at least reduced in motivational force. Let us call this valued state of affairs "motivational integrity."

(ii) He believes that the way to achieve motivational integrity is to form a habit of performing specific actions in line with his *evaluative* reasons despite the baleful influence of desires to act otherwise. One might usefully compare Aristotle's account of the acquisition of the virtues: in order to acquire a habit of right desire when one is afflicted with wrong desires, one must repeatedly act enkratically, i.e., perform actions conforming to those of the virtuous person despite the existence of temptations to act otherwise.

J_3 is rationally formed, however, on the basis of the same set of reasons as J_4. The utility of attaining the good of motivational integrity is not a linear function of the individual utilities of the individual acts that contribute to that good. Since, I hypothesize, the marginal contribution of each refraining from brushing to motivational integrity is outweighed by the nonevaluative reasons for acting, the toothbrusher is also disposed to accept that the optimistic action is to get up and brush.

I have argued, then, that Davidson's case of the weak-willed toothbrusher can be seen as analogous to the case of the nontoothbrusher earlier described. In brief, the nontoothbrusher is disposed to accept that the thing to do is to act in line with each of J_1 and J_2. The toothbrusher is disposed to accept that the thing to do is to act in line with each of J_3 and J_4. J_1 and J_2, however, prescribe conflicting courses of action, as do J_3 and J_4.

It will be objected that I have not described the case of *Davidson's* weak-willed toothbrusher, for Davidson's toothbrusher acts against a single best judgment. This is not at all obvious, however, for Davidson's description of the case suggests an unnoticed ambiguity in the notion of "acting against one's better judgment." In Davidson's description, the better judgment

Chapter 10   Executive Failure

appears to be based on evaluative reasons only: my teeth are strong, decay is slow, I will probably get a bad night's sleep. The nonevaluative reasons in favor of getting up are relegated to mere desire: ". . . my *feeling* that I ought to brush my teeth is too strong for me" (*op. cit.*, pp. 101–2; italics added). There is, however, an ambiguity in the notion of "best judgment," namely, between an evaluative judgment about what is best based solely on evaluative reasons, and a judgment about the thing to do based on a wider set of reasons, viz., both evaluative and nonevaluative reasons. Once the ambiguity is revealed, it is not at all obvious that Davidson's case could not be redescribed in the way I have suggested.

Let us summarize. The simple case differs from the complex case in this respect. In the simple case, the good directly aimed at by the relevant continent actions are "vaguely defined gestalts" (e.g., the good of sound teeth, the good of being a partygoer, etc.). In the complex case, the good directly aimed at by the relevant continent actions are not vaguely defined gestalts but, e.g., staying in bed and getting a good night's sleep, feeling better after a run. In the complex case, however, there is another "vaguely defined gestalt" desired by the agent, which is secured by a sufficient number of relevant actions, viz., the good of motivational integrity. In the complex case, the distinction between evaluative and nonevaluative reasons becomes important. The dilemma can be seen as occurring only if there is a perceived tension between actions suggested by evaluative reasons and those suggested by nonevaluative ones.

I think that many cases of weakness of will described in the literature can be understood as involving the good of motivational integrity.[14] There are cases of weak-willed acts, however, where there is no "vaguely defined gestalt" in the offing—there is no such good aimed at directly or indirectly by relevantly continent actions. Perhaps, it will be claimed, Peacocke's account of weakness of will applies at least to these cases. But this is not at all obvious. A different kind of dilemma may afflict these weak-willed agents.

---

14. See, e.g., Robert Audi's example of the adulterer in "Weakness of Will and Practical Judgment," *Noûs*, XIII (1979): 173–95; and Thalberg's example of the curious landlady in "Acting against One's Better Judgment," in G. W. Mortimore, ed., *Weakness of Will* (New York: Macmillan, 1971), pp. 233–53.

Type B Examples

I discuss now the second type of example that casts doubt on the orthodox view outlined by Peacocke. In these cases, the agent is disposed to accept on rational grounds two candidates for an all-things-considered judgment, one of which embraces a narrower set of reasons than the other.

Consider the following example. I hail from subtropical climes, but currently find myself in a foreign, miserably cold place. I have no reason to believe that I will ever be in such a place again. I know that I will feel better if I get up early and go for a run. (I have no other opportunity to go for a run.) Where I come from, getting up early to go for a run presents no hardship. Here, however, I feel apathetic and wretched, and am disinclined toward making the effort to get up. Concerning *this* occasion, I make the following judgments.

J_5: (Considering evaluative reasons only) I judge it best to get up and go for a run.

J_6: (Considering evaluative and nonevaluative reasons) I judge it best to stay in bed.

I shall assume that there is no good in the offing having the characteristics of a "vaguely defined gestalt." I am not interested in developing motivational integrity with respect to getting up early to go for runs in cold climes, for I do not expect to be in my current predicament again. Nor do I subscribe to the belief that it is good for one generally to do unpleasant things, since that is "character building." I don't believe in that nonsense.

Davidson may well analyze the above case as follows. For him, all-things-considered judgments are judgments of *desirability*: hence, *the* all-things-considered judgment would be J_5. He would relegate the nonevaluative reasons in favor of staying in bed to the realm of desire or feeling: my desire to stay in bed "is too strong for me." On my account, however, the agent is disposed to claim both that the thing to do is to act on J_5 and the thing to do is to act on J_6.

Here, too, the agent is in the grip of a dilemma. Normally, it is rational to act on an all-things-considered judgment that is relative to the widest set of reasons considered by the agent. Where one such judgment takes into account set S_1 of reasons (evaluative reasons) and another takes into account S_1 and S_2 (non-

Chapter 10 Executive Failure

evaluative reasons), then, it appears, the agent ought to act from the latter judgment.

Our agent, however, though mindful of this, is also high-minded. She feels that the addition of S_2 somehow contaminates the weighing of the reasons included in S_1. From the point of view of assessing agent *utilities*, the reasons contained in S_1 and S_2 are all of a piece; however, from the point of view of weighing agent utilities and the desirability of the objects of the agent's desires, the reasons contained in S_1 and S_2 are not all of a piece. Consider the desire to stay in bed. The satisfaction of this desire produces some agent utility (its nonsatisfaction requires unpleasant effort). Let us say, however, its object does not feature at all on the agent's desirability matrix. She may not value at all a state of affairs in which she stays in bed. Now, since the agent would rather be free of the feelings of apathy and wretchedness that cause the disinclination to get out of bed, she may, through high-mindedness, judge it to be a good thing to act from the *narrower* set of reasons considered in J_5. The high-minded *weak-willed* agent, however, fails to act from that narrower set of reasons, and instead acts on J_6. She takes the "line of least resistance" and is weak; but, again, it is not clear that her action is irrational.

I now propose an analysis of weakness of will as a certain kind of response to the dilemmas identified above. The analysis satisfies the two desiderata mentioned above. First, it understands the phenomenon to be neither absurd, nor irrational, nor mysterious. Second, it adheres to the core ideas of weakness of will as being a weakness, and as being in some sense action against a perceived requirement endorsed by the agent herself. These desiderata are satisfied by a certain understanding of this requirement, and what it is to act against it. On this understanding, I shall argue, weakness of will is not an irrational bypassing of an all-things-considered best judgment.

An account that appears to satisfy these desiderata is that of Schiffer. I shall argue, however, this account fails to do justice to the root idea of weakness of will, viz., that it is action against a perceived requirement. A critique of Schiffer's view leads to my own account of action "against the will."

According to Schiffer, weak-willed agents act on their strongest first-order desires but against their strongest second-order desires. The "will" is weak because the agent's will (the strongest second-order desire) is not the agent's motivationally strongest desire. In his article "Intention and Akrasia," Peacocke argues that a theory such as Schiffer's fails to account for the irrationality of the akrates. This criticism has bite, however, only on the assumption that the akrates *is* irrational in the sense defined by Peacocke (see above, p. 139–40). The problem with Schiffer's account is not that it fails to account for the irrationality of the akrates, but that it fails to account for the philosophical puzzlement that generates the analysis of weak-willed behavior as a species of irrationality. What is puzzling about weak-willed behavior is that something perceived as required in some sense is nonetheless not motivationally most powerful. On the Davidsonian view, that perceived requirement is given by the agent's single all-things-considered judgment about what is best. Perhaps on Schiffer's account the perceived requirement is given by the content of one's second-order desires. But these desires need not be based on judgments about the thing to do, and it is for this reason that Schiffer's account seems to embrace phenomena other than weakness of will.

Consider the following example. I have a first-order desire to partake of a healthy dish, but, due to an ascetic distaste for eating, I have a second-order desire not to act on that desire. Let us assume that this second-order desire is based not on an assessment about what is best, but on a groundless semineurotic fear of getting fat. In this case, acting against the second-order desire is not to be seen as acting against a perceived requirement; hence, it is puzzling why acting against it should be regarded as weak-willed. Why should, after all, a semineurotic yielding to one's second-order desires be an action coincident with a perceived requirement? The presumption that one's second-order desires coincide with perceived requirements seems necessary to Schiffer's account if it is to succeed as an account of weakness of will: however, the presumption is suspect.

On my account, I aim to do justice to the intuition that weakness of will is acting against a perceived requirement, while denying that it is acting against an all-things-considered best (or superior) judgment.

How can this be done? I shall argue that the problem with Schiffer's account is its identification of the will simply with the motivationally strongest second-order desire. A more promising approach is to identify the will with a second-order volition

Chapter 10 Executive Failure

based on an *evaluative* second-order desire. That is, the will is identified with that evaluative second-order desire which the agent wants to move him all the way to action. I shall later argue that this evaluative desire is not an all-things-considered best judgment.

What is the nature of this evaluative second-order desire? Such a desire is in Taylor's[15] terminology a strong evaluation. According to Taylor, strong evaluation of first-order desires is concerned with their "qualitative worth," which is not assessable by "simple weighing." The dimension of evaluation at issue here is not the weighing of outcomes of action, but the assessment of the type of person one wants to be or, more narrowly, the type of dispositions one wishes to have. One aspect of this is the type of desires by which one wants to be motivated. Hence, one considers evaluation of desire in terms of noble or base, courageous or cowardly, dignified or degrading, strong or weak (with respect to resisting the sensuous desires), and so forth. In contrasting qualitative evaluation with quantitative evaluation of alternatives, Taylor alludes to the breakdown of the latter in the face of incommensurabilities. He argues, for example, that, in assessing the desirability of two holidays, one of which is exhilarating, the other of which is relaxing, it is not necessarily the case that the choice is amenable to calculation: frequently, one has to opt for the one rather than the other on other grounds. These other grounds of choice may be what Taylor calls weak evaluation, i.e., an assessment of desire based on brute preference: "I feel like an exhilarating holiday." Alternatively, they may be based on strong evaluations.

It is my contention that, in the context of weakness of will, the will should be identified with strong evaluation. *Weakness* of will, I shall argue, is a certain kind of action against strong evaluation (see further below). As I have said, the problem with Schiffer's account of weakness of will is that in some cases it is unclear why a motivationally stronger second-order desire should have more claim to being the agent's will than a motivationally stronger first-order desire. Once strong evaluation enters the picture, however, the agent's will can be identified with an evaluatively based second-order volition. Evaluation plays a key role in identifying the agent's will just as in the more tradi-

---

15. "Agency and the Self," in his *Human Agency and Language: Philosophical Papers* I (New York: Cambridge, 1985), pp. 15–44.

tional accounts evaluation plays a key role in identifying the will with the all-things-considered best judgment.

The proposed account of the will enables us to understand why in Schiffer's example (see above, p. 138) the smoker has no *will* to give up even though he acts against his better judgment. He has no will to give up since he has not formed a strong evaluation to give up. He is happy to be the sort of person who is self-indulgent rather than rational. Hence he is not *weak-willed*. The neurotic dieter of my example is not weak-willed even though she acts contrary to her second-order desire. She is not weak-willed because her second-order desire is not a strong evaluation, and hence is not identified with her will.

It must be emphasized that strong evaluations of first-order desires do not necessarily yield a second-order volition to act in accordance with one's *evaluative* reasons. Strong evaluations are judgments about the kind of dispositions one wants to have, and one may not want always to be disposed to act on the basis of evaluative reasons. The exclusive concern in the literature with what I call "high-minded" weakness of will should not blind one to the possibility of "low-minded" varieties. Consider again Davidson's toothbrusher. This person as I have described him is high-minded. His acting on *non*-evaluative reasons is weak-willed. But consider a low-minded analogue. This person's strong evaluation is not to promote the best state of affairs from the perspective of evaluative reasons. While staying in bed, agitating away, striving to conquer his semineurotic tendencies to get up, he is also saying to himself, "Stop being so masochistic—just get up." As Davidson might put it, however, his feeling that he ought to stay in bed, based on his drive for self-improvement inherited from his perfectionist parents, is just too strong for him. His first-order desire to lie in bed (based on evaluative reasons) is stronger than his second-order volition to give in to his nonevaluative reasons. Hence, his acting on his evaluative reasons is weak-willed.

Let us consider further the nature of *weakness* of will. The following question arises. It may appear that a second-order desire that is a strong evaluation must be an all-things-considered best judgment that the best thing to do is to act on that first-order desire having a certain quality. Hence, it may appear, if weakness of will is acting against a strong evaluation, is it not irrational? The suggestion is that a strong evaluation is a

Chapter 10 Executive Failure

kind of super all-things-considered judgment used to resolve the dilemmas described above. I now challenge that suggestion.

The view that a strong evaluation is a super all-things-considered judgment misrepresents its nature. A strong evaluation is not a judgment about the thing to do *here and now*: it is a "background" judgment about the kind of dispositions and character one wishes to have and to cultivate (e.g., a character of temperance with respect to food, drink, or sex; a courageous character with respect to one's dealings with one's Head of Department or authority figures generally, or more generally a character disposed to act from evaluative rather than from nonevaluative reasons). Such evaluations do not necessarily flow into judgments about what to do here and now precisely because of the dilemmas outlined above: dilemmas that occur because the agent has *not yet* acquired the relevant desired character or dispositions.

It will be replied that there must be some connection between strong evaluations and judgments about the thing to do here and now. Indeed, there is. But the way to forge this connection is to eschew the model of practical rationality that suggests that practical judgments—including strong evaluations—are necessarily based on, or are, judgments about the best, or a best, thing to do.

Pettit and Brennan offer a model of practical reasoning that enables us to understand the role of strong evaluation. They suggest that, in certain kinds of situation, one should eschew calculative strategies according to which one attempts to optimize. Rather, one applies the following kind of rule: do A in C except where there is a "(loosely specified sort of) emergency" (*op. cit.*, p. 447). Hence, (i) one checks that circumstances C obtain (e.g., this is the standard time for cleaning teeth); (ii) one checks that "the escape condition" is unrealized (e.g., it is not too inconvenient right now. It would be too inconvenient if, e.g., the water is outside, and it is hailing). In particular, the agent is ". . . not to try to identify and weigh the pro's and con's of doing A in that particular instance of C" (*op cit.*, p. 447).

One of the kinds of situation in which one eschews calculative strategies is when one is beset by the kinds of dilemmas described earlier. In these kinds of situations, the rational agent acts in accordance with the following rule: act in line with a relevant strong evaluation (e.g., be temperate with respect to chocolate eclairs or gin and tonics, clean teeth at the standard times) unless there is an "emergency."

What, then, is weakness of will? Weak-willed action is not action against one's strong evaluation *simpliciter*, for there may indeed be an "emergency." Weakness of will occurs when the emergency occurs *all too readily*. For the weak-willed agent, evaluations such as the appropriateness of cleaning one's teeth at standard times is all too readily disregarded as a result of appeal to escape clauses which are, as Pettit and Brennan claim, "loosely specified." The repertoire of escapes available to the weak-willed is depressingly familiar: I am particularly tired, apathetic, edgy, in need of solace, in need of excitement, in need of relaxation, and so on. It is the mark of the weak-willed to set aside maxims at the slightest pretext presented by such escape clauses. To appeal to such escape conditions is not irrational, for the appeal is not backed up by a judgment that it is an inferior course of action. Nonetheless, the disposition to appeal to such "escapes" too readily is a defect of character, and a weak-willed act on a specific occasion is either a manifestation of that defect, or an "out of character" lapse. A judgment that an agent was weak-willed on a particular occasion is a normative judgment, where there are no hard or fast rules determining when the judgment is correct or reasonable.

My conclusion, then, is this. A weak-willed failure to act in line with a strong evaluation is not an irrational bypassing of an all-things-considered best (or superior) judgment. At worst, weakness of will merely betrays a defect of character. A detailed account of the nature of that defect is presented in section (iii).

(iii) *The Virtue of Executive Courage*

I have said that weakness of will betrays, at worst, weakness of character. In this section, I discuss the nature of this weakness, and generalize the idea of executive failure as a manifestation of weakness of character. The weakness can be characterized generally as a lack of what I shall term "executive courage." Although courage is often thought of as a virtue involving a rather settled disposition of character, I shall not make that assumption here. Lack of executive courage can be manifested even where there is not, or not as yet, a settled disposition of character. Nonetheless, for convenience, I shall use the term 'virtue' to describe the desirable trait of executive courage.

To describe the virtue of executive courage, one needs the concepts of the *field* of the virtue, and the *goal* of the virtue. The field of a virtue relates to the desires, emotions, feelings, and attitudes for which the particular virtue is, to use Philippa Foot's[16] terminology, a corrective. That is, the point of the virtue is the "schooling" of these emotions so that temptation, deficiency of motivation, or other character failures are avoided: more generally, the emotions must occur to the right degree in the right circumstances. The goal of a virtue is that for the sake of which the virtue exists. The goal of executive courage is executive success—the avoidance of the two varieties of mismatch mentioned above, between action and relevant intentional states of the agent (be they espoused principles, commitments, practical judgments, desires, or intentions).

Let us consider in more detail the goal of executive courage, before discussing the field of the virtue. To do that, I need to specify the situations in which exercise of the virtue is called for, and to specify what counts as a successful or appropriate response to those situations.

A virtue in general is a disposition of the agent, viz., a natural tendency to behave appropriately and with reason, in both problematic and ordinary situations. Thus, temperance is manifested where temptations of the flesh are in the offing, courage where the agent faces dangerous or otherwise fearful situations. Agents of virtue, unlike enkratic agents, have a *natural* tendency to behave appropriately, because their desires are not in conflict with the appropriate course of action. The virtuous agent also acts "with reason," unlike those whose behavior, though correct, is unthinking or unprincipled. I do not mean to imply that a virtuous agent need deliberate where virtue is exercised in perfectly standard situations.

The situations in which the virtue of executive courage is required are those where the agent is or could be beset by the various indeterminacies of reason characteristic of the practical activity of human beings. In general terms, indeterminacy arises when the agent is faced with a need to weigh and balance reasons for action, but reason dictates no clear-cut best course of action, or none may commend itself to the agent in a way stable enough to dictate action. This failure may be due to a

---

16. "Virtues and Vices," in her *Virtues and Vices and Other Essays* (New York: Blackwell, 1978), pp. 1–18.

fault of the agent, or it may simply be due to the nature of the reasons to be weighed. I shall presently consider more detailed examples, but for the moment let us say that phenomena involving indeterminacy of reason include: dilemmas (such as those described in section (ii)); instability (where the agent, weighing incommensurables, changes her mind back and forth about which option to choose); a failure to order alternatives at all; incomplete orderings of alternatives (where the agent is a maximizer, where the agent is committed to not choosing an inferior alternative and is worried that a better option may be "just around the corner," or where the agent judges it appropriate to choose any adequate alternative but, like Buridan's ass, lacks sufficient reason to go for *this* one rather than *that* one).

Let us turn now to the notion of an *appropriate* response to the occasions on which exercise of executive courage is called for. Executive courage is demanded when the agent is threatened by indeterminacy of reason. But what is the response of the agent of executive courage?

In general terms, the goal of executive courage is served when indeterminacy is both resolved, and resolved in a way that avoids mismatch between action and relevant intentional states. We will gain a clearer picture of what counts as mismatch by considering the types of indeterminacy that afflict the agent, and the distinctive types of responses required if the associated kinds of executive failure are to be avoided.

Weakness of Will. As we have seen, the weak-willed person is faced with practical dilemmas according to which each of two actions, including the "weak" action, is seen as reasonable. A response to this indeterminacy is appropriate when the agent balances and weighs reasons for action in a way that appropriately resolves the dilemma, and then acts accordingly. This weighing has two aspects.

  (i) An assessment of the appropriateness of making a strong evaluation in order to resolve the dilemma. For example, does the agent of case 1 above think it best to develop a habit of cleaning teeth at certain standard times, or does the agent of case 2 think it best to develop a habit of not getting up when he has forgotten to clean his teeth?
  (ii) An assessment of the appropriateness of acting on that strong evaluation (if there is one) here and now.

There is a mismatch of the kind characteristic of *weakness of will* between an appropriate practical attitude (viz., one that resolves the dilemma) and action, when the following occurs. The agent forms a strong evaluation but fails to act on it—pleading "emergency" and acting weakly—when it is inappropriate to do so. Acting *weakly* involves taking the line of least resistance, succumbing to temptation, habit, apathy, laziness, and so on.

There is another executive failure analogous to weakness of will when there is a failure in (i) above. That is, the agent fails to form a strong evaluation when it is appropriate to do so, and acts weakly. I shall not call this failure weakness *of will*, since there is no perceived requirement against which the agent acts. Rather, one might call the failure simply "weakness."

Further remarks need to be made about the notions of "appropriate" and "inappropriate." First, it need not always be necessary or even important to form a strong evaluation when faced with dilemmas of practical reason of the sort described in section (ii). The issues may be insufficiently significant, insufficiently pervasive, and may occur insufficiently frequently. The agent may simply have a natural tendency to act in line with one salient desire, and this may be all right from the point of view of what Young has called "dispositional autonomy." Even if such action is regarded as "weak," it is not an executive failure—a manifestation of executive vice.

Second, "pleading emergency" is appropriate when the emergency is "genuine." Needless to say, there are no hard and fast rules for what counts as a genuine emergency. This is not to say, of course, that there are no standards for *reasonable* assessments. The vices associated with unreasonable assessments will be discussed when I consider the *field* of executive courage. Suffice it to say here that acting in line with a strong evaluation may, indeed, on occasion be inappropriate—one may cause oneself too much stress, too much tiredness, too little joy. In those cases, one may manifest the vice of excessive *strength* of will.

It is time now to say more about executive failures other than weakness of will, the indeterminacies of reason characterizing them, and the goal of executive courage with respect to those indeterminacies.

Anomie. "Anomie," in the sense of a state of mind or character, refers to the undisciplined state of a person's desires. These desires are not only unlimited and unstable, they are also unregulated. That is, the individual does not subject them to the ordering process of deliberation culminating in the kind of practical judgments and intentions that allow desires to be focused on the world in a disciplined way. Such a state may manifest itself in a variety of executive defects. Anomic individuals may frenetically switch from pursuit to pursuit, rapidly becoming bored with any long-term activity. Alternatively, they may become indecisive and vacillating. Again, such individuals may suffer the "malady of infinite aspiration"[17] and be fated to a life of continual dissatisfaction and restlessness. And, finally, since the anomic individual can attain no deep long-term satisfaction by an ordered pursuit of goals, he can suffer from disillusionment, apathy, and a weariness with life.

The indeterminacies facing the weak-willed may also be at least partly due to a failure to discipline desires; but the weak-willed, unlike the anomic, has at least formed practical judgments as a result of deliberation. The dilemmas in which the conflicting desires appear are both rational options. The failure in weakness of will is not essentially failure to evaluate and thence control desires; it is a failure to resolve adequately dilemmas arising from that evaluation.

Lack of resolve. In lack of resolve, there is a breakdown between judgments about the thing to do and the formation of an intention. Irresolute persons either fail to form a proximate intention to do something here and now, or fail to form *specific* action plans so that remote intentions can be transformed into proximate intentions. Thus, for example, I judge that the thing to do is to read in the not too distant future several important philosophical works that have recently been published. But I fail to set myself to read them, because my attention, for one reason or another, is always drawn to other things.

Irresolution differs from weakness of will because there is no perceived requirement against which the agent acts. In weakness of will, the perceived requirement is to act in line with strong evaluations except in "genuine" emergency. The weak-willed agent takes advantage of leeway in the notion of "genuine" to plead "emergency" all too readily. There is a different latitude involved in irresolution: the practical judgment allows for indeterminate delay in the formation of specific intentions.

---

17. Emile Durkheim, *Suicide.*

Chapter 10 Executive Failure

But, at some stage, the delay might rightly be censured as involving the character defect of irresolution.

Irresolution can be thought of as a stage prior to that of weakness of will: the agent has not yet perceived herself to be in a dilemma resolvable by the formation of a strong evaluation. The dilemma may, for example, have the form: it is best for me to read this philosophy book sometime, and now is an appropriate time not to allow my attention to be drawn to other things. It is best for me not to read this philosophy book now, because right now I am drawn to the more attractive novel by my bedside.

What is an appropriate response to the indeterminacy or latitude facing the irresolute agent? The appropriate response is not to search in vain for a best time to read this book or that book (for it may always be the case that a better time may be "just around the corner"). There are only appropriate times, and inappropriate times, where the boundary between these is very fuzzy at that. The resolute person is the one with the strength of character—the courage, if you like—to read the book *now*, where now is an appropriate time (and the threshold of appropriateness, though fuzzy, is set clearly neither too high nor too low). The resolute person can do this, even though reason does not dictate that now is the *best* time to read the book.

In brief, the goal of executive courage in situations where irresolution threatens is to act on a recognition that, in the words of Raz, "Rational action is action for (what the agent takes to be) an undefeated reason. It is not necessarily action for a reason which defeats all others."[18]

Vacillation. The vacillator, unlike the irresolute, keeps changing his mind about the thing to do. Reason does not yield a stable ordering of options when weighing incommensurables: different desiderata assume different levels of salience at different times. Yet the vacillator acts as though reason should provide a clearly correct and hence stable ordering, as though there should be a reason that clearly defeats all others. The increased or decreased salience of various desiderata is interpreted as evidence of *mistake*, instead of, e.g., incommensurability. The vacillator lacks the courage to act on one *satisfactory* option, even though it is not fully sanctioned by reason as the *best*.

Moral cowardice. In moral cowardice, the mismatch between relevant intentional states of the agent and action is not due to

---

18. *The Morality of Freedom*, p. 339.

incompletion of the practical process; it is completed but in the wrong way. Like other executive failures, moral cowardice is characterized by an indeterminacy of reason. Moral cowardice is a response to the same kind of dilemmas as those facing the weak-willed. The dilemmas have the following general form:

P_1: Considering all evaluative reasons only, I ought to φ.
P_2: Considering all evaluative and nonevaluative reasons, I ought not to φ.

The moral coward, like the "low-minded" weak-willed, is the person who habitually acts on P_2 rather than P_1. Unlike the weak-willed, however, the moral coward identifies with that course of action: she has not formed a strong evaluation to act in line with P_1 (except in emergency).

In moral cowardice, there is a mismatch between actions and relevant intentional states—a mismatch that is not in the traditional sense irrational. Indeed, on the traditional view, the rational agent acts on P_2 since P_2 contains the widest set of reasons. The mismatch consists in the failure to balance reasons for action with integrity—with due regard to the agent's own principles. It is not *irrational* for a man who seeks dishonorable safety to reason thus: "Although I am not acting in such a way as to realize the most valuable state of affairs (victory in a just cause), I am not lucky enough to be endowed with courageous instincts, so it is acceptable for me to succumb to my fears." Nonetheless, such a coward manifests a defect of character.

I do not wish to imply that all cases of acting against evaluative reasons exhibit a character defect. It may be appropriate to set aside options featuring on one's "desirability matrix" when the psychic costs (expressed by nonevaluative reasons) are too high relative to the desirability of the rejected option. Of course, there are no hard and fast rules for determining when moral cowardice is thereby exhibited, any more than there are such rules for determining when weakness of will is exhibited.

I turn our attention now to the *field* of executive courage, viz., those desires, emotions, feelings, and attitudes which may militate against a natural reasoned tendency to behave appropriately where the exercise of the virtue is called for, and to which the virtue of executive courage is a "corrective."

It will be useful to compare the field of executive courage with that of normal courage. In normal courage, the emotions and attitudes to which the virtue is a corrective form two types.

Chapter 10 Executive Failure

First, there is the emotion of fear: fear of pain, fear of injury, fear of death, fear of ostracism, fear of mice, fear of the unknown. Fear of these things must be neither excessive, nor deficient, nor otherwise inappropriate to the circumstances. Second, there are the tendencies to make overly cautious or overly incautious assessments of the appropriate course of action when faced with danger and other feared situations. Acquiring courage may not just be a question of reducing fear: it may also involve eliminating rashness.

Similarly, the tendencies to which the virtue of executive courage is a corrective form two types. First, there are the tendencies for desires, emotions, and feelings to be excessive, deficient, or felt in the wrong circumstances. These include such potentially damaging tendencies as laziness, curiosity, desire for sensuous pleasure, fear, desire for a life of ease and comfort. Examples of weakness of will tend to focus exclusively on *excessive* feeling and desire where these are regarded as temptations: one feels too much passion, and in the wrong bedroom. In much executive vice, however, including weakness of will, relevant emotions may be felt too weakly. The apathetic depressed person may fail to make practical judgments, or fail to transform practical judgment into action, because the world seems lacklustre and grey.[19]

Second, there are the tendencies to make overly cautious or overly incautious assessments of the appropriate course of action when faced with indeterminacies of reason. As with normal courage, there are several factors to be weighed in assessing an appropriate course of action on a given occasion, viz., the nature of the valuable alternatives that might be furthered on that occasion, the nature of the costs of achieving them, the odds of achieving them, the odds of bearing the expected costs. Let me illustrate with weakness/strength of will. In this area, the agent of executive courage will characteristically aim to attain the objects of strong evaluation. These goals may be highly important, such as motivational integrity with respect to a central area of one's life, e.g., overcoming the inertia that threatens one's career ambitions. Or they may be relatively trivial, such as curbing a nail-biting habit. Now the costs of furthering those

---

19. It is refreshing to see Amelie Oksenberg Rorty discuss accidie or melancholia in the context of akrasia; "Where Does the Akratic Break Take Place?" *Australasian Journal of Philosophy*, LVIII (1980): 333–46.

goals on a particular occasion may be high: it may be that the only way I can stop biting my fingernails *today*, given the stress I am under, is by suffering the humiliation of wearing woollen mittens. The costs of overcoming melancholia, laziness, boredom *whenever* they occur may be constant and tiresome monitoring of inner states, anxiety, fatigue, and lack of spontaneity. When there are relatively high costs, and relatively low odds of achieving goals, not all cases of failure to act in line with strong evaluation will manifest the character defect of weakness of will. Obviously, there are no clearcut guidelines as to the kind of weighing of odds, costs, and goals that an agent of executive courage would perform. We can, however, gain insight by considering the associated vices: excessive caution and excessive incaution.

First, executive vice may involve an excessively cautious attitude toward the weighing of relevant factors. For example, the procrastinator may fail to seize an adequate opportunity for writing the letter, not because he is lazy, but because he wonders (all too often) if a better opportunity will present itself later (he may feel more inspired, be under less pressure, and so on). Again, a weak-willed person, having formed a strong evaluation to adopt a more exciting life style, turns down an opportunity for a trip to a remote Pacific island because, excessively fearful of risk, he overestimates the discomforts and dangers of the boat trip, disease, and stone fish. In general, one will manifest the character defect of weakness of will if there is excessive caution: though the expected contribution of an action to a goal is significant relative to the expected costs of that contribution, one nevertheless pleads the existence of an "emergency" and does not perform the action. Negative features, such as the nature of the costs, the risk of incurring them, the risk of the action being ineffective in the realization of the goal, have become overly salient in one's assessments.

The other kind of vice, incaution, comes in two types. First, there is impetuosity: incaution resulting from insufficient deliberation. Excessive reaction against decision phobia and the various paralyses affecting practical activity may lead to plumping for an alternative without due consideration. For example, aware of the evils of procrastination, I start reading the difficult and lengthy philosophy book I had been planning to read for ages, at precisely the time I should be getting the students' tests marked. The vice of incaution can be seen in its most obvious manifestations as an over corrective to vacillation, irresolution, and anomie, but it can also be seen as a vice opposed to weakness of will. The weak-willed person, faced with dilemmas, makes a strong evaluation but, taking the "line of least resistance," acts against it. The undeliberated person, on the other hand, with those same dilemmas, plumps for an option without searching for deeper evaluations on which commitments could be based. That person, like the weak-willed person, lacks executive courage.

The second type of incaution is rashness: after due deliberation, the importance of the goal (relative to the costs of attaining it, and the odds against attaining it) becomes overly salient in the mind of the agent. Here is a third vice opposed to the virtue of strength of will. Where the goal is insufficiently important (relative to costs and odds), an agent may nonetheless fail to plead "emergency" where it is appropriate to do so, and doggedly remain strong-willed, causing himself and his friends to suffer. Interestingly, there appears to be no name for the vice of *excessive* strength of will.

Chapter 11

Significance of Actions

(i) *Freedom and Interests*

Our account of freedom so far is incomplete in a vital respect. There is a very important endoxon that the theory has so far recognized but not yet fully discussed. This is the view that the extent of our freedom depends on the *significance* of the alternatives with respect to which we are more or less free or unfree. In chapter 6, I concluded that the role played by the significance of action in the assessment of overall freedom could be expressed in the following proposition.

> P_5: An agent is the freer overall, ceteris paribus, the less significant are the actions with respect to which practical activity is flawed in the ways described in P_1-P_4 (see above, p. 80).

On one view of freedom—that which emphasizes potential in agency as *propensity*—"significance" should be interpreted simply in terms of agents' wants. The more an agent wants a restricted option, the less free she is, *ceteris paribus*. My aim in this chapter, however, is to pay attention to the third aspect of potential identified in chapter 3—that which identified realization of potential with flourishing in agency. It may appear obvious that "significance" in this respect should be connected with self-realization, and this would be so if we were dealing with ideal-world scenarios. My interest in this chapter, however, is to develop a notion of signficance that connects with "flourishing" in imperfect worlds—worlds in which agents may be quite unable to attain self-realization in a relatively context-independent sense, but can only "make the best of a bad job." To make this clear, I shall interpret the notion of significance in terms of interests: an option is the more significant to an agent the more it is in his interests for it to be available and eligible. The notion of interests, unlike that of self-realization, clearly relates to the actual worlds in which agents find themselves.

In keeping with the methodology of this work, I shall develop a concept of interests that does justice to two important but conflicting endoxa about the nature of interests. These are

E_{21}: The person to whom interests are ascribed is the final arbiter of her interests in the sense that they are not ultimately determined by certain ideals of justifiability, right, good, that are not necessarily espoused by herself.

E_{22}: A person's interests promote in some sense her "good."

Emphasis of E_{21} leads to the idea that the concept of interests is essentially descriptive: there is a conceptual link between a person's interests and her wants or preferences. Emphasis of E_{22} leads to the idea that the notion of interests is essentially normative, and that there is no conceptual link between a person's interests and her stated wants or preferences. Examples of the first emphasis are analyses of "x is in A's interest" as "A wants x"[1] or "A expresses a policy preference for x."[2] An example of the second is an analysis of "x is in A's interest" in terms of wants that it would be good for A to have. Thus, Benn[3] claims in "Interests in Politics" that "It might be in [a] child's interests to deny him satisfaction of some of his desires to save him from becoming the sort of person who habitually desires the wrong sort of thing" (*ibid.*, p. 131). Inasmuch as I distinguish between realization of propensity and flourishing (even in imperfect worlds), I cannot adopt the first alternative. But, on the other hand, it seems that a notion of flourishing *entirely* disconnected from the mature agent's *own* perceptions of her situation in the world in which she finds herself is problematic, even if we are to distrust certain of those perceptions.

(ii) *The Concept of Interests*

Before embarking on the task of reconciling the conflicting endoxa E_{21} and E_{22} about the nature of interests, I should indicate

---

1. See, e.g., C. B. Hagan, "The Group in Political Science," in Roland Young, ed., *Approaches to the Study of Politics* (London: Stevens, 1958).
2. See J. D. B. Miller, *The Nature of Politics* (London: Duckworth, 1962). Miller's concept of interests is criticized by Barry in "The Public Interest," repr. in Quinton, ed., *Political Philosophy* (New York: Oxford, 1967), pp. 112–26.
3. *Proceedings of the Aristotelian Society*, LX (1960): 123–40.

my reasons for not accepting certain analyses that appear to come close to achieving this task.

Theodore M. Benditt,[4] taking his cue from E_{22}, claims that the good of a person "may plausibly be taken to consist in his being sufficiently satisfied in as many departments of his life as are necessary to make him happy" (*ibid.*, p. 254), and that something is in a person's interests if it improves his position with respect to being happy. Happiness is defined in terms of mental and emotional well-being, which in turn is defined "in terms of states and/or conditions which enable [a person] to feel satisfied with what life brings" (*ibid.*, p. 255).

Benditt's account appears to accommodate E_{21} and E_{22}: Does not everyone want to be happy, and is not happiness the good of human beings? That the good of human beings is happiness in Benditt's sense would be disputed by, e.g., Maslow, for whom that good is "self-actualization." Self-actualization is a complex ideal, the realization of which may in certain circumstances be incompatible with a contentful adjustment to "what life brings" (*op. cit.*, pp. 5–8). Furthermore, not everyone may *want* to be happy at a given time in a given place. Someone living in Nazi Germany might see his good in terms of remaining sensitive to the suffering of others, and would not want to be happy in such an environment. Many policies promoting his happiness (e.g., brainwashing to accept Nazi doctrine) would not be considered *by him* to be in his interests, for they would involve him in a betrayal of his ideals.

Virginia Held[5] claims explicitly to have found a middle road between normative and descriptive conceptions of interests by providing a conception that places interests somewhere between wants, on the one hand, and rights on the other. For her, "x is in a person's interests" is equivalent to "a claim by or in behalf of that person for x is asserted as justifiable" (*ibid.*, p. 31).

This middle road, however, conforms neither to E_{21} nor to E_{22}. It does not conform to E_{22} for the following reasons. A claim for x might be asserted as justifiable without its promoting a person's good or advantage; it may even be inimical to it. For example, x could be an explosive device, in dangerous condition, unwanted by the person who has right of ownership over it.

---

4. "The Concept of Interest in Political Theory," *Political Theory*, III (1975): 245–58.

5. *The Public Interest and Individual Interests* (New York: Basic, 1970), p. 33.

Second, a policy could promote a person's good without there being any assertion or even belief that effecting that policy is justifiable. Held's concept also moves too far from E_{21}: a person is not in any sense the final arbiter of his interests when claims on behalf of him for x are automatically in his interests if they are asserted as justifiable.

I feel that Held's concept of "being in a person's interests" is too close to the notion of "having an interest in," which might be described as "the relation of being objectively concerned in something by having a right or title to, a claim upon, or a share in," and not close enough to the notion of "being in the interests of," which means "on the side of what is advantageous or beneficial to."[6] The former notion, unlike the latter, is not intimately connected with E_{21} and E_{22} about the nature of interest.

A concept of interests that perhaps comes closer to reconciling E_{21} and E_{22} is that of Connolly.[7] Since his concept has certain affinities with my own, to be developed below, discussion of a problem with Connolly's concept is best deferred.

My attempt to harmonize the E_{21} and E_{22} involves an explication of a complex relation between a person's interests and her wants. I see my account of this relation as a further development of the sophisticated and thoroughgoing analysis in Barry's writings on the subject of interests,[8] though my account will differ significantly from Barry's. In important respects, Barry's analysis fails to conform to the nature of interests specified as E_{21} and E_{22}. It is my hope that a discussion of problems in Barry's account, leading to further development in the theory of the relation between interests and wants, will effect a reconciliation between those endoxa.

Barry's concept of interests is defined by him as follows: "a policy, law or institution is in someone's interest if it increases his opportunities to get what he wants."[9] Before problems with Barry's account of interests can be discussed, clarification is needed of the notion of a want presupposed in the definition.

---

6. *Oxford English Dictionary* (Oxford, 1933), cited in *ibid.*, Held, p. 20.
7. See his "On Interests in Politics," *Politics and Society*, II (1972): 459–77.
8. See especially *Political Argument* and "The Public Interest."
9. "The Public Interest," p. 115. In Barry's discussion of the concept of an interest, it is clear that he extends the notion of policy to include actions in general. See, for example, *Political Argument*, pp. 180, 182. I shall follow suit in my discussion.

Barry makes it clear that it is "self-affecting"[10] or self-regarding wants that are relevant in the ascriptions of interests to people. I shall take self-regarding wants to include any want that is a want for *oneself* to do, have, or be certain things. The wants of a person A for *others* to have or do certain things and "results concerning people other than A are not directly relevant" (*ibid.*, p. 182) in the assessment of A's interests. For example, satisfaction of A's desire to give his salary increase to someone else, for the sake of improving that person's welfare, or for the sake of furthering equality, does not enhance A's *interests*. Barry claims that ". . . although one could say that under such circumstances [a] man *wants* his assets to be reduced, this does not in the least entail that he thinks *it is in his interests* for them to be reduced. Rather, it is to be described as a case where he allows his principles to override his interests (*ibid.*, p. 177).

There is a problem in interpreting Barry's claim that "other-regarding" wants are not "directly relevant" in the calculation of a person's interests. I take other-regarding wants to include any wants for *another* to do, have, or be certain things. Barry could be making one of two claims about the nonrelevance of other-regarding wants. These claims I shall call interpretation (a) and interpretation (b).

   (a) In the assessment of a person's interests, other-regarding wants should be excluded *ab initio*. Thus, we can never properly say that satisfaction of an other-regarding want enhances a person's interest.

   (b) In Barry's definition of an interest, cited above, the term 'wants' ranges only over wants for *oneself* to do, have, or be certain things. Nonetheless, a consideration of other-regarding wants is "indirectly" relevant in the assessment of a person's interests: they cannot be excluded *ab initio*. It is possible that satisfaction of an other-regarding want increases A's opportunities to satisfy wants for himself to do, have, or be certain things. Therefore, actions satisfying an other-regarding want can be in A's interest. For example, A's giving his salary increase to B will be in A's interest if this action enhances A's relationship with B, A finds this relationship gratifying, and A values the enhancement of this rela-

---

10. *Political Argument*, p. 185, fn. 1.

tionship more than his possession of the salary increase.[11]

Interpretation (b) fits in better with Barry's conceptual framework, since he does not explicitly limit the concept of opportunity in the way he limits the concept of a want in his definition of interests. Presumably, all kinds of things can increase one's opportunities to satisfy self-regarding wants, including the satisfaction of other-regarding wants.[12]

I now discuss a case which presents problems for Barry's concept of interests, and which indicates how his concept comes adrift from E_{21} and E_{22}. A solution of these problems will lead to further development in the theory of the relation between interests and wants, and a reconciliation of E_{21} and E_{22}.

Consider the following case. In the past, a person, A, had a large range of wants $[x, y, z \ldots]$ that were satisfiable. A now acquires an overriding want w, which she strives to satisfy. The acquisition of this new want is accompanied by a marked decline in the range of wants $[x, y, z \ldots]$. An example might be: A wishes to get married, and simultaneously ceases to wish to go frequently to the tavern, to be out with her friends at the weekend, to travel, and so on.

The question is whether policies or actions leading to the acquisition and/or satisfaction of w can be against one's interests. For Barry, it is in a person's interests to increase her opportunities to get what she wants. This, of course, does not entail that it is against her interests to diminish the range of her wants. Therefore, it would seem that actions leading to the acquisition and/or satisfaction of w are not, on Barry's account, against a

---

11. Compare Feinberg's notion of an interest as having a stake in something. The satisfaction of a want that *another* be well-off enhances one's *own* interests if one has a stake in the well-being of that person.
12. It might be noted that, if interpretation (b) rather than interpretation (a) is favored, a major criticism of Barry's concept, advanced by Connolly, can be undercut. Connolly claims that, according to Barry, only *privately* oriented wants are relevant in the ascriptions of interests to people—"the satisfactions" that enhance my interests "do not themselves involve a reference to other people" ("On Interests in Politics," p. 467). He thinks that, on Barry's account, one cannot have interests as a social being. According to interpretation (b), however, one can have interests as a social being. The account of the relation between other-regarding wants and interests, specified as interpretation (b), is the one I shall favor in my own account of interests.

person's interests. This seems perfectly uncontroversial in the example of marriage given above.

The problem becomes acute, however, in extreme cases. Let us assume that w is the want to be under the influence of a pleasure-producing drug, or to have electrical stimulation of the pleasure centers of the brain. Furthermore, when w is satisfied, one's wants are restricted to such an extent that one's sole want, w', is for the pleasurable sensations to continue. Does the state of being perpetually connected to a pleasure-producing machine maximize one's interests? It would seem so, once one has acquired the sole want w'. For being permanently connected to such a machine maximizes one's opportunities to get what one wants, viz., to satisfy the want w'. In the calculation of interests, wants are not weighted or eliminated by reference to factors such as their origin or desirability. As I mentioned earlier, according to Barry, the concept of an interest is firmly embedded in want-regarding theory.

Furthermore, on Barry's definition of an interest, it appears that satisfying one's first want to connect oneself to a pleasure-producing machine, which leads to the acquisition of w', is not an action against one's interest. For Barry, it is against one's interests to satisfy a present want if satisfaction of that want drastically curtails one's opportunities to satisfy future wants. The putative future wants that A is *predicted* to have *before* he acquires the want to connect himself, however, will not exist after he connects himself. Can mere "possible" wants, as opposed to wants that do or will exist, enter into assessments of a person's interests? If possible wants can enter into a calculation of interests, then the concept of an interest is not strictly want-regarding in the sense defined by Barry.

What about wants that a person has *now*, to do, be, or have certain things in the future? Does not connecting oneself to a pleasure-producing machine drastically curtail one's opportunities to satisfy *those* wants? It would appear not, if we assume that one always has the opportunity to disconnect oneself. Satisfaction of those wants can only occur in the future, and in the future the opportunity to satisfy them will remain. By hypothesis, one will not avail oneself of this opportunity because those wants will no longer exist.

Unfortunately, Barry does not adequately distinguish between wants that a person now has to do, have, or be things in the future, wants that a person will have in the future, wants that a person is predicted to have in the future, and wants that a person might have in the future under certain circumstances. Hence, it is unclear which of these kinds of wants may legitimately enter into a calculation of a person's interests. He says:

> The kind of example we are thinking of when we speak of limiting a man's opportunities to get what he wants "in his own (best) interests" is surely one where by doing what he wants now he will produce results that he doesn't want in the future (including, very commonly, a lack of opportunity to satisfy *whatever* wants he may have in the future). The contrast is thus not between want-satisfaction and something other than want-satisfaction, but rather between want-satisfaction now and want-satisfaction later.[13]

The last sentence especially suggests that actions leading to the acquisition of the sole want w' cannot be against a person's interests. By hypothesis, he gains both want satisfaction now and want satisfaction later: the wants he *will* have in the future will be satisfied.

This consequence of Barry's account indicates that his conception of interests does not conform to E_{22}. The acquisition of a severely restricted range of wants of the kind w' is not normally thought to further a person's good, especially if satisfaction of those wants limits one's capacity or motivation to acquire a broader range of wants. The problem to be addressed now is this: How can one assert that actions leading to the acquisition of w', may not be in A's interests, while at the same time asserting that in some sense the person to whom interests are ascribed is the ultimate arbiter of his interests?

As a first step to resolving this problem posed by Barry's account, one must think of assessments of persons' interests as necessitating the arrangement of their wants in a means-end hierarchy. This hierarchy would terminate with fundamental self-regarding wants, such as wants to be happy, to live a comfortable and secure life, to live a certain kind of ideal life, e.g., a life devoted to the service of God. As in Barry's account, one can mistake one's interests by being in error about the means to satisfy one's wants. Since fundamental wants have to be taken into account, however, it is possible that certain things that max-

13. *Political Argument*, p. 185.

imize *opportunities*, e.g., acquisition of assets, could be against one's interest, for one may have a fundamental want to abandon the acquisitive attitude.[14]

This consideration suggests a refinement of Barry's definition of interests by a specification of the types of wants referred to in the definiens. These would be fundamental self-regarding wants of the sort described above.

(1) A policy, law, or institution is in a person's interest if it furthers the extent to which she can satisfy her fundamental self-regarding wants.[15]

Although this definition conforms to E_{21} by placing the concept of an interest firmly in the want-regarding category, according to Barry's definition cited above,[16] it still does not do justice to E_{22}, which states that a person's interests promote her good.

On the other hand, if the concept of an interest is to remain in the want-regarding category, the notion of what is good for a person cannot be explicated in terms of ideals. How can one walk such a tightrope? Take the case of a person who as a result of being connected to a "pleasure-experience machine" acquires a fundamental self-regarding want to seek pleasure at all times and at any cost in terms of ideals. How can we say that remaining connected may not be in that person's interests because it is

---

14. For Barry, opportunities for want satisfaction could "be expressed in a common medium such as money."

15. In one place Barry briefly considers the status played by what I have called fundamental wants in the ascriptions of interests to people. He considers the want of people to go to heaven rather than to hell (*Political Argument*, p. 182). He denies that such a want could feature in an assessment of interests on the grounds apparently that "tremendously illiberal" policies, such as the Inquisition, could then be said (by some) to be in people's interests. He concludes that any analysis of interests in terms of "wants for results" of actions or policies must be limited to results of a "short-run kind." My answer to Barry's point is this. The fact that a given analysis of a concept allows leeway for political abuse is not a sufficient reason for rejecting that analysis. Second, if we are to treat "all moments [of a person's life] as equally part of one life" (Rawls, *TJ*, p. 295), then long-run results of policies should be taken into account. Otherwise, we should be discounting the interests of the distant-future self, and we could not say, for example, that taking up smoking was against a person's interest.

16. But note the subsequent restriction imposed by Barry: "pretty clearly if the interpretation of the 'want-regarding' category in terms of wants for results is to be tolerable the 'results' must be of a short-run kind" (*Political Argument*, p. 182; cf. preceding note).

not good for that person in some sense, and yet maintain that the notion of an interest is a want-regarding notion? I shall suggest a conception of interests that at least partially resolves the above problem. I say "partially" because, although the concept will be want-based in some sense, it may not strictly be "want-regarding" in the sense defined by Barry. Ascriptions of interests to people, however, will not rest on judgments made by other persons about ideals of character, life style, what is justifiable, right, and so on.

One of the grounds for ascriptions of interests, which does not make reference to an ideal, is the hypothesized preferences of people were they to be placed under certain conditions of choice, such as actual experience of certain alternatives. On this view, a judgment of persons' interests solely by reference to the wants they actually have or will have in the future is unwarrantedly biased toward their actual or predicted life style and environmental circumstances. These considerations suggest the following definition of interests:

> (2) A policy, law, or institution is in a person's interests if it furthers the extent to which she can first (if necessary) acquire and then satisfy that fundamental self-regarding want she would prefer to have were she to experience alternative life styles appropriate to the possession of different fundamental wants.

On this definition, for example, replacing the acquisitive attitude with a desire to "lead the simple life" might be in a person's interests. Having acquired the latter desire, it might then be in her interests to give away her assets.

A view related to definition (2) is put forward by Connolly, whose definition of interests is as follows:

> Policy x is more in A's interests than policy y if A, were he to experience the results of both x and y, would choose x as the result he would rather have for himself.[17]

One problem, shared by both definition (2) above and Connolly's definition, is this: Should the conditions under which preferences are hypothetically possessed be specified in terms

---

17. "On Interests in Politics," p. 472.

of experience of alternatives? I shall claim that a more complex set of "hypothetical conditions" needs to be specified.

According to both definition (2) and Connolly's definition, "the key criterion" in the ascription of interests to people is "the choice of the agent involved, but the privileged choice is one made after the fact, [of experience] so to speak, rather than before it" (*ibid.*). Under certain circumstances, however, the preference expressed before the experience of an alternative may be the privileged one in a judgment of interests. For example, a preference expressed before one has become connected to a "pleasure-experience machine" may be more privileged than one expressed after one has become connected. Experiences may so distort, or limit, one's memories of previous life styles that judgments of one's interests "after the fact" may be suspect. Indeed, there are several conditions that need to be satisfied in order for preferences expressed after experience of alternatives to be privileged in an assessment of interests. These are:

(i) The person expressing the preference after the fact is sufficiently integrated with the person expressing the preference before the fact. It is especially important that significant memories of the old life not be lost.

Clearly, one cannot state in advance precisely what degree of psychological integration between the person before and after experience of alternative is necessary in order to satisfy condition (i). There are clear cases, however, in which the condition has not been satisfied. A case in which a change in fundamental want occurs after experience of alternatives, where there is no loss or distortion of memory, no change of character, and no change in fundamental beliefs (except those directly relevant to the change in want), may be contrasted with the following kind of case. Consider the man who does not want to be happy in Nazi Germany. Suppose that this person is brainwashed into believing the fundamental tenets of the regime. He now acquires the want to be happy, satisfies this want, and declares that he is glad of the change. Was the brainwashing, leading to a change in fundamental want, in that person's interests? Although his memories of his past life are veridical, and his judgment of being glad of the change is made in a spirit of calm rational detachment, we may find it impossible to affirm or deny that a change to a want to be happy (and all that is involved in that change) was in that person's interests. For the change has

hese wants, once acquired, could not be satisfied, or
an be satisfied only at too great a cost.

t, the hypothetical experience test described under (3)
ed to yield wants that one would prefer to have and
l things considered, i.e., when all costs of acquiring,
and satisfying those wants are taken into account.

how has my concept of interests reconciled the en-
and E_{22}? Significance of actions is not interpreted
terms of the want regarding, but neither is it inter-
rely in terms of ideals. Let me elaborate. It is true that
of interests is outside the realm of want regarding if
rding principles are to make reference only to wants
 will exist. Since, on my account, interests must be
ccording to preferences predicted to occur under cer-
thetical conditions (e.g., experience of alternative life
en interests can be judged according to preferences
t actually occur, now or in the future. There are two
nake about this, however. First, judgments about what
terests are based on hypotheses about which prefer-
ld be possessed by A himself under certain condi-
hermore, these conditions are not described in terms
essing or conforming to ideals of life style or charac-
ed by people other than A himself.

the interests that can be ascribed to people by refer-
nts that do not or will not exist are very limited. They
to the acquisition of the fundamental self-regarding
would prefer to have, all things considered, under
ditions. To take an example: it may be in A's interests
a want to lead the simple life, even if ascription of
st cannot be justified in terms of any wants that A
 have. It is not necessarily in A's interest, however, to
 extent to which he can lead the simple life in ad-
is acquiring the want to lead the simple life. For
is not automatically in A's interest to give away his
ose circumstances. Giving away his assets is in A's
ly if it would enable him to acquire the want to lead
ife.

nt of interests is want-regarding, however, in the
vhat is in a person's interests is not defined in terms
at ideal or characteristic human agents would pos-
 the conditions stated in definition (3) of interests.

involved, let us say, not only a radical change in belief structure, but a radical change in character. The man sensitive to the sufferings of others has become a man insensitive to the sufferings of large classes of persons.

Under these conditions of radical change, mere experience of alternatives is not sufficient grounds for asserting that expression of preference made after the change is more privileged in an assessment of what was in the man's interests than that expressed before the change. What would constitute evidence for an assertion that a change to a new want, by brainwashing, say, was in the man's interest? How would evidence for the claim that the man had mistaken his interests before being brainwashed differ from evidence for the claim that the interests of the man after being brainwashed had simply changed? Where a person before a change of fundamental want is sufficiently integrated with the person after the change, we can and do regard preferences expressed after actual experience of alternatives as evidence in favor of claims that mistakes of interests had been made. For example, we may say of a man who wants nothing more than to be successful that a change of want would be in his interests because a new life appropriate to this change would better suit his existing character, temperament, and abilities. Suppose that, having experienced that new life, the man's fundamental want is changed, and he expresses a preference for a life governed by that want without undergoing major changes in character or beliefs. We could then regard the expressed preference as evidence for the truth of our hypothesis that the man had hitherto mistaken his interests rather than as evidence for the view that his interests had merely changed.

(ii) One's preference for having a certain fundamental want, expressed after experiencing alternative life styles, is privileged only if the following condition holds. The memories of the old life style must not be distorted and colored by the new perspective on life acquired after experience of the new life style. Judgments of interests cannot be based on preferences colored by the following kinds of belief: "I could not have been really happy doing those kinds of things, no matter what I thought, because life was then without Christ." This situation is different, however, if one remembers experiencing an aimless empty existence, and these memories are involved, let us say, not only a radical change in belief structure, but a radical change in character. The man sensitive to the sufferings of others has become a man insensitive to the sufferings of large classes of persons.

Under these conditions of radical change, mere experience of alternatives is not sufficient grounds for asserting that expression of preference made after the change is more privileged in an assessment of what was in the man's interests than that expressed before the change. What would constitute evidence for an assertion that a change to a new want, by brainwashing, say, was in the man's interest? How would evidence for the claim that the man had mistaken his interests before being brainwashed differ from evidence for the claim that the interests of the man after being brainwashed had simply changed? Where a person before a change of fundamental want is sufficiently integrated with the person after the change, we can and do regard preferences expressed after actual experience of alternatives as evidence in favor of claims that mistakes of interests had been made. For example, we may say of a man who wants nothing more than to be successful that a change of want would be in his interests because a new life appropriate to this change would better suit his existing character, temperament, and abilities. Suppose that, having experienced that new life, the man's fundamental want is changed, and he expresses a preference for a life governed by that want without undergoing major changes in character or beliefs. We could then regard the expressed preference as evidence for the truth of our hypothesis that the man had hitherto mistaken his interests rather than as evidence for the view that his interests had merely changed.

> (ii) One's preference for having a certain fundamental want, expressed after experiencing alternative life styles, is privileged only if the following condition holds. The memories of the old life style must not be distorted and colored by the new perspective on life acquired after experience of the new life style. Judgments of interests cannot be based on preferences colored by the following kinds of belief: "I could not have been really happy doing those kinds of things, no matter what I thought, because life was then without Christ." This situation is different, however, if one remembers experiencing an aimless empty existence, and these memories are

corroborated by the testimony of friends who recall repeated laments of boredom and aimlessness.

(iii) One's preferences for having certain fundamental wants, expressed after experiencing alternative life styles appropriate to them, must be made in a spirit of rational detachment. For this reason, one is liable to distrust the preferences expressed by people in the grip of addictive cravings, religious hysteria, and so on.

The addition of the above three conditions for expressions of preference being privileged suggests the following modification to Connolly's account of interests, viz.,

(3) Policy x is more in A's interests than policy y if A, were she to experience the results of both x and y, and were she to experience those results under the conditions of integration, nondistortion, and detachment described under (i)–(iii) above, would choose x as the policy she would rather have for herself.

The following criticism may be leveled against definition (3). It may be thought that a virtue-oriented conception of freedom would regard the above analysis of interests as inadequate as an explication of significance of options. Could it not be that a life ruled by a fundamental want, or set of wants, suits one's existing character, but that it is in one's interests to change one's character in a more virtuous direction? Definition (3) of interests can accommodate this point. "Policy x" could include policies of character change.

It may be further objected: Why not simply argue that it is in one's interests to become virtuous and acquire wants commensurate with virtue? Why all this business about hypothetical wants? The answer to this objection, of course, is that in imperfect worlds it is not always in one's interests to acquire a virtuous character and commensurate wants. In this I disagree with those such as Grenville Wall,[18] who wholly rejects the view that actual and hypothetical preferences determine interests. Wall discusses the case of the heroin addict who would prefer the life of addiction to alternatives. It is possible that, under hypothetical conditions such as those being described, a person

---

18. "The Concept of Interests in Politics," in *Politics and Society*, V (1975): 487–510.

would not express a preference for a life governed by a want to live a "worthwhile" life of achievement, say. Let us suppose that this person would not care to live a long life, that he would do anything to avoid pain, frustration, anxiety. Finally, let us suppose that his character is such that he finds the stresses of modern life intolerable and that there is no real prospect of being able to change his character. On my account of interests, it is possible for it to be in that person's interests to remain an addict.

Wall claims that this kind of consequence of "subjectivist" accounts of interests clearly demonstrates that a person's interests lie in his "good" or "advantage" understood objectively (*ibid.*, pp. 503–4). Those who emphasize E_{21}, viz., that in some sense people are the ultimate arbiters of their interests, would be prepared, however, to swallow the consequence that, for some persons, in some circumstances, a life of addiction may be in their interests. Where a person's good is defined in terms of satisfaction of those fundamental wants preferred under certain hypothetical conditions, it may not be the case that physical health, longevity, a life of achievement in accordance with virtue constitute every person's good.

The point of the experience test outlined in (3) now becomes clearer. In imperfect worlds, it may be impossible, very difficult, or very costly to become virtuous, and to acquire and/or satisfy those fundamental wants that are commensurate with a life of virtue. Life may be short, society "nasty and brutish"; one may be dogged by ill fortune and tragedy; one may have been badly brought up, traumatized, ill-educated, and so on. The experience test allows the agent herself, under idealized conditions, to determine just what sacrifices and costs are to be borne in the pursuit of an ideal life in the various complex and deficient circumstances in which she finds herself. In general, it may not be in one's interests to pursue a virtuous life if that is too costly. It is not in one's interests to acquire those fundamental wants commensurate with a life of virtue, under the following conditions:

(i) Acquisition of those wants is too costly in terms of expenditure of time and energy, and frustration of, e.g., existing wants.
(ii) The causal consequences of possessing those wants are too costly.

(iii) These wants, once acquired, could not be satisfied, or can be satisfied only at too great a cost.

In short, the hypothetical experience test described under (3) is intended to yield wants that one would prefer to have and satisfy, *all things considered*, i.e., when all costs of acquiring, pursuing, and satisfying those wants are taken into account.

Finally, how has my concept of interests reconciled the endoxa E_{21} and E_{22}? Significance of actions is not interpreted purely in terms of the want regarding, but neither is it interpreted purely in terms of ideals. Let me elaborate. It is true that my notion of interests is outside the realm of want regarding if want-regarding principles are to make reference only to wants that do or will exist. Since, on my account, interests must be assessed according to preferences predicted to occur under certain hypothetical conditions (e.g., experience of alternative life styles), then interests can be judged according to preferences that do not actually occur, now or in the future. There are two points to make about this, however. First, judgments about what is in A's interests are based on hypotheses about which preferences would be possessed by A himself under certain conditions. Furthermore, these conditions are not described in terms of A's possessing or conforming to ideals of life style or character espoused by people other than A himself.

Second, the interests that can be ascribed to people by reference to wants that do not or will not exist are very limited. They are limited to the acquisition of the fundamental self-regarding wants one would prefer to have, all things considered, under certain conditions. To take an example: it may be in A's interests to acquire a want to lead the simple life, even if ascription of that interest cannot be justified in terms of any wants that A does or will have. It is not necessarily in A's interest, however, to further the extent to which he can lead the simple life in advance of his acquiring the want to lead the simple life. For example, it is not automatically in A's interest to give away his assets in those circumstances. Giving away his assets is in A's interests only if it would enable him to acquire the want to lead the simple life.

My account of interests is want-regarding, however, in the sense that what is in a person's interests is not defined in terms of wants that ideal or characteristic human agents would possess under the conditions stated in definition (3) of interests.

My notion of interest is not defined in a way that entails that in any empirically realizable situation, the freedom of any agent is maximized only if she attains virtue. On the Aristotelian view, a virtue is a disposition that it is good for the characteristic mature human being to possess in environments conducive to flourishing. But some agents may not be characteristic (being defective, already ingrained in vice) and some may find themselves in Hobbesian "states of nature" where possession and exercise of the standard human virtues is not for their good. My account is compatible with Gibbs's notion of freedom, however, for his view that only the virtuous agent is *perfectly* free is compatible with its *not* being the case that, in *any* empirically realizable situation, the freedom of any agent is maximized only where she attains virtue.

CHAPTER 12

Conflicts of Freedom

(i) *The Nature of Conflicts*

In the foregoing chapters, I have accommodated a variety of apparently conflicting endoxa about the nature of freedom. As a result of this accommodation, my theory satisfies requirement (d) for a superior coherence theory (see above, p. 28), namely that the endoxa should be as far as possible preserved by the theory. It may be, however, that the satisfaction of this desideratum has costs. Pluralistic conceptions of value may fail requirement (a): that is, they may lack coherence in the sense of satisfying broad standards of rationality. In short, a pluralistic conception of freedom permits the possibility of conflict within the dimensions of freedom. This possibility raises the problem of the rational basis of claims that certain freedom packages enhance, or diminish, the level of overall freedom. That problem is addressed in the next sections; here I discuss the nature and structure of conflicts of freedom.

One type of conflict of freedom is familiar—the conflict between the freedom of one individual and that of another. I shall focus on conflicts within the freedom of one individual. On our conception, such conflicts are of two types.

(1) Increasing the severity of restrictions (and other flaws or breakdowns) on an agent's freedom with respect to a set of actions on the one dimension may decrease the severity of restrictions on the same dimension with respect to another set of actions. Whether or not an agent's overall freedom *on that dimension* has been thereby increased depends on two factors.

  (i) Whether or not the severity of restriction has undergone a net increase or decrease.
  (ii) Whether or not the actions to which decreased restrictions are attached are on average more significant than the ones to which increased restrictions are attached.

Chapter 12 Conflicts of Freedom

MacCallum produces a good example in "Negative and Positive Freedom":

> ... suppose that Smith, who always walks to where he needs to go, lives in a tiny town where there have been no pedestrian crosswalks and where automobiles have had right of way over pedestrians. Suppose further that a series of pedestrian crosswalks is instituted along with the regulation that pedestrians must use only these walks when crossing, but while in these walks pedestrians have right of way over automobiles. The regulation restrains Smith (he can no longer legally cross streets where he pleases) but it also frees him (while in crosswalks he no longer has a duty to defer to automobile traffic) (*op. cit.*, p. 190).

It is, of course, not immediately clear whether the regulation increases Smith's overall freedom relative to the status quo. That depends on the severity of the restraints imposed and removed by the regulation, and on the significance of the actions restrained and freed from restraint.

The second type of conflict of freedom is this:

> (2) Increasing the severity of restrictions, flaws, etc., on an agent's freedom with respect to a set of actions on the one dimension may decrease the severity of restrictions on another dimension with respect to the same or another set of actions.

Barber's apparently paradoxical claim that the maximization of options can be deleterious to freedom ceases to be paradoxical when seen in the context of his assignment of greater weight to another dimension of freedom, viz., autonomy. According to Barber, a superabundance of options can dictate significant wants, thereby reducing autonomy:

> Multiplying superficial options may actually obscure significant alternatives. The American consumer's freedom to choose between thirty-seven brands of deodorant may be repressive of true consciousness in that the choice between brands conceals the more significant choice of whether to mask natural odours or not. ... (*op. cit.*, p. 75).

Compulsory schooling is another example of conflict between dimensions. When children are confined within the walls of their classroom, surfing and playing space-invader games become unavailable options to them. But the justification for compulsion is enhanced freedom: the expansion of the child's rational capacities and thereby increased autonomy.

This second type of conflict poses serious problems for the justification of claims that one freedom package comprises greater or lesser overall freedom than another. As I admitted earlier, Feinberg was absolutely right to affirm that the relations between aspects of freedom is not like the relation between the height, breadth, and depth of a physical object (*op. cit.*, p. 19). This fact does not, however, preclude the possibility of a rational basis for judgments about overall freedom. In section (ii), I consider the rational basis for ordinal comparison. In section (iii), I address the issue of deeper incommensurability, where ordinal rankings are out of place.

(ii) *The Rationality of Ordinal Judgments about Overall Freedom*

Consider a case of conflict between the dimensions of freedom. The problem is: Which freedoms should be given more weight? The natural reply is that the application of a rule determines those weightings, and yields a judgment about which freedom packages constitute higher levels of overall freedom. Given that the freedom phenomena are highly varied and complex, however, it is difficult to see how there could be an applicable rule, or lexicographical ordering of rules, that justifies the weightings assigned in any potential conflicts. In the remainder of this chapter, I shall develop the view that weightings can be justified in the absence of such rules.

It might be thought that the first requirement of rationality to be sacrificed in such a system would be consistency. Nonetheless, the indifference-curve approach[1] allows for the possibility of consistency in the absence of rules *justifying* weightings. Weightings can be determined by sheer preference, but preference can be demonstrably consistent.

According to the indifference-curve approach, the dimen-

1. See Barry, *Political Argument*, pp. 4–8.

sions of freedom are substitutable in the following way. An evaluator can be prepared to trade off given reductions in freedom on one dimension for given increases in freedom on the same or other dimension, until she reaches a point of indifference between the levels of freedom in the freedom packages. A consistent pattern in these trade-offs is ideally demonstrated if the evaluator is armed with an indifference map whose coordinates represent combinations of degrees of reduction or increase between which the evaluator is indifferent. There is no need for degrees of increase to be quantified: comparisons can be stated in terms of greater or lesser increases of freedom, or slight versus considerable increase (*ibid.*, p. 6).

Further development of my theory of overall freedom could contain the conceptual resources for an indifference-curve analysis: all one needs is an ordinal conception of degree of freedom along any given aspect of freedom. I have briefly discussed the basis of judgments of degree of availability of actions in terms of number and variety, and, in chapter 8, I discussed also the notion of degree of restraint, thereby providing the conceptual basis for talk of degree of eligibility of action. My notion of interests permits talk of degree of significance of actions, and, as far as autonomy is concerned, conceptions of degree of rationality and degree of authenticity could be developed. Indeed, a fine-grained analysis would show that each "dimension" of freedom is itself composed of several "dimensions": rationality, for example, is not just distinct from authenticity, but itself includes several aspects.

The indifference-curve approach shows that, despite conflict, and despite the lack of a common unit of measurement of the "dimensions" of freedom, ordinal comparisons of overall freedom can be made. But does the approach solve the problem of the rational basis for such comparisons? The approach, ideally, allows for the possibility of rationality as consistency of evaluation. But a consistent pattern of evaluations, where the latter are based on sheer preference, is not tantamount to a rational basis. What *underpins* the evaluations?

It appears that the analysis so far is vulnerable to the kind of criticism leveled at intuitionists in ethics, namely, that, at rock bottom, justification is a matter of subjective preference. This is essentially Rawls's criticism of intuitionism made in his *A Theory of Justice*. He claims that the intuitionist assigns weights in moral conflict, but ". . . contends that there exists no expressible ethical conception which underlies these weights. A geometrical figure or a mathematical function may describe them, but there are no constructive moral criteria that establish their reasonableness" (TJ, 39). Rawls concludes that intuitionists "can only say that it seems to us more correct to balance this way rather than that" (TJ, 39).

In reply it must be stated that *on Rawls's own definition of intuitionism*, intuitionists merely deny the existence of a "decision procedure"[2] for resolving conflicts. It does not follow from this that the intuitionist cannot avail himself of an underlying conception that demonstrates the reasonableness of the assignment of weights. I, too, have eschewed a decision procedure; nonetheless, a conception of the free person could rationalize the favored trade-offs.

Could our theory be expanded to provide such a conception? A rationalization of the assignment of weights to various aspects of freedom would necessitate the expansion of the background theory, so that it is recognized not merely that a variety of flaws, limitations, and breakdowns in practical activity impairs freedom, but also that some impairments are more serious, vis-à-vis overall freedom, than others.

Such an expanded background theory would assign varying degrees of importance to the various aspects of individual human potential in agency. The theory would comprise an enriched (but not necessarily complete) conception of human flourishing wherein these weightings would be justified. I say not necessarily complete, because it is recognized that freedom is but one aspect of flourishing in general.

There is no shortage of conceptions of human good as it relates to individual potential in agency. Differing accounts of that good can accord most weight to, respectively, minimization of obstacles to desire, choice maximization, consciousness maximization, and virtue. On one view, the aspect of potential most highly valued is the achievement of one's goals—the realization of one's potential as propensity. Absence of frustration, presence of a sense of self-respect arising from the successful realization of one's aims, is the major point and value of freedom.

Another conception of the paradigmatically free person is that afforded by the maximizing-options model. On this view,

---

2. See J. O. Urmson, "A Defence of Intuitionism," *Proceedings of the Aristotelian Society*, LXXV (1975): 111–9.

even more important than realizing one's desires is maximizing one's alternatives, for one's potential as an agent in the sense of expanding and realizing one's *capacities* for action may be severely reduced by the tailoring of goals and even desires to suit the narrowness of eligible options. For example, if one lacks the motivation to go to the university because of the ineligibility of attendance, one's capacities are even further reduced. Attention to phenomena such as this reduces the temptation to give greatest weight to freedom as absence of obstacles to the realization of desire.

This kind of phenomenon has been explored by W. G. Runciman,[3] who comes to the surprising conclusion that those who are least likely to want consumer goods that they do not have are, in general, those at the bottom level of income in manual and nonmanual strata (*ibid.*, p. 209). Where options are limited, one is inclined to tailor one's expectations to a "realistic" low level. This in turn causes a choice of limited comparative reference groups (*ibid.*, p. 62): those with considerably greater options are beyond the social vision of the worse off. A choice of limited reference groups will impede the assessment of the intrinsic merits of achieving or obtaining certain things (such as a university education), and prevent the realization that people like yourself in relevant respects are enjoying and benefiting from things that you yourself would enjoy and benefit from.

Such limited comparisons, in turn, prevent the upward spiral of wants, thus aiding the strategy of accommodation, acceptance, and frustration avoidance.[4] At the same time, however, this strategy limits the motivation to break down barriers to the enhancement of capacities.

The tailoring of goals and even wants to suit the narrowness of eligible options may be mediated also by another phenomenon: normative socialization. Socialization that instills the

---

3. *Relative Deprivation and Social Justice* (New York: Routledge and Kegan Paul, 1966).

4. See further Frank Parkin, *Class Inequality and Political Order: Social Stratification in Capitalist and Communist Societies* (London: Paladin, 1972), p. 61. See also Herbert H. Hyman, according to whom the lower-class individual does not want as much success, knows he could not get it even if he wanted to, and does not want what might help him get success; "The Value Systems of Different Classes: A Social Psychological Contribution to the Analysis of Stratification," in Reinhard Bendix and Seymour Martin Lipset, *Class Status and Power* (Glencoe, IL.: Free Press, 1953).

belief that one has no right to a considerably expanded set of options will forestall feelings of resentment and emulative envy, and thereby fosters contentment with one's lot. In brief, those wishing to give high weight to maximizing options can point to the deleterious effects on potential in agency of a variety of phenomena directly or indirectly causally related to limited options, even where existing goals or wants are largely realized. Socialization, strategies for avoiding frustration and failure, habituation, lack of experience of alternatives, and ignorance may all condition a person's wants to be in line with her limited opportunities and abilities.

Those giving more weight to the minimizing of obstacles on *desired* options, however, can point to a variety of ways in which maximizing options does not conduce to flourishing qua agent. Consider, for example, the explosion in consumer choice. With an increase in consumption possibilities comes an increased cost in consumption, namely, the costs of time, effort, and stress in purchasing items. The multiplication of types, brands, and models of goods, as well as the trend toward more rapid obsolescence and differences in packaging and sizes increase the costs in time, effort, and stress of making a rational choice. If one attempts to avoid these costs by choosing from habit, or making no choice at all, one suffers the anxiety of making the wrong choice, of being unfashionable, and so on. Furthermore, an increase in consumption possibilities increases the frequency of facing these sorts of cost. All these points are noted by E. J. Mishan:[5]

> If, beginning with a situation in which only one kind of shirt were available, a man was transposed to another in which ten different kinds were offered to him, including the old kind, he could of course continue to buy the old kind of shirt. But it does not follow that, if he elects to do this, he is no worse off in the new situation. In the first place, he is aware that he is now *rejecting* nine different kinds of shirts whose qualities he has not compared. The decision to ignore the other nine shirts is itself a cost, and inasmuch as additional shirts continue to come on to the market, and some are withdrawn, he

---

5. *The Costs of Economic Growth* (London: Staples, 1967). See further, Gerald Dworkin, "Is More Choice Better than Less?"

is being subjected to a continual process of decision-taking even though he is able, and willing, to buy the same shirt. In the second place, unless he is impervious to fashion, he will feel increasingly uncomfortable in the old shirt. It is more likely that he will be tempted, then, to risk spending an unpredictable amount of time and trouble in the hope of finding a more suitable shirt (*ibid.*, p. 118).

As we have seen also, choice maximization can limit critical consciousness by reducing the motivation, capacity, and energy to assess *important* options. Further, choice maximization can limit the *availability* of important options—a phenomenon to which Gerald Dworkin[6] draws attention. He cites the example of marriage, an institution that limits options to pursue sexual liaisons. At the same time, it offers the opportunity of not merely eschewing such relationships, but of putting oneself under an institutionally derived *obligation* not to pursue such relationships. Thus, an institution or practice of restricting choices may in some contexts permit an option of entering a relationship with a special, valuable, moral character.

Barber is vigorously opposed to both paradigms of the free agent considered above. Criticizing Oscar and Mary Handlin's[7] paradigm of the "free American" as the person who wants to "expand his capacity for action by increasing the number of choices available to him" (*ibid.*, pp. 74–5), Barber proposes the "intentionalist" model of freedom where "maximization of consciousness" is opposed to "maximization of options." In assessing the extent of an individual's freedom, the question "Are his options increased?" is of less importance than the questions: "Does he seem more or less able to resist particular environmental stimuli . . . ?"; "Is he a creature of habits, or does he face events and situations as possibilities for creation?"; "To what extent can he articulate reasons and grounds for his actions?"[8] For Barber, the expansion of options is not as important for agency as the expansion of the capacity and motivation to assess the influences operating on one, and critically to examine beliefs and wants with a full appreciation of alternative value

6. "Is More Choice Better than Less?" pp. 56–7.
7. *The Dimensions of Liberty* (Cambridge: Harvard, 1961).
8. *Superman and Common Men*, p. 74.

systems and of the conceptual apparatus within which those beliefs and wants are formed. Although a massive bribe increases the range of options open to one, Barber claims it may actually restrict conscious (i.e., deliberated) choice: "A massive bribe in the face of abject poverty . . . operates not to increase the range of choice open to the conscious actor but to preclude choice altogether in favour of an immediate gratification of the drive for security unmediated by any form of intentionality" (*ibid.*, p. 65).

Finally, those for whom "only the virtuous are perfectly free" see freedom as more than the "maximization of consciousness." Freedom involves not merely the enhancement of critical consciousness and deliberation, it also involves the schooling of desire so that, unlike the anomic, desires are ordered, and unlike the intemperate, the apathetic, or the melancholic, desires are appropriate to circumstance. There is appropriate anger (and not indifference or violent rage); desire is not passion for the wrong objects. Furthermore, where appropriate, behavior is regulated by principle rather than desire: instrumental rationality is augmented by a proper conception of ends. Finally, principle is not at war with desire: unlike the enkratic, the desires of the virtuous are in line with their practical judgments.

Even where it is recognized that states of mind and character are crucial to freedom, there is, however, debate about the social conditions conducive to virtue, particularly the extent to which choice expansion or imposition of regulation promote virtue. In his "Alienation and Anomie," Steven Lukes[9] highlights an important contrast of view—that between the Durkheimian view of human nature and the Marxian. According to the former, anomie is a serious obstacle to flourishing in agency and must be countered by the imposition of suitable constraint, regulation, and order: "To limit man, to place obstacles in the path of his free development, is this not to prevent him from fulfilling himself? But . . . this limitation is a condition of our happiness and moral health. Man, in fact, is made for life in a determinate, limited environment. . . ." (*ibid.*, p. 144). On the Marxian view, by contrast, the existence of regulation, constraint, and enforced roles produces alienation and limits potentiality. Lukes concludes: "Social constraint is for Marx a denial and for Durkheim

---

9. In Peter Laslett and W. G. Runciman, eds., *Philosophy, Politics and Society*, Third Series (New York: Blackwell, 1967), pp. 134–56.

Chapter 12 Conflicts of Freedom   187

a condition of human freedom and self realization" (*ibid.*, p. 142). Alienation and anomie are both destructive of autonomy, but it is a moot point whether both can be removed. If they cannot, there is a problem of weighting within a virtue-centered conception of freedom itself.

(iii) *Deep Incommensurability*

We have argued that the assignment of weights to various freedom packages can be justified by augmenting our background theory. Such a theory would provide an underlying conception of the free person that rationalizes varying emphases on different aspects of freedom. In this case, the assignment of weights is not just a matter of preference: consistent or nonconsistent. A new problem emerges, however. Is it possible for an augmented theory to provide a justification for all assignments of weightings, or would such a theory underdetermine such assignments? Indeed, is there a uniquely justifiable conception of the free person at all?

I have already cast doubt on this possibility in chapter 3, but let us here further develop this skeptical thought before assessing its implications. It may be claimed that a suitably augmented background theory would give most weight to the fourth conception of the free person outlined above, viz., a virtue-oriented conception. Indeed, I have already argued for the correctness of Gibbs's view that only those who are virtuous (in the relevant agency-related respects) are perfectly free. This route is, however, too easy. In a perfect world, there is harmony between the various elements of freedom. From the truth that only the virtuous (in relevant respects) are *perfectly* free, it does not follow that the path to maximal freedom in an imperfect world is the single-minded pursuit of virtue. Is virtue a state of freedom in a world that allows only virtuous actions? Again, in an imperfect world of nonvirtuous agents, where option expansion can reduce virtue but increase a sense of success in the realization of goals and of doors being open for future activity, it is not obvious that giving most weight to the virtue element of freedom is the correct view. Emphasizing virtue will be rational in a world where becoming virtuous is relatively costless in terms of other freedom values, and expansion of options may not be rational in a world such as the ones Durkheim and Mishan describe.

Expansion of options will be rational, however, where there is a deep sense of frustration at the lack of options, or where horizons have been narrowed in ways harmful to development of potential. In general, the nature and severity of conflicts between the various elements of freedom will vary, and in complicated ways. It is unlikely that a single conception of flourishing in agency will generate a set of rules determining correct weightings in all conceivable situations. The augmented background theory, yielding a fuller conception of flourishing in practical activity, will underdetermine assignments of weights. Different but adequate conceptions will yield different emphases, each of which will constitute a reasonable response to a conflict of freedom, and none of which will offer a fully determinate answer to all questions about weightings.

In this case, it may be argued, the problem of subjectivism re-emerges: there is a residue of conflicts of freedom—perhaps a very large residue—of which an intuitionist can only say, "It seems to me more correct to balance this way rather than that."

In the remainder of this section, I shall consider a response to this final charge of subjectivism. In this "residue" of conflict, the intuitionist can claim, the options are incommensurable in a sense defined by Raz which precludes even ordinal comparison: "Two valuable options are incommensurable if (1) neither is better than the other, and (2) there is (or could be) another option which is better than one but is not better than the other."[10] If two options are incommensurable in this sense, it is not the case that there is an objectively correct ranking, for ranking is "out of place"; hence, it cannot be the case that the intuitionist can only form an unjustified assessment about such a ranking. It may be retorted that the subjectivism criticism is not thereby answered: either incommensurability is simply "rough equality," in which case there is an objectively correct ranking within limits of vagueness, or the preference for a freedom package is without good reason.

The first horn of this dilemma is apparently supported by the following plausible-looking argument cited by Raz:

---

10. *The Morality of Freedom*, p. 325.

(1) Two options are roughly equal if and only if it does not matter which one is chosen, if it is right to be indifferent between them.

(2) What rightly makes one care about which option to choose is that one is better supported by reason than the other.

(3) There is no reason to prefer either of two incommensurable options.

Therefore, all incommensurables are of roughly equal value (*ibid.*, p. 331). As Raz points out, however, the argument is flawed, since the plausibility of premise (2) relies on a confusion between it, and

"(2') What rightly makes one care about which option to choose is that each is supported by weighty, and very different, reasons" (*ibid.*, p. 332).

The acceptance of Raz's position here, though, exposes one to the second horn of the dilemma—choice between freedom packages must be without good reason. The argument for this is as follows. If reason provides no better case for one option than for the other, then, it may be suggested, choice between those options is insignificant—one should be indifferent between them. This may, in turn, suggest that one does not have good reason for a choice. Both these suggestions are mistaken. The subjectivism criticism is countered by the fact that one may have good reason for a significant choice without those reasons outweighing the reasons for the alternative.

But how does one rationally choose? The answer to this problem is contained in Raz's discussion of personal value. The function of choice when faced with incommensurability is to determine what was previously underdetermined by reason. Once the choice has been made, we have additional and often very weighty reasons for pursuing and fostering the outcomes of that choice. These reasons are provided by commitment to that choice, and obligations to honor expectations and foster values created by that choice. In this way value is created "through choice among an adequate range of options" (*ibid.*, p. 389).

This kind of "self creation" is discussed by Raz in the context of personal choices such as career, life styles, whether or not to have children; and virtues such as friendship, loyalty, and integrity. Raz's insights should be extended to the arena of social choice, however. The choice about which freedoms to foster is a social choice, and the way it is made will determine whether the society is dominated by the pursuit of virtue, the cult of the market, the revolutionary spirit, the advocacy of self-criticism, and so on. Again, the model is *societal* self-creation of value through choice among an adequate and reasonable set of incommensurable options.

The following fascinating question arises: Which virtues should be cultivated by the government and powerful groups within society vis-à-vis those created values? The work of Raz and others has deepened our understanding of the virtues associated with self-creation in the personal sphere: integrity, loyalty, constancy, fidelity. In the area of societal self-creation, where choice between incommensurables has been made, the issue has been much less explored. For example, what should be society's attitude to change in this area? Should fidelity to a "commitment" be regarded as a virtue, or should the powerful be constantly responsive to the changing wants or interests of the changing dominant or majority groups? To what extent should societal self-creation of value be regarded as a commitment at all? Given the often terrible dislocation to individual lives by frequent or widespread social change, should commitment to a mode of freedom, for example, be regarded as analogous to commitment to one's children? To what extent are other societies morally permitted to interfere with, or even influence, those self-creating choices?

The answers to these questions lie beyond the scope of this book. Whatever the answers, choice between incommensurable freedom packages can be made for good reason, even where that choice is underdetermined by the underlying conception of the free person. Not only may choice in accordance with an undefeated reason be rational even where the reason does not defeat the reasons for the alternatives, but the choice itself has value by determining what was previously undetermined, and by creation of further value.

Conclusion

My theory of freedom is marked by its liberality: a wide variety of incompatible conceptions of freedom have been accommodated by it. The charitability of my approach may be criticized. It is all too easy, it may be claimed, to survey a set of conceptions that have been regarded by various theorists as *the* conception of freedom, and to regard them all as sensible and worthwhile conceptions. To adopt "a principle of charity" is in itself no more satisfying than to be a narrow dogmatist making distinctions, on the basis of dubious appeals to "ordinary language," between freedom and, e.g., ability, opportunity, strength of will, want satisfaction, and so on. My coherence theory is not merely a "principle of charity," however. It shows not only that incompatible conceptions *can* be coherently regarded as aspects of freedom within the one theory, but that there is a powerful rationale for so regarding them. This rationale is the background theory that, like MacCallum's triadic schema of freedom, provides a unifying mechanism: it explains why it is sensible to regard disparate conceptions as all conceptions of freedom.

My theory goes further than MacCallum's in two ways, however. First, it shows not merely that disparate conceptions are genuine and sensible conceptions of *freedom*: it shows how these conceptions can be accommodated within the one theory. There is no need to *choose* between them. MacCallum's theory, unlike a coherence theory, does not "prune and adjust" these conceptions in order to render them part of a coherent whole.

Secondly, as I have just suggested, MacCallum's theory is not a coherence theory. It relies on the optimistic assumption that there is a single uncontested core concept of freedom underlying the contested conceptions. I rejected this assumption. What unifying feature then could warrant the view that a justified single conception of freedom is there to be explicated?

The answer, I claimed, lies with the endoxa: those particular judgments about freedom accepted by the many or the wise. The problem with this focus in the search for unity, however, is that the endoxa themselves do not provide a unified front, even if, as I claimed, they provide the materials for a unified theory.

The tensions among the endoxa are to be resolved by the provisions of a background theory that rationalizes the imposition of unity on the recalcitrant endoxa. In doing this, it goes further than MacCallum's theory. For it not only rationalizes the schema of overall freedom into which all rival conceptions can be *fitted*, but provides a theory of the perceived point or value of freedom which shows why it is *important* to accommodate them somehow within a single theory of freedom. This feature is crucial, for I have not assumed that the schema of overall freedom is an *uncontested* core concept of freedom. It is not, as it were, a descriptive given: it, too, stands in need of justification within a broader coherence theory as a whole.

The background theory permits the achievement of this justificatory goal in two major ways. First, the defeasibility account, which views freedom as absences of various kinds of infelicities in the practical process, provides a structure which *permits* the *required charity*: the accommodation of a wide range of endoxa. Secondly, the specific account of the perceived point or value of freedom permits a reply to the criticism of *excessive* charity: the account of this value provides the *required constraints*. Not any infelicity in the practical process can count as a freedom-related infelicity. Those relating to freedom pertain to the limitation of individual potential in practical activity, and not to the limitation of holistic social goals, goals relating to relationships between individuals, e.g., justice, or suprahuman goals, e.g., service or obedience to God. At the same time, however, my account of the perceived point of freedom shows not only that inclusion of a wide variety of endoxa is possible—a possibility provided by the defeasibility conception—but also that it is justified. For it provides a framework within which arguments can be mounted *justifying* the inclusion of controversial conceptions. For example, it permits counterargument to Flathman's claim that, despite their powerful hold on the endoxa, virtue-oriented conceptions of freedom fail to be genuine conceptions of freedom because they do not fit neatly into some putative core schema.

Finally, the theory does not pretend to offer the only possible or sensible way to cohere the freedom phenomena. The theory is a more or less adequate way of effecting this coherence. The extent to which it is adequate and superior to rival conceptions can be gauged in the light of the standards of appropriate coherence (set out in chapter 2, section (iv)).

Endoxa Concerning Freedom

E_1: He who is a slave to his passions (e.g., the compulsive gambler) is not free.

E_2: "A person cannot be unfree to do something he actually does."

E_3: In New Zealand, a person is not free to commit acts of murder.

E_4: The man who hands over his money, having yielded to credible threat at gun point, does not perform a free act.

E_5: To assert that "I freely did what I was not free to do" is paradoxical.

E_6: Those who can achieve their goals without interference are free.

E_7: The individuals in *Brave New World* are not free.

E_8: "The people who are especially resistant to threats have the widest freedom, though they may have to suffer for it, heroes, criminals, saints."

E_9: "[A person is] unfree when he is restrained from doing anything that it is in his power to do, regardless of whether he wants to do it or not."

E_{10}: Those in prison are not free regardless of their desires, goals, or choices.

E_{11}: If the first individual feels adequate opportunity to achieve his goals among the ten choices he has, whereas the second feels frustrated because the thousand choices he has are trivial, then the second individual is not necessarily freer than the first.

E_{12}: An all-consuming desire to complete a great work of art does not limit an agent's freedom, even though it renders the option of wasting time very difficult to entertain.

E_{13}: "The autonomous person is the one who makes his own life and he may choose the path of self-realization or reject it."

E_{14}: The person who is protected by a high fence from going over the edge of the cliff has not had his freedom impaired by the existence of the fence.

E_{15}: "If I am free to be a pitcher or a poet, I am freer than if my options are being a pitcher or a shortstop."

E_{16}: The professional tennis player who accepts the promoter's offer of $50,000 merely to appear in a tournament in which he otherwise would not have appeared performs a free act, even though he could not be reasonably expected to turn down the offer.

E_{17}: Legal sanctions that are standardly enforced limit the freedom of those who perform the sanctioned actions and are not caught.

E_{18}: Laws with associated sanctions restrict an agent's freedom even if she is ignorant of the law.

E_{19}: Anticipated punishment limits one's freedom inasmuch as it constitutes a threat that *inhibits* agents performing actions.

E_{20}: A smoker who does not want to have the desire to smoke in a sense smokes unwillingly; his first-order desire, being a fetter to willing action, limits his freedom.

E_{21}: The person to whom interests are ascribed is the final arbiter of her interests in the sense that they are not ultimately determined by certain ideals of justifiability, right, good, that are not necessarily espoused by herself.

E_{22}: A person's interests promote in some sense her "good."

Index

Ability versus freedom, vii, 95
Actions
  availability, 59–60, 91–95
  deterrents and inducements, 90
  evaluative and nonevaluative reasons, 143–46
  free equals virtuous, 82
  ineligibility limitations, 59–60, 84
  impediments, 90
  ineligibility, 104
  insignificant course restraints, 73–75
  mismatch with practical attitudes, 71–72
  overall freedom, 79–80, 84–86
  person-relative impossibility, 92–94
  restraints, 89–91, 113–17
  significance, 162–77
  unavailability, 89–91, 94–103
  value, 80
Advice, 126
Agency connection with freedom, 97–98
All-things-considered judgment, 146–47
Anomie, 156
Anscombe, G.E.M., 33–34, 51–53, 55–56
Aristotle, 7, 23–26
  acquisition of virtues, 144
  criticizing theorists, 28
  deliberation in practical reasoning, 91
  rationality, 42
  wants eminating from virtuous dispositions, 131
Attitudes, inner-directed nonauthenticity, 130
Audi, Robert, 145n
Austin, J. L., 32–35, 37–38, 107n
  breakdowns in machinery of action, 37
Authenticity, 118–19
  non-inner-directedness, 123, 129–35
  nonvicariousness, 123–29

Autonomy
  See also freedom
  as authenticity, 124
  higher-order desires, 132–34
  independence of desires and practical judgments, 124
  nonalien origin of desires, 134
  rationality, 120–23

Background theory and endoxa, 29–30
Barber, Benjamin, 126, 130, 179–80, 185–86
Barnes, Jonathan, 7n
Barry, Brian, 8, 28, 70, 165–70, 180n
Barwell, Ismay, 58n
Bay, Christian, 124
Behavior modification, 126
Beliefs
  coherence, 27–30
  of the many or wise, 7, 23–26
Benditt, Theodore M., 164
Bendix, Reinhard, 183n
Benn, S. I., vii, 50–51, 68–71, 91–92, 94, 98–99n, 111, 163
Bentham, Jeremy, 87
Berlin, Isaiah, ix, 96n, 97–98, 100–101
Bermant, G., 101n
Brandt, Richard B., 123n
Bratman, Michael, 137
Breakdowns in machinery of action, 37
Breathing-space model, 73, 85
Brennan, Geoffrey, 139, 151–52
Bronaugh, Richard N., 37
Brown, P., 101n

Campbell, John, 18–19
Cassinelli, C. W., 67–68
Caution, 160
Chapman, John W., 95n, 111n
Christman, John, 123, 132n, 134
Coherence theory, 62, 191
Common core concept, 6
Common referents, 7
Concept of item x, 1–3
Conception of x, 1–3

195

Conee, Earl, 140n
Conflicts, 188–90
　between individuals, 178–79
　dimensions, 178–80
　nature of, 178–80
　severity of restrictions, 179
Connolly, W. E., 50–51, 165, 167n, 171–72, 174
Considered judgments, 23
Contestedness thesis, 3–4
Cooper, W. E., 26n
Copp, David, 12n, 26
Core area
　accommodating endoxa, 81–88
　coherence, 76–77
Core concept, 62
　disputes, 63–64
Course of action limitations, 67–69
Cranston, Maurice, vii
Crocker, Lawrence, 103n, 120

Dahl, Robert A., 74–75
Daniels, Norman, 11–12, 26, 61
Davidson, Donald, 137–38, 140–46, 148, 150
Day, J. P., 73, 85
Dearden, R. F., 120–21
Deliberation, 55
　objects, 59–60
Desirability, 146
Desires, 53–54
　effective and noneffective, 53
　evaluative second-order, 148–50
　first- and second-order, 131–32
　flawed, 64–57, 81–82
　higher-order, 132–34
　mismatches between, 136
　nonalien origin, 134
　objects, 59–60
　prioritizing, 55
　strong evaluation of first-order, 149–52
　versus idle wishes, 53–54
Deterrents, 90, 115–17
Dewey, John, vii, 65
Dispositional autonomy, 155
Dryer, V.D.P., 73–74, 85
Durkheim, Emile, 44, 156n, 188
Dworkin, Gerald, 9, 101–2, 133, 184n, 185

Ellis, Brian, 27n
Endoxa, 7, 23–26, 61, 76, 78
　accommodating in core area, 81–88
　as reasonable collocation, 32–33
　background theory and, 29–30
　incompatible, 29
English, Jane, 23
Erwin, Robert, 18–19
Essential contestedness thesis, 1–10
　common core concept, 6
　common referents, 7
　epistemological version, 4–5
　favored conception of freedom, 8–9
　ontological version, 4–5
　truth of C, 5–6
Executive courage
　appropriate responses, 154
　field, 158–60
　goal, 153–54
　virtue, 152–61
Executive failures, 71–73
　anomie, 156
　defining, 136
　lack of resolve, 156–57
　manifestation of cowardice, 72–73
　moral cowardice, 158
　vacillation, 157–58
　versus heteronomy, 118
　weakness of character, 152–61
　weakness of will, 72, 137–52, 154–55
Executive vices
　caution, 160
　incaution, 160–61
External restraints, 90

F phenomena, 16–20, 22
　answering particular classifactory interest, 17–19
　causally related to F, 17–20
　considered judgments, 23
Feinberg, Joel, 73–74, 85–87, 90–91, 167n, 180
Flathman, Richard E., 40, 66, 88, 192
Flew, Anthony, 83
Flourishing, 41–48
　norms, 42–43
　optimum conditions for the individual, 42–44
　value-impregnated concepts, 44–46

Index

value, 41
virtues, 44
Foot, Philippa, 153
Formal property, 36–37
Formation of attitudes limitations, 69–71
Frankfurt, Harry, 53, 132, 135
  first- and second-order desires, 131–32
Freedom, 21–22
  See also autonomy and overall freedom
  absences, 33, 35, 37
  action, 37, 68, 73–75, 84, 100–103
  agency, 97–98
  autonomy, 69–71, 119
  background theory, 31–32
  barriers and obstacles, 50
  breathing space model, 85
  coherence theory, 62, 192
  conceptions, 2, 8, 61–64
  conflicts, 178–90
  consensus on paradigm cases, 24
  core concept, viii–ix, 62–64
  defeasibility account, 31–37
  dyadic relation between agents and obstacles, viii–ix
  effect of threats and offers, 104
  endoxa, 7, 28, 61, 76, 78
  essential contestedness, 1–10
  executive failure limitations, 72–73
  flawed desires, 64–67, 81–82
  formal property, 36–37, 111
  human potential in agency versus limitations, 38–48
  identification, 132–33
  implementation of desires, 70
  inability and ability, 95–96
  indifference-curve approach, 180–82
  individual flourishing, 43
  intentionalist model, 185–86
  interests, 162–77
  invariability, 91–92
  limitations, 38
  machinery of the successful act, 34
  material properties, 36, 111
  maximizing-options model, 183–85
  methodology problems, ix
  monadic property of agents, ix
  nonhuman deprivation, vii
  normality, 98–99
  normative socialization, 184
  options, 67–69, 188–90
  peripheral disputes, 63–64
  practical activity, 49–52
  principle of charity, 191–92
  propensity, 162
  rationality, 50–51, 120, 122–23
  right desire, 65
  rule-derived, 92
  severity of restrictions, 179–80
  significant courses of action restraints, 73–75
  societal value, 40–41
  states of mind and character, 186–87
  threats and offers limitations, 109–13
  unavailable actions, 67–68, 95–100
  values, 38, 40–41, 47, 80, 192
  various and complex standards, 34–35
  versus ability, vii, 95
  virtue, 82–83, 187–88
  virtue-oriented, 64–67, 81–84
Freedom phenomena, 38
French, Peter A., 12n, 101n
Friedman, Marilyn, 132n, 133–34
Full virtue, 64

Gallie, W. B., 1–5, 22n
Gert, Bernard, 95
Gibbs, Benjamin, 65, 83, 177, 187
Goldman, Alvin, 12
Good, 182
  happiness and self-actualization, 164
Griffiths, A. Phillips, 65n

Hagan, C. B., 163n
Haksar, Vinit, 35, 37
Haller, Rudolph, 133
Hampshire, Stuart, 56
Handlin, Mary, 185
Handlin, Oscar, 185
Happiness, 164
Hare, R. M., 118n, 125–26, 128, 137
Hedonic calculus, 87
Held, Virginia, 111n, 113, 164–65
Helvetius, 98n
Heteronomy
  as inauthenticity, 124–27
  limitation in practical activity, 124

Heteronomy *(cont.)*
  nature of, 118–20
  versus executive failure, 118
Hintikka, Merril B., 139
Hirst, Paul H., 120n, 127
Hobbes, T., 51
Hollins, T.H.B., 128n
Human potential in agency, 47
  versus limitations, 38–48
Hyman, Herbert H., 183n

Identification, 132–33
Impediments, 90
Impetuosity, 160–61
Impossible intentions, 56–57
Impulsiveness, 131
Incaution, 160
  impetuosity, 160–61
  rashness, 161
Indeterminacy, 154–55
Indifference-curve approach, 180–82
Individual flourishing, 43
Indoctrination, 127–29
Inducements, 90
Intentional action, 33–35, 51–52
  forming intentions, 57–58
Intentionalist model, 185–86
Intentions, 55–60
Interests, 162–63
  ascriptions, 171–72
  concept, 164–77
  costs of acquiring, 175–76
  means-end hierarchy, 169–70
  mistaken, 173–74
  other-regarding wants, 166–67
  person's good, 175
  preferences expressed, 172
  radical change, 172–74
  satisfying one's want, 167–69
  self-regarding wants, 166–67
  want-reguarding, 176–77
Internal restraints, 91
Interventions, 105
Invariability, 91–92

Judgments
  the thing to do, 54–55
  what is good and fitting, 54
Justice, 99–100
  common element in conceptions, viiin

Kant, I., 120–21
Kovesi, Julius, 18, 36

Lack of resolve, 156–57
Lankshear, Colin, 51n
Laslett, Peter, 186n
Limitations
  action, 67–69
  construction of reason-giving links, 58–59
  converting judgments and intentions into action, 59
  formation of attitudes, 69–71
  objects, 58–60
  practical activity, 58–60
  versus human potential in agency, 38–48
Lindblom, Charles E., 74–75
Lipset, Seymour Martin, 183n
Locke, Don, 135n
Locke, John, 112n
Louden, Robert B., 45n
Lucas, J. R., 97
Lukes, Steven, viii, 2–6, 8–9, 22n, 24, 186–87
Lycan, William G., 13

MacCallum, Gerald, viii, 24, 62–66, 76–77, 179
  triadic relation of freedom, 2, 76–77, 191–92
McGinn, Colin, 72n
McMurrin, Sterling M., 121n
Manipulation, 125
Maslow, Abraham, 45n, 164
Material properties, 36
Maximizing-options model, 183–85
Means-end hierarchy, 169–70
Mill, J. S., 39, 86
Miller, David, 98n
Miller, J.D.B., 163n
Mishan, E. J., 184–85, 188
Moral cowardice, 158
Mortimore, G. W., 145

Narrow reflective equilibrium (NRE), 15
Negative restraints, 90
Nielsen, Kai, 11–12, 16, 17n, 20, 23
Non-inner-directedness, 129–35
Non-relative truth conditions, 4

Index

Nonvicariousness, 123–29
Normal courage, 159–60
Normality, connection with freedom, 98–99
Normative socialization, 184
Nozick, Robert, 29, 110n
Nussbaum, Martha Craven, 7n, 24–25, 28

Offers
  limiting freedom, 109–13
  limiting options, 111–13
  nature of, 104–9
Oppenheim, Felix, 96n, 101, 116, 125
Options, 188–90
Ordinal judgments rationality, 180–87
Other-regarding wants, 166–67
Overall freedom, 77–80, 192
  See also freedom
  freedom-limiting obstacles, 80
  given set of actions, 79
  pluralism, 88
  rationality of ordinal judgments, 180–87
  significance of actions in assessment, 79–80, 84–86
  soundness of concept, 86–88
Owen, G.E.L., 7n

Parent, W. A., 7n, 24, 28, 62, 67–68, 94–96
Pargetter, Robert, 18–19
Parkin, Frank, 183n
Peacocke, Christopher, 138–40, 146, 148
Pears, 137
Pennock, Roland J., 95n, 111n
Peripheral disputes, 63–64
Personal value, 189–90
Persuasion, 125–26
Peters, R. S., vii, 120n, 127n–28n
Pettit, Philipp, 139, 151–52
Plato, 64
Pluralism, 88
Positive restraints, 90
Power and common core, viiin
Practical activity, 33–35
  connection with freedom, 49–52
  deliberation, 55
  desires, 53–54
  forming intentions, 55–58

  limitations, 58–60
  nature of, 52–58
  practical judgments, 54
Practical judgments, See judgments
Principle of charity, 191–92

Raphael, D. D., vii, 97
Rashness, 161
Rational unsettlability thesis, 8–9
Rationality, 42, 118–23
  consistency, 180–82
  ends, 42
Rawls, John, viiin, 2, 9, 13n, 14, 21–22, 24, 27, 31–32, 61–62, 170n
  intuitionism, 182
Raz, Joseph, 21–22, 83–84, 157, 188–90
  personal value, 189–90
Restraints, 89–91
  degree of ineligibility, 113–17
Rorty, Amelie Oksenberg, 159n
Runciman, W. G., 110n, 183, 186n
Russell, Bertrand, 51, 74, 80
Ryan, Alan, 65n, 96n

Schiffer, Peter, 137, 147–50
Schofield, Malcolm, 7n
Scott, K. J., 70–71, 96, 117
Searle, John, 107n
Self actualization, 164
Self realization, 83–84
Self-regarding wants, 166–67
Silverstein, Harry S., 140n
Singer, Peter, 101–2
Skinner, Quentin, 110n
Slote, Michael, 121n
Smith, Nowell, 37
Smith, Peter, 7n
Sorabji, Richard, 7n
Steiner, Hillel, 67, 104–6, 110–11
  standard of normalcy, 105
Stevens, Robert, 104–6, 108–9
  standards of normalcy, 108
Sylvan, Richard, 140n

Tawney, R. H., vii
Taylor, Charles, 65, 79–81, 83, 149
  first- and second-order desires, 132
Thagard, Paul, 13
Thalberg, Irving, 56, 145n

Threats
  limiting freedom, 109–13
  limiting options, 110–11
  nature of, 104–9
Triadic schema of freedom, viii, 191–92
Trianosky, Gregory W., 67n

Uehling, Theodore E., Jr., 12n, 101n
Unfreedom, 119
  as heteronomy, 118
  executive failure, 72
  limitations, 33, 35–37
  thwarted tendencies, 70–71
Untoward events, 93
Urmson, J. O., 32, 107n, 182n

Vacillation, 157–58
Vaguely defined gestalt, 139–45
  motivational integrity, 141–42
  non-party-goer, 141
  sound teeth, 141
Value and flourishing, 41
Value terms, 15–16
Vermazen, Bruce, 139n
Virtue, 44, 186–88, 190
  field, 153
  goal, 153
Virtuous dispositions, 82–83
Vlastos, Gregory, 123

Waldron, Jeremy, 100n
Wall, Grenville, 174–75

Warnock, G. J., 32
Watson, Gary, 137, 142–43
Weakness of character, 152–61
Weakness of will, 137–55
  high-minded versus low-minded, 150
  structurally similar paradoxes, 140
  type A examples, 140–46
  type B examples, 146–52
Weinstein, W. L., 68, 91–92, 94, 98n–99n, 111
Wettstein, Howard K., 12n, 101n
White, J. P., 128
Wide reflective equilibrium (WRE), ix–x, 11–30
  coherence of beliefs, 26–30
  considered judgments, 23
  epistemological role, 12–22
  F phenomena, 16–23
  internal realists, 15
  justification for moral concepts, 13
  moral theorists, 22
  nature, 23–26
  rival moral conceptions, 14
  value terms, 15–16
Williams, Bernard, 41, 45, 140n
Wilson, John, 128
World relation with value terms, 15–16

Young, Robert, 37, 72, 133, 155, 163n

Zimmerman, David, 12n, 26n, 112–13